JERUSALEM

JERUSALEM

A GUIDE TO THE SACRED PLACES OF JERUSALEM

MARTIN LEV

Alfred A. Knopf   New York   1989

THIS IS A BORZOI BOOK
PUBLISHED BY ALFRED A. KNOPF, INC.

Copyright © 1989 by Martin Lev

All rights reserved under International and Pan-American
Copyright Conventions. Published in the United States by
Alfred A. Knopf, Inc., New York, and simultaneously in
Canada by Random House of Canada Limited, Toronto.
Distributed by Random House, Inc., New York.

Library of Congress Cataloging-in-Publication Data

Lev, Martin.
    The traveler's key to Jerusalem: a guide to the sacred places of
Jerusalem / Martin Lev.—1st ed.
        p.   cm.
    Bibliography: p.
    Includes index.
    ISBN 0-394-55635-6
    1. Jerusalem—Description—1981- —Guide-books. 2. Shrines—
Jerusalem. I. Title. II. Title: Traveler's key to Jerusalem.
DS109.15.L48   1989   88-45491
915.694′40454—dc19   CIP

Manufactured in the United States of America
First Edition

CONTENTS

ACKNOWLEDGMENTS

Jerusalem does not yield its secrets easily, and I have been overwhelmed by all the help I have received in the attempt to unravel its mysteries. First of all, I would like to acknowledge and thank Pol and Noel Pilven, who taught me how to look at sacred places. Mr. Yusuf Natsheh, Director of the Department of Islamic Archeology of the Waqf, and Mr. Issa Baidun, of the Department of Islamic Archeology of the Waqf, made it possible for me to study the monuments of the Temple Mount (Al Haram es-Sharif). Special thanks are due the following: Mr. Kevork Hintlian, Secretary to the Armenian Patriarch; Father Niceforos, Greek Orthodox Superior, Church of the Holy Sepulchre; Father Claudio Barrato, Director, Christian Information Center; Mr. Daniel Rossing, Ministry for Religious Affairs; Mr. Moshe Ben-Haim, Ministry for Religious Affairs; Father Bargil Pixner, Dormition Abbey; Mr. Kristos Skouros, Greek Orthodox Patriarchate; Bishop Guregh Kapikian, Church of the Holy Sepulchre; Sister Joachim, Sisters of Zion; Father Francis Bowen, Church of St. Anne; Father Claudio Bottini, Studium Biblicum Franciscanum; Archbishop Benham Jajjawi, Syrian Orthodox Convent; Archbishop Athanasius, Ethiopian Monastery; Father Alphonse Meyer, St. Peter in Gallicantu.

I would like to thank Miss Sivan Ben-Mayor, who took the photographs for this book. I would also like to thank my children, Abigail and Boaz, who suffered their father's long absences with constant love and understanding. My special appreciation goes to the Friedman family of New York, Alan, Deborah, and Alek, who made it physically possible for me to finish this book.

No acknowledgments could be complete without mentioning my editor, and editor of the Traveler's Key series, Mrs. Toinette Lippe. I have enjoyed every minute of my work with her, and my only regret is that the first two years of our association was by mail. The loss was mine.

JERUSALEM

INTRODUCTION

What is a sacred place?

There are probably as many answers to this question as there are people who write about it. But all seem to be in agreement on one point. The sacred manifests at the meeting place between heaven and earth, where the divine touches and enters the human world. Life at this point is always described as being of a different nature and quality from the profane world which surrounds it. Thus, when Moses encounters the divine in the midst of the burning bush he is told, "put off thy shoes from off thy feet, for the place whereon thou standest is holy ground" (Exodus 3:5). But what does this mean for us today, when the divine seems to hide its face, and all that remains is monuments commemorating the sites of former glories? Is the sacred still to be found?

This question is especially poignant in Jerusalem. Pilgrims and visitors to the city come here with expectations they bring to no other sacred place. For Jerusalem is not just a city of the past. It is here that the Divine Presence has promised it will one day renew its ties with men, bring them eternal salvation, and reestablish God's kingdom on earth. Each visitor, consciously or unconsciously, seeks a confirmation of this promise. Even the most rational of men hopes to find here some indication that will bridge the gap between his outer material world and the world of his deepest beliefs and hopes. In other words, he secretly seeks some kind of real contact with another level of being.

What form can such a contact take in a Jerusalem where the divine no longer lives openly in the midst of men? Theories run the entire spectrum from the excesses of religious emotion to the coldness of pure intellectual speculation. Each approach contains a fragment of the truth. No one can doubt, for example, the sincerity of an aged Jewish woman overcome as she prays at the Tomb of David, but when we learn that this is not the real site of David's Tomb and that the tradition here is Christian in origin, we are forced to question the nature of the experience. The same can be said about the places of devotion along the Via Dolorosa, which is now known not to have been the route taken by Jesus, nor the one commemorated in the first eleven centuries of Christianity.

Some contend that sacred buildings and sites arise at places on the earth which exhibit especially strong energies. It is claimed that Jerusalem, especially the area of the Temple Mount, is such a place. While this may be true, and there may be people who are sensitive to such forces, for the normal visitor it must remain in the realm of theory. He may choose to believe it, but intellectual belief is far from the real contact that he seeks.

A much more interesting approach is taken by a number of scholars who have noted that structures built on sacred sites are invariably repositories of great knowledge. Thus, for example, the construction of pyramids and stone circles and the orientation of certain churches and ancient temples have been shown to be intimately related to the recording of astronomical phenomena. The incredible accuracy with which the ancients were capable of measuring both the earth's surface and the heavens often astounds modern man, who has been taught to think of his ancient counterpart as primitive. But the concentration of such seemingly profane knowledge at sites held to be sacred should come as no surprise. These sites were often believed to lie along a vertical line of descent which connected the heavenly world above with the earthly world below. They thus became centers where the divine manifested itself in earthly form and from which, under favorable conditions, its influence could spread outward to the profane world. The divine was seen as a well-defined world of order, while the profane was an endless sea of chaos. The form taken by the sacred site, which was an earthly, material reflection of the divine world above, invariably manifested some aspect of this heavenly order. The simplest of these reflected the outer physical order of the heavens and were astronomical in nature. But there were others which reflected some aspect of the inner nature of divine order in the universe. Jerusalem was just such a sacred place. The city's monuments consistently demonstrate the laws concerning man's relation to the divine—from his fall to the inner spiritual evolution that leads to his eventual salvation and return. What is remarkable is that no one building or sacred site in Jerusalem contains all this great knowledge. Rather, different places combine with certain of the city's traditions, legends, history, religions, and art to record in permanent architectural form particular aspects of these laws, and the cumulative story is Jerusalem's heritage to the world.

The opening chapter of the book gives a somewhat unconventional picture of the history and geography of the city in its different periods. It also treats a number of sites of lesser importance not dealt with in the other parts of the book. All this is indispensable for understanding the relationship between the different parts of the Jerusalem mosaic. In succeeding chapters we will be visiting a number of sites where great truths entered the world. Many of the structures built at these sites were designed in such a way as to be the symbolic expressions of these truths. Schools of great knowledge often existed at these sacred places. Their purpose was not to impart facts but to help a man to awaken to the inner meaning of the symbols before him. In the spirit of these ancient schools, this book invites the visitor to view Jerusalem in such a way as to stimulate his own inner understanding.

A guidebook on Jerusalem can be an encyclopedia, listing and naming all existing sites, or it can choose a number of these in order to study them in depth. Encyclopedic guidebooks are plentiful because they seem to offer the visitor tangible advantages. Simply knowing the name of something often gives us the illusion that we understand it, and such books provide all the names. But true understanding may come from the sustained pursuit of a specific line of inquiry. This presents both the author and the visitor with a more challenging task, but the rewards are well worth the effort. *The Traveler's Key to Jerusalem*, then, addresses the question "What is a sacred place?"

HISTORY AND BACKGROUND

Jerusalem is a city with more than one hundred names. The rabbis of old claimed that the city had seventy names, which were equivalent in number to the names of God. The Hebrew word for Jerusalem itself appears 656 times in the Old Testament—almost always in its singular form, Yerushalem. Only three times does it appear as Yerushalayim, the fuller plural form it has today. The earliest historical record of the city is in Egyptian texts of the eighteenth to nineteenth centuries B.C., where it is mentioned as a Canaanite city-state called Ushalmes. In the later (fourteenth-century B.C. Egyptian) Tel el Amarna letters it is called Ruschalim, while in an Assyrian inscription the name occurs as Urusalimmu. The Greeks of a later period called it Hierosolyma, in which can be found the word *hieros*, "holy." The Christians of the Middle Ages called it Jerosolyma or Hierosalem, from which derives the French and English Jerusalem.

BEFORE THE DESTRUCTION OF THE FIRST TEMPLE, 586 B.C.

Much of Jerusalem's history from this earliest period (from the time of the patriarchs to the fall of the Kingdom of Judah) is not history at all, but traditions surrounding its biblical and mythological origins. These traditions are reflected in the meanings of a number of the city's earliest names.

Shalem (English: Salem)

According to tradition, the Hebrew name Yerushalem is a combination of two separate names, Yeru or Yir'eh, and Shalem (English: Jeru and Salem). Shalem is one of the city's seventy names mentioned by the rabbis, and first appears in connection with Abraham's defeat of the confederation of kings and his meeting with Melchizedek. "And the king of Sodom went out to meet him after his return from the slaughter of Chedorlaomer, and of the kings that were with him. . . . And Melchizedek king of Salem brought forth bread

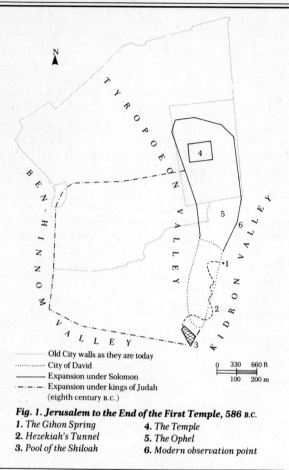

Fig. 1. Jerusalem to the End of the First Temple, 586 B.C.
1. *The Gihon Spring*   4. *The Temple*
2. *Hezekiah's Tunnel*   5. *The Ophel*
3. *Pool of the Shiloah*   6. *Modern observation point*

and wine: and he was the priest of the most high God. And he blessed him, and said, Blessed be Abram of the most high God, possessor of heaven and earth: and blessed be the most high God, which hath delivered thine enemies into thy hand. And he [Abraham] gave him [Melchizedek] tithes of all" (Genesis 14:17–20).

In rabbinic literature Melchizedek is identified with Shem, the son of Noah. It was he who founded the city of Shalem, whose three consonants, *sh, l,* and *m* (the Hebrew of the Old Testament is written without vowels), mean "perfect" or "whole" (*shalem*) or "peace" (*shalom*). His name is composed of two words, *melech,* meaning "king," and *zedek,* meaning "justice" or "righteousness." He is thus the king of justice, as well as the king of Shalem, meaning "peace" or "perfect." He is also the priest of the most high God (Hebrew: El Elyon). In Psalms 110:4 it is written, "The Lord hath sworn, and will not repent, Thou art a priest forever after the order of Melchizedek." Melchizedek's immortal nature, hinted at in Psalms, is emphasized by St. Paul, who identifies him with the Messiah (Jesus). "For this Melchizedek ... without father, without mother, without descent, having neither beginning of days, nor end of life; but made like unto the Son of God; abideth a priest continually" (Epistle to the Hebrews 7:1–3).

Jewish tradition further states that it was at Shalem that Shem (Melchizedek) established an academy or school to instruct the people of the world in the ways of God. This picture of an immortal priest who rules a city of perfect peace and instructs the nations of the world in the ways of the most high God, is reminiscent of Isaiah's prophecy concerning Jerusalem at the end of time: "And it shall come to pass in the last days, that the mountain of the Lord's house shall be established in the top of the mountains, and shall be exalted above the hills; and all nations shall flow unto it. And many people shall go and say, Come ye, and let us go up to the mountain of the Lord, to the house of the God of Jacob; and he will teach us of his ways, and we will walk in his paths: for out of Zion shall go forth the law, and the word of the Lord from Jerusalem. And he shall judge among the nations, and shall rebuke many people: and they shall beat their swords into plowshares, and their spears into pruninghooks: nation shall not lift up sword against nation, neither shall they learn war any more" (Isaiah 2:1–4).

Yeru or Yir'eh (English: Jeru or Jireh)

The meeting between Melchizedek and Abraham must be recognized as an investiture ceremony in which the priesthood of a higher spiritual plane is passed on to the earthly Abraham. It is through Abraham that the reflection of the true Shalem first becomes established on earth. The earthly site where this act takes place will later be called Yeru or, more precisely, Yir'eh, by Abraham. Yir'eh was also one of Jerusalem's seventy names, and its origin lies in the story of the binding of Isaac. After Abraham had bound his son and laid him on the altar and took hold of the knife to sacrifice him, an angel called to him out of heaven, saying, "Lay not thine hand upon the lad, neither do thou anything unto him. ... And Abraham lifted up his eyes, and looked, and behold behind him a ram caught in the thicket by his horns: And Abraham went and took the ram, and offered him up for a burnt offering in the stead of his son. And Abraham called the name of that place Jehovah-jireh [God will show]: as it is said to this day, In the mount of the Lord it shall be seen" (Genesis 22:12–14).

A rabbinical commentary on Genesis says the following: "Abraham called it Yir'eh [will show]. ... Shem [Melchizedek] called it Shalem. ... Said the Holy One Blessed be He: If I call it Yir'eh as did Abraham, Shem, a righteous man, will complain. If I call it Shalem, as did Shem, Abraham, a righteous man, will complain. I shall therefore call it as both of them called it: Yerushalem, that is, Yir'eh-Shalem." The name of the place as well as its location is significant. The "mount of the Lord" that is spoken of above is located in the "land of Moriah" (Genesis 22:2), the place later identified with the site of the Temple. It is the place where later God will show (*yir'eh*), or make known on earth, the fullness and perfection (*shalem*) of what is above.

Tsiyon (English: Zion)

Another name for Jerusalem is the Hebrew Tsiyon, or, in English, Zion. The source of the name is unknown. The original Fortress of Zion was the hilltop city captured by David. When the city expanded northward under Solomon, Zion came to be identified with the Temple Mount. Eventually this name came to encompass all of Jerusalem, then all of Israel, and finally the Jewish people itself. In the Prophets and in the Book of Psalms, these three elements, city, land, and people, became symbolically united into a single entity. For the prophets Jeremiah and Isaiah, Zion came to be seen as a mother who mourns the fate of her children: "But Zion said, the Lord hath forsaken me, and my Lord hath forgotten me. Can a woman forget her sucking child, that she should not have compassion on the son of her womb? Yea, they may forget, yet I will not forget thee" (Isaiah 49:14–15). In Psalms too, Jerusalem as Zion mourns the exile of her children but will one day find joy when they are returned to her bosom.

The idea of a return to an earthly Zion typifies Jewish belief and thought. Jewish tradition, like Christianity, developed the idea of a celestial Jerusalem. But unlike in Christian tradition, where the celestial city predominated, Jewish messianic thought centered on a terrestrial Jerusalem which united the historical reality of the exile and dispersion of a people with a promised renewed and restored social, religious, and political entity in the promised land of Israel and its city of election, Jerusalem. We thus see that the national Jewish movement known as Zionism is not something new, but is rooted deep in Jewish memory and consciousness. Jewish mystical thought concerning the celestial city never lost sight of this. In Judaism, terrestrial Jerusalem was not simply a reflection of its celestial counterpart. On the contrary, Jewish tradition held that God had built the upper city out of His great love for the one below. The earthly city thus had a value in itself, expressed by the suffering of Zion and the historic hopes of her children. On the heavenly plane it was expressed by God's promise not to enter the upper city until the lower one had been rebuilt.

To some extent the idea of Jerusalem as the mother of the Jewish people can be related to the Jewish idea of the Shechinah, the Divine Presence on earth. The development of the idea of the Shechinah runs counter to all logic and all norms of religious evolution. In the opening lines of Genesis, God is described as the creator and master of the universe, unlimited by time and space. Even today the Jewish concept of God is of a being so great, so unimaginably vast and unknowable, that there is no way to bridge the gap between the human and the divine. As a man approaches the border between these two worlds, he can experience only the depth of his own nothingness. Yet the history of the Jewish people is the story of this God's seemingly self-imposed limitation. This universal God intervenes on the stage of world history and influences particular events by choosing Abraham and his descendants as His special people. He leads the Children of Israel out of bondage in Egypt and causes them to build a portable tabernacle for Him to dwell in during their wanderings. But even this tabernacle is not limited enough. When Solomon builds what is finally God's permanent and fixed abode on earth, the Temple in Jerusalem, he asks the question that still bothers us today. "Then said Solomon, the Lord hath said that he would dwell in thick darkness. But I have built an house of habitation for thee, and a place for thy dwelling for ever. . . . But will God in very deed dwell with men on earth? behold, heaven, and the heaven of heavens cannot contain thee; how much less this house which I have built!" (II Chronicles 6:1–2, 18). "And the glory of the Lord filled the house. And the priests could not enter into the house of the Lord, because the glory of the Lord had filled the Lord's house" (II Chronicles 7:1–2). The Divine Presence that filled the Holy of Holies came to be known as the Shechinah. The name is important because its form is feminine. It is said of Moses, for example, that in his later years he had no intimate relations with his wife because he was preparing for the moment of his death, which would be brought by the kiss of the Shechinah. We can also understand better Solomon's Song of Songs, which talks of love in such intimate and sensuous terms that we forget that this love is the love of God. The destruction of the Temple brought with it the dispersion of the Jewish people and the exile of the Shechinah, though tradition holds that the Shechinah has never left the Western Wall. Yet there can be no question regarding the bond that has always remained between the two and the promise that it will one day be restored. This relationship took the form of Israel and the Shechinah, and also Jerusalem (Zion) and her children. For Jews the place chosen by God for this restoration and return is the terrestrial city of Jerusalem, where the divine and the human are destined to reunite in a real and material world.

For Christians, the significance of earthly Jerusalem has always been a far more complicated question, if not an actual dilemma. It was the site of the most important events in the history of the world: Christ's ministry, his Passion, Resurrection, and Ascension, as well as the birth of the Church at Pentecost. Christian pilgrims have always come to Jerusalem to pray at the sites associated with the mystery of salvation. At the same time, great figures of the Church throughout the ages have expressed severe doubts concerning such acts of pilgrimage to Jerusalem, often declaring them to be devoid of spiritual value. While the earthly Jerusalem was not despised or even rejected, it was believed that only the celestial Jerusalem was real and essential.

Christian ideas regarding celestial Jerusalem took root in the Second Temple period, and in the period following its destruction. Many of these ideas are found in the Jewish thought of the day, especially those of the Essenes. This Jewish sect had rejected the Temple while it still stood, claiming it to be defiled. For the Essenes the holiness of the Temple and its sacrifice was replaced by the holiness of the community which lived together in ritual purity, and dreamt of a new Temple that would be built by the hands of God. Their beliefs in election, baptism, and the coming of the Messiah, who would lead the forces of the Sons of Light against the Sons of Darkness, are reminiscent of early Christian thought. But while the Essenes were essentially Jews, and their visions of a new Temple and of Jerusalem were earthly in character, the early Christian community placed their emphasis on Jerusalem's celestial, and purely spiritual, counterpart.

However, even this celestial counterpart was different from the one envisioned by Jews. At its center stood not the Temple or the Holy of Holies, but Christ. The essence of this belief was found in Christ's name of Immanuel ("Behold, a virgin shall conceive, and bear a son, and shall call his name Immanuel"—Isaiah 7:14). In Hebrew the name means "God is with us." Celestial Jerusalem was believed to be the body of Christ, which contained the totality of grace that had spread throughout the universe at the moment of creation when God said "Let there be light!" According to St. Paul, part of this spirit dwelt in man ("Know ye not that ye are the temple of God, and that the Spirit of God dwelleth in you?"— I Corinthians 3:16). The physical body thus contained the true Temple, in which dwelt the Holy Spirit, and new Jerusalem became the community of Christians united through the Christ within. True Jerusalem was the heavenly one. Terrestrial Jerusalem, the one united to the Jerusalem above, became any place where a perfect Christian life was lived. It no longer depended on any one geographical location but was reflected in the united body of the Church, in whose midst God reigned over a faithful and sanctified people.

The Jewish idea of Zion mourning for her children also underwent a transformation in Christian thought. Zion was no longer abandoned and forgotten by God (". . . but ye are come unto Mt. Zion, and unto the city of the living God, the heavenly Jerusalem"—Hebrews 12:22), and her children could now return to her, not in the world below, but through the Church to the world above (". . . Jerusalem which now is, . . . is in bondage with her children. But Jerusalem which is above is free, which is the mother of us all"—Galatians 4:25–6).

In spite of the new doctrine, the earthly Jerusalem remained a center of Christian pilgrimage and devotion. St.

Augustine wrote of two types of pilgrimage: "It is one thing to walk with our body, and another to walk with our heart. He who walks with the body changes his place by the movement of the body; he who walks with his heart changes his sentiment by the movement of his heart." As early as the fourth century, St. Jerome, who spent most of his life in Bethlehem, wrote: "The sanctuary is open to you as much in England as in Jerusalem, for the kingdom of heaven is within you." In the Middle Ages many spiritual pilgrimages were indeed made without ever leaving Europe since the pilgrim was seeking the Jerusalem of the heart. Yet for many modern Christians, the experience of actually being at the sacred sites stimulates the heart.

Jebus

Another name for Jerusalem was Jebus, the city of the Jebusites. This was the hilltop fortress captured by David early in the tenth century B.C. Jerusalem is one of Israel's oldest cities, whose remains can be traced back some five thousand years. By the early second millennium B.C. Jerusalem was under Egyptian suzerainty and played an important role in the region's military and trade routes. Jebus itself was probably little more than a large agricultural town or village of some 10 acres (4 hectares). It was this agricultural basis that had no doubt permitted it for centuries to service the caravans and armies passing through it. The city was located on a hill whose choice was originally determined by the presence on its eastern slope of a freshwater spring, the Gihon. Besides the city's artificial defenses, it was naturally defended on the east by the valley of the Kidron, and on the west by a narrow but deep valley called the Tyropoeon. The two met at the city's southern tip. (The Tyropoeon, which was filled in as the city expanded westward, is still one of Jerusalem's major thoroughfares, running from the Damascus Gate in the north to the Pool of Shiloah in the south). It was only in the north that the city lacked any natural defenses, and it was probably here that was situated the citadel later known as the Fortress of Zion.

The Old Testament account concerning the conquest of Jerusalem by the invading Hebrews is confusing. We are told that it was captured by Joshua, but when we hear of it again it is once more a Canaanite city. Apparently the city was captured by the Israelites but not held. At about the same time that the Israelites began their conquest of Canaan, a Hittite tribe, the Jebusites, also entered the country. It was they who finally captured the city and managed to hold on to it for some two hundred years until it was taken by David.

An interesting addition to the story of the city of Jebus is that of the threshing floor of Araunah the Jebusite, on Mt. Moriah, later bought by David as the site where Solomon would one day build the Temple. There are a number of peculiarities about this site which leave the impression that it was more than a simple threshing floor. First of all, there is the question why the threshing floor lay outside the city proper, unprotected by its walls. Second is the matter of the purchase itself. The city had been conquered by David in war, and no other part of it had been purchased; why, then, the threshing floor? The third peculiarity concerns the threshing floor's location at the summit of Mt. Moriah. Threshing floors require a certain amount of wind for the winnowing of the wheat. In Israel they are invariably found on the upper slopes of hills—but never at their highest points, where the winds are generally too strong for such purposes. These strange circumstances, together with the sacred history that would later be associated with Mt. Moriah, suggest that Araunah was perhaps the last priest-king of the Jebusite city, and the threshing floor a sacred site, not only of the Jebusite city but of the Canaanite cities before it.

The City of David

Following the capture of Jebus, Jerusalem came to be known as the City of David ("Nevertheless David took the stronghold of Zion: the same is the city of David"—II Samuel 5:7). In size it remained essentially the Jebusite city described above, though David developed it by strengthening fortifications, erecting public buildings, and making it the political capital of a united Israel, which in his lifetime extended from the Red Sea, in the south, to the Euphrates, in the north.

The establishment of Jerusalem as the permanent capital of a united kingdom ushered in a new era in Jewish history. The Shechinah, the Divine Presence, which had traveled with Israel in its wanderings, had been associated with two sacred objects: the Ark of the Covenant, and the Tabernacle, a portable sanctuary. On top of the ark there was what was described as a "mercy seat" flanked by two golden cherubim with outstretched wings. In later mystical thought these cherubim served as the chariot of God. The role of the ark and the mercy seat are made clear in God's instructions to Moses concerning their construction: "And thou shalt put the mercy seat above upon the ark; and in the ark thou shalt put the testimony that I shall give thee. And there I will meet with thee, and I will commune with thee from above the mercy seat, from between the two cherubims which are upon the ark of the testimony, of all things which I will give thee in commandment unto the children of Israel" (Exodus 25:21–22). With the Israelite conquest of Canaan the sanctuary was established at Shiloh, some 12 miles (19 kilometers) south of Shechem. When Shiloh was attacked by the Philistines, the surviving priests settled at Nob, possibly on the Mt. Scopus ridge. Later the sanctuary was moved to Kiryat Ye'arim, from which David brought it to Jerusalem. The move has been described as David's establishment of Jerusalem as the religious as well as the political center of the country. But it was much more than that. At no time during Israel's wanderings is Jerusalem ever mentioned by

God as the place to which he is leading them. Their objective
is always called "the place that I will show you." Even with
the conquest of Canaan, there is no indication that Jerusalem will be the center of God's chosen kingdom on earth.
And when the city finally is chosen, as described in II Samuel 7, the choice is made discreetly and indirectly: "And it
came to pass, when the king [David] sat in his house [the
royal palace in Jerusalem], and the Lord had given him rest
round about from all his enemies; that the king said unto
Nathan the prophet, See now, I dwell in an house of cedar,
but the ark of God dwelleth within curtains [verses 1–2]. . . .
And it came to pass that night, that the word of the Lord
came unto Nathan, saying, Go and tell my servant David,
Thus saith the Lord [verse 4]. . . . I will appoint a place for
my people Israel, and will plant them, that they may dwell in
a place of their own [verse 10]. . . . I will set up thy seed after
thee, which shall proceed out of thy bowels, and I will establish his kingdom. He shall build an house [the Temple]
for my name, and I will establish the throne of his kingdom
for ever [verses 12–13]." Thus there was established the
permanence of Jerusalem, the future Temple, and the Davidic line. This event, of an infinite God's limiting of himself
for all time to a particular city, sacred site, and royal line is of
the utmost significance, not in terms of the time in which it
occurred but in terms of eschatological history. By this act a
particular earthly stage was set for the great events that will
take place here at the end of time.

THE CITY OF DAVID *(Hebrew: Ir David)*

If you have the time, pay a visit to the ancient City of David.
Although there are no sacred sites to see here, the visit will
help you place Jerusalem in its proper geographical and
historical perspective. It is also valuable in understanding
the relationship between the City of David and the Temple
Mount. The area is relatively small, but requires a great deal
of walking up and down hills and can be tiring, especially in
the hot summer months.

Begin your visit on the road overlooking the large parking
lot just to the south of the Dung Gate. Looking south, you
can get a certain impression of the remains of the Tyropoeon
Valley, which bordered the City of David on the west. Walk
eastward as far as you can and you will find a sign marking
the entranceway to the City of David Archeological Garden.
Here you have a natural observation point overlooking the
Kidron Valley. This was the City of David's eastern boundary, and it is easy to see the natural defenses it afforded.
Across the valley is the village of Silwan. In the lower part of
the hill you can see a number of large rectangular or square
openings cut into the rock. These are burial chambers from
the First Temple period. Jews have always buried their dead
outside of Jerusalem's walls. Burials from this period are also
found in the west in the Ben-Hinnom Valley, and to the

north. The only burials within the city were those of members of the royal house of David. These were located somewhere in the City of David, but have never been found.

Monumental Tombs of the Kidron Valley

About a three-minute walk to the north of the observation point, there is a good view of the area of the Kidron, where a number of monumental tombs are hewn out of the rock. Although these are not within the City of David, they are some of Jerusalem's most famous landmarks, and from here you have a perfect view of them.

Monumental tombs of the Kidron Valley.

Absalom's Pillar (*Hebrew: Yad Avshalom*) The monument furthest to the north is called Absalom's Pillar. There is every reason to believe that there was once a monument here dedicated to this favorite son of King David ("Now Absalom in his lifetime had taken and reared up for himself a pillar, which is in the king's dale: for he said, I have no son to keep my name in remembrance: and he called the pillar after his own name: and it is called unto this day, Absalom's place"— II Samuel 18:18). In Hebrew it is known as Yad Avshalom, "the Hand of Absalom." According to tradition, a stone hand once surmounted the pillar. This was associated with Absalom, who had raised his hand against his father by rebelling against him. The present structure, however, is not a monument but a tomb dating to the first century B.C., some nine hundred years after the time of David's son.

Tomb of Bnei Hezir (*Hebrew: Ma'arat Bnei Ḥezir*) Just to the south is the tomb of the Bnei Hezir family, mentioned in I Chronicles 24:15 as the priestly family that drew the seventeenth watch in the Temple service. On the architrave is a Hebrew inscription which translates as "This is the grave and the memorial of Eliezer, Hania, Yoezen, Shimon, Yohanan, the sons of Yoseph, son of Oved; Yoseph and Eliezer, sons of Hania, priest of the House of Hezir." The burial vault dates from the second century B.C. Christians called it the Grotto of St. James, whose remains were said to have been found here in the fourth century A.D.

Tomb of Zechariah (*Hebrew: Kever Zechariah HaNavi*) The third tomb, with the pyramidal roof, dates from the first century B.C. and not from the time of the prophet Zechariah (sixth century B.C.). Perhaps the association with the prophet comes from the belief that this was the burial place of Zecharius, the father of John the Baptist.

The City of David Archeological Garden

Returning southward, take the path and stairs descending to the City of David Archeological Garden. The gate at the entranceway marks the approximate northern boundary of the City of David. While the eastern and western sides of the city were protected by deep valleys, which converged and met in the area of the Shiloah, the northern side of the triangle was vulnerable to attack, and it was here that was probably located the tower or fortress that protected the city. A small depression separated this northern boundary from a slightly higher hill called the Ophel. This was also called the Millo, which comes from a Hebrew word meaning "to fill," hinting that the depression was filled in to form one continuous level with the City of David. This took place during the reign of David's son Solomon and became the site of his administrative offices. Solomon then extended the city's boundaries further north to include Mt. Moriah (which towered above the Ophel and the City of David), where he constructed the Temple. The city's plan in Solomon's time thus reflected Israel's relationship to God. In the lower city (the City of David) were the dwelling places of the common people. Above this, in the Ophel, were the royal offices. And towering above them all was the Temple in which dwelt the Divine Presence.

Numerous excavations have taken place in the City of David during this century and are still going on today. The present site, representing a small portion of the northern part of the city, has been opened by the Israeli government as an archeological garden. As with all endeavors of this sort, the Israelis do an exceptional job. The path through the garden is clear, signposted, and well explained. Portions of every layer of settlement have been preserved for viewing. This can be a little confusing, since some twenty layers have been uncovered. Keep in mind, however, that in the pre-Israelite period the walls of the city were located on the upper part of the hill while in the First Temple period they were on the lower slopes. When the walls were rebuilt after the return from the Babylonian exile in the sixth century B.C.

(and also in later periods), they were again built higher up. So when you see remains of houses built just outside walls it generally means that the building was from an earlier period when the city walls were further down, while the wall you see was from a subsequent period when they were again built higher up. One of the more significant finds is the House of Bullae, a central archive where over fifty clay seals were discovered. This confirms that from the period of David onward the royal administration was located in the northern or upper part of the city.

Warren's Shaft (Hebrew: Pir Warren)

At the southern end of the archeological garden is a path that leads down to Warren's Shaft, named after Charles Warren, who discovered it in 1867. One of the most important problems of any ancient city was its water supply. We have already mentioned that Jerusalem's location was largely determined by the spring called the Gihon, which once gushed forth just below at the base of the hill in the Valley of the Kidron. About halfway down the hill Warren discovered a shaft which was used for drawing water up from the Gihon. Both the shaft and the construction of the tunnel leading to it are very impressive. It was originally believed that the shaft was of Canaanite or Jebusite origin, but today it is known to have been built in the Israelite period, when it lay well within the city walls.

Hezekiah's Tunnel (Hebrew: Minharat Ḥizkiyahu)

Continue down past the remains of some of the Israelite defenses below the level of Warren's Shaft. At the bottom of the hill in the Kidron Valley you will come to a structure covering the source of the Gihon and one end of Hezekiah's Tunnel. By the reign of King Hezekiah in the eighth century B.C., the City of David had already spread across the Tyropoeon Valley to the western hill. Two circumstances at that time required a radical change in the city's water supply. The first was the necessity of making water more easily available to the newer parts of the city. The second, and even more pressing, stemmed from the current political and military situation. During Hezekiah's reign the Kingdom of Judah was faced with a serious attack from the Assyrian king Sennacherib. One problem was the safety of the city's water supply in the event of siege. The Gihon had always presented a problem. In other Israelite cities where a well inside the city was supplied from a spring lying outside it, the quantity of water the spring provided was generally quite small, perhaps no more than 175 cubic feet (5 cubic meters) a day. This relatively small quantity insured that the water supplied daily by the spring would be used up. The spring would thus never overflow and its location be made known to the enemy. This was not true of the Gihon, which gushed forth hundreds of cubic yards of water daily, and whose source could not be hidden or dammed up. In the early

Israelite period a channel had been cut along the base of the western slope, which allowed the excess waters to flow into Solomon's fields in the southern part of the city. But until the reign of Hezekiah the city's water supply was never in any real danger. Sennacherib's imminent attack presented the possibility that the water supply could be cut off. In order to solve both problems (a more readily available water supply for the western part of the city, and defense against an impending siege), Hezekiah built an underground tunnel that conducted the waters of the Gihon to the southeastern tip of the hill, to an artificial reservoir or pool called the Shiloah. Its construction was an engineering miracle. The work was begun by two teams, one beginning at the source of the Gihon and one at the Shiloah. It was cut through solid rock, and though it followed a zigzag course both teams met up and joined. Warren's Shaft was blocked off, the source of the Gihon covered up, and all its water flowed to the new artificial pool. It is still possible to walk through Hezekiah's Tunnel the short distance to the Shiloah, though you have to wade through water that at times comes up to your knees. (You will need a flashlight if you decide to take the plunge.)

The Gardens of Solomon
If you wish to keep your feet dry, continue along the road to the southern tip of the City of David. On the hill above, you will see excavations in progress. Eventually, on the right, you will see a tunnel about the size of a man cut into the rock with water flowing out of it. It flows onto the road and then into the fields to the left. This is not the Shiloah. Even with an artificial pool there was still often too much water. When the tunnel was built, an extension was constructed here to take the overflow, which was thus diverted out of the city and onto the fields. The Old Testament reminds us of the king's gardens that once existed here.

The Pool of the Shiloah
Walk around the southern tip of the city and up the hill to the right. A short way up the hill is the entrance to the Shiloah. Here the water of the Gihon left the tunnel to fill the pool. In Hebrew the pool is called Breichat HaShiloah, which probably means "Pool of the Conducted (Waters)." The name Shiloah was later corrupted to Siloam. In Arabic it is called Ain Silwan, "Spring of Consolation." It is said that anyone who is sad and drinks of its waters will be consoled because the spring derives its waters from the Garden of Eden. Indeed, its source, the Gihon, bears the name of one of the rivers mentioned in Genesis as flowing out of Eden. For Christians it is the site where Jesus cured the blind man (John 9:11). Return up the hill to the point of departure. The distance is not great, but the climb is rather steep.

The CITY OF DAVID ARCHEOLOGICAL GARDEN is open to the public daily except Saturday, 9 A.M.–5 P.M.; on Friday, closing time is 4 P.M.

THE SECOND TEMPLE PERIOD, 538 B.C.–70 A.D.

In 586 B.C. the Kingdom of Judah was overthrown and Solomon's Temple destroyed by the Babylonian Nebuchadnezzar. Only some fifty years later Babylon itself was conquered by the Persian Empire, and the Jews who had been taken into exile following the fall of Jerusalem were permitted to return to their homeland. The next six hundred years, from 538 B.C. to 70 A.D., comprised the Second Temple period. This period can be divided into three parts. The first was the

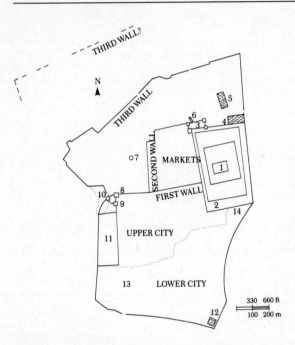

Fig. 2. *Jerusalem in the Second Temple Period, 538 B.C.–70 A.D.*

1. *The Temple*
2. *The Royal Stoa*
3. *The Antonia Fortress*
4. *Pool of Israel*
5. *The Sheep Pool (Bethesda)*
6. *The Struthion Pool*
7. *Golgotha (Calvary)*
8. *Tower of Hippicus*
9. *Tower of Mariamne*
10. *Tower of Phasael*
11. *Herod's Palace*
12. *Pool of the Shiloah*
13. *Palace of the High Priest*
14. *The Hulda Gates*
    (the main entranceway to the Temple Mount)

era of Persian rule, which began in 538 B.C. and ended in 332 B.C. with Alexander the Great's conquest of the east. It included: the Return to Zion movement led by "Sheshbazzar, prince of Judah," then by his nephew Zerubbabel, who followed him as "governor of Judah"; the rebuilding of the Temple, which was completed in 515 B.C.; and the reconstruction of the city and its wall under Ezra and Nehemiah in the mid-fifth century. It would seem that the Jerusalem of Nehemiah's day was greatly reduced in size, consisting—as it had in the days of Solomon—only of the City of David and the Temple Mount.

The second part comprised the period of Hellenistic rule under the successors of Alexander the Great (first by the Ptolemies of Egypt until 198 B.C., then by the Seleucids of Syria until 167 B.C.), and the first century of restored Jewish independence under a priestly family, the Hasmoneans. The relative religious freedom enjoyed by the Jews under the Persians and the Ptolemies came to an end with the Seleucid ruler Antiochus IV Epiphanes. It was this ruler's desecration of the Temple that finally sparked the successful rebellion led by the Hasmoneans (more popularly known as the Maccabees). The Temple was purified and rededicated (today commemorated by the festival of Hanukah), the Temple area was fortified, and a fortress called the Baris was constructed to the north of the Temple Mount. But it would seem that Jerusalem itself did not undergo any major changes, and retained the same geographical boundaries as before, that is, the City of David and the Temple Mount. It was in this period that the rock-cut monuments in the Kidron Valley were built.

It was in the following period, starting with the rule of the Hasmonean king Alexander Janneus (first century B.C.), that Jerusalem broke out of its narrow geographical confines and expanded westward across the Tyropoeon Valley to the western hill known today as Mt. Zion. The newly expanded city was surrounded by a fortification known as the First Wall, which followed the approximate lines of the wall that had existed in the days of the kings of Judah. One of the extraordinary things about Jerusalem is how faithfully it has maintained its geographical integrity throughout the ages, especially the lines of the walls and the thoroughfares within the city. The First Wall's northern border, for example, has always determined the city's main east-west route. Today this corresponds to David Street, which begins near the Jaffa Gate and runs eastward until it meets its eastern extension, the Street of the Chain, which in turn continues on to the Temple Mount. The marketplace with its numerous small shops that exist along today's route no doubt existed at all times, even during the period of the First Wall. The city's most spectacular expansion, however, took place in the Herodian period (37 B.C.–70 A.D.). It was in this period that the city's population began to spread northward, and was surrounded by a fortification known as the Second Wall. These were the two walls present at the time of Jesus's ministry. In approximately 44 A.D., King Agrippa built the city's Third Wall. Most identify it with the city's present-day northern wall. Remains of walls from the Herodian period, however, have also been found further north. On this ground, some claim that the city's northern boundary extended much further than it does today, though the prevailing view is that this was no more than a forward defense of the city's real Third Wall.

In Herod's time the internal face of the city also underwent enormous changes. Notwithstanding the low esteem in which Herod is held today by both Jew and Christian, he was a good soldier and an outstanding administrator, and had an enormous passion and talent for monumental building projects. Along the western wall of the city he built a huge royal palace, at the north end of which there was a fortress with three large towers called Phasael, Hippicus, and Mariamne. These towers were located near the site of today's Jaffa Gate, and some remains of the Hippicus are still visible. The fortress with its towers became a castle under the Byzantines, a fortress under the Muslims, David's Tower under the Crusaders, and the Citadel under the Turks. Today it is still called either David's Tower or the Citadel. Herod's most important work, however, was the repair and reconstruction of the Temple and the expansion of the Temple Mount. There was apparently nothing to compare with it in the classical world, and it was often written that he who had not seen Herod's Temple had never beheld true beauty. At the northwest corner of the Temple Mount, Herod replaced the Hasmonean Baris with a new fortress called the Antonia, named after his friend Mark Antony. Both the Antonia and the Citadel were built at the city's two weak points, where there were almost no natural defenses (deep escarpments).

Despite the external splendor of Herodian times, there were many who decried the moral and religious corruption of the age and predicted the downfall of Jerusalem and its Temple. In 6 A.D. Herod's son, Archelaus, was deposed and Judah became a Roman province. The subsequent decades of misrule and insensitivity to Jewish religious sensibilities finally sparked the rebellion against Rome known as the First Jewish War (66–70 A.D.). The capture of Jerusalem and the destruction of the Temple by Rome in 70 A.D. brought the rebellion to an end, and marked the end of Jewish control of the city for nearly two thousand years.

There can be no question that in terms of subsequent world history the single most significant event of this period was the birth and ministry of Jesus of Nazareth. The early Hellenistic Church constantly linked this event to the destruction of the Temple and the dispersion of the Jewish people. For them it was the end of the old and the beginning of the new. But Jesus's ministry was intended for Jews and depended upon a world view that had taken the Jewish people centuries to develop. All other religions of the ancient Near East were dualistic in nature. (Scholars today often claim that ancient religions were not really polytheistic or dualistic, and that the many gods of these religions were often merely attributes of the One God. While this may be so, it is also true that it was the dualistic nature of these religions which was emphasized, and most deeply burned into the mentality of their adherents.) Good and evil, light and darkness, were pitted against each other in constant warfare. The Jewish concept of the One God differed in that it contained within itself all these opposing elements. Today this idea seems commonplace, but initially it was a revolution. Once it had become part of the mentality of the Jews, it was possible to go on to the next stage. What was true on a larger, macrocosmic scale was also true for the microcosm, man. This was the teaching Jesus brought: to show "the Way" to the reconciling God within that could englobe the dualistic elements of each man's own nature. After Jesus's death, when the teaching passed to the Hellenistic world, it quickly fell to the level of that world, where spiritual awareness had not developed beyond dualistic concepts. And it was the Hellenistic Church, in its various forms, which was eventually to spread throughout the world.

This was the milieu that saw the birth of the Christian Church, though the earliest followers of Jesus of Nazareth could hardly be called Christians. Like Jesus and the Apostles, they were observant Jews who adhered to Mosaic law and did not at all consider Jesus's ministry to be the herald of a new religion. Today they are called by scholars Judeo-Christians to differentiate them from their Hellenistic counterparts who did consider Christianity to be a new religion and who converted to it from paganism without first passing through the fold of Judaism. The rivalry between these two groups was settled only some three hundred years later (in favor of the latter) with the conversion of the emperor Constantine to the Hellenistic Church, or, as it has come to be known, the Church of the Gentiles.

A valuable impression of HEROD'S JERUSALEM can be gained from the extensive and, for the most part, accurate scale model of the ancient city, on the grounds of the Holyland Hotel at 1 Bayit VeGan. Open daily.

THE ROMAN PERIOD, 70–330 A.D.

Following Rome's victory in 70 A.D., a major part of Jerusalem's population consisted of a garrison force of Rome's Tenth Legion. In addition to these, Rome sent some eight hundred retired soldiers to Jerusalem to help repopulate the city. The Roman force was garrisoned in the western part of the city, in the area today known as the Armenian Gardens, and in the three towers, Phasael, Hippicus, and Mariamne, which were apparently not destroyed during the siege of the city. The city itself lay in ruins. The Christian community, which had fled Jerusalem during the siege, returned and settled round the camp of the Roman legion. Little is known of the Jewish population of Jerusalem following the war. Seven synagogues on Mt. Zion were reported to have survived the destruction of the city, one of which still existed in the time of the emperor Constantine in the fourth century, but whether these were Jewish or Judeo-Christian houses of worship is difficult to say.

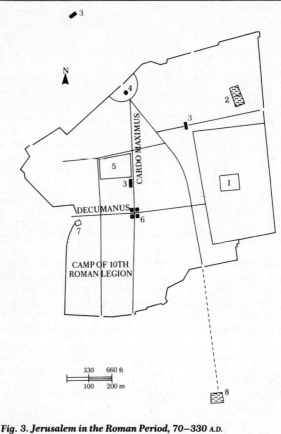

Fig. 3. Jerusalem in the Roman Period, 70–330 A.D.
1. *Temple of Jupiter*
2. *Healing pools*
3. *Triumphal gates*
4. *Column*
5. *Temple of Venus*
6. *Tetrapylon*
7. *Headquarters of the Roman Legion*
8. *Pool of the Shiloah*

In the year 130 A.D., the emperor Hadrian visited Jerusalem and decided to build a provincial Roman colony on the ruins of the city. It was to be called Aelia Capitolina—"Aelia" in honor of the emperor himself, whose full name was Publius Aelius Hadrianus; "Capitolina" after the Capitoline triad, Jupiter, Juno, and Minerva, who were to be the patrons of the new city (the triad was worshipped on the Capitoline Hill in Rome). The founding of the new colony and the proposed building of a pagan temple on the Temple Mount sparked the outbreak of the Second Jewish War, also known as the

Bar-Kochba rebellion. The insurgents managed to capture the city in 132 A.D. and held it for three years. But in 135 the rebellion was crushed, and Hadrian decreed that thenceforth no circumcised person was to be allowed entry into Jerusalem on pain of death. The main effect of this edict was to change for all time the balance of power between the Judeo-Christians (the Church of the Circumcision) and the Hellenistic Christians (the Church of the Gentiles), and there ensued the election of the city's first Christian bishop not of Jewish origin.

Hadrian's city was laid out more or less along the lines of a square-shaped Roman camp. The eastern, northern, and western walls followed the same line as they had in the Herodian period, while a new wall was added in the south, excluding the City of David and Mt. Zion. This is the shape the city still retains today. Inside the city there were two main colonnaded roads, which bisected each other and divided the city into four parts, reflecting today's Jewish, Armenian, Christian, and Muslim quarters. The main north-south road was called the Cardo Maximus. It began at the Damascus Gate, ran south joining the route once taken by the "second wall," then continued south to the Zion Gate. A second north-south road also began at the Damascus Gate, ran southward along the Tyropoeon Valley, and exited through the Dung Gate. The main east-west road was called the Decumanus. This followed the route of the old First Wall. These three roads exist today and are still the city's main thoroughfares. The Cardo Maximus runs along the Suq Khan es-Zeit, crosses David Street, and continues southward along the excavated and reconstructed section of the Cardo. The Decumanus runs along David Street and its eastern extension, the Street of the Chain (Hebrew, Rehov HaShalshelet). The second (eastern) north-south route is today's Valley Street (Hebrew, Rehov HaGai; Arabic, el Wad).

There is one other feature of Hadrian's city that has an important bearing on understanding today's Jerusalem. This was the construction called the "triumphal gate." Four such are known to have been built here—gateways of a special type, consisting of one large central arch and two lower flanking ones. A triumphal gate might be built to commemorate the founding of a city and to mark the limit of its jurisdiction, in which case it would be a good distance from the city's wall. It might also serve as entranceway to the city's forum or marketplace, or simply as the city's main gate. Remains of one triumphal gate have been found to the north of the Damascus Gate, and this was almost certainly the one commemorating the founding of Aelia Capitolina. Remains of a second can be seen today below the entranceway to the Damascus Gate. You will also find here a reconstruction of the Roman guardroom, and large flagstones marking the beginning of the Cardo Maximus. Remains of a third triumphal gate can be seen on the Via Dolorosa. This is the structure known as the Ecce Homo Arch, where it was believed that Pontius Pilate presented Jesus to the people with the words "*Ecce Homo*," "Behold the man." Today it is known that it was built some hundred years after the death of Jesus and was the entranceway to a Roman market built on the site. Remains of a fourth triumphal gate can be seen in the basement of the Russian Hospice and Alexander Church. This was the gate that stood at the entranceway to the Roman Forum in the area known as the Muristan. "Muristan" is a Persian word meaning "hospital." In the Crusader period, this was the site of the headquarters of the Knights Hospitalers, who maintained hospices and hospitals there for Christian pilgrims.

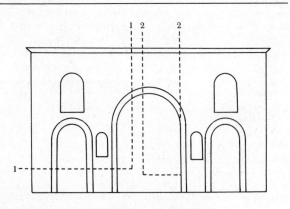

Fig. 4. Triumphal Gate of the second century A.D.
Section 1. Section of arch in the Ecce Homo Basilica.
Section 2. The Ecce Homo Arch, on the present-day Via Dolorosa.

Alongside the Muristan, and just to the west of the Cardo, Hadrian constructed a temple dedicated to Venus. Some claim that he purposely chose this location because it was known to be the site of Jesus's crucifixion, burial, and resurrection, and the emperor wished to discourage Christian worship there. It cannot be ignored, however, that the Middle Eastern equivalent of Venus was the goddess Astarte, who entered the underworld to bring the dead god Tammuz back to the world of the living. Thus, for the Romans, too, this was a sacred site intimately connected with the mysteries of resurrection. A second temple, one dedicated to Jupiter, was constructed on the Temple Mount, again reflecting the Romans' appreciation of the site's sacred nature.

THE BYZANTINE PERIOD, 330–638 A.D.

Byzantine Jerusalem followed the outline and internal structure of the Roman city that had preceded it. The vast changes that Jerusalem underwent during this period were not the result of political or military upheavals, but of events of a completely different nature.

In 312 A.D., Constantine became emperor of the Western Roman Empire by defeating Maxentius, his last serious rival for the throne. Legend holds that before the battle the emperor-to-be looked into the sky and saw a cross of light with the words "In this sign conquer." Constantine converted to Christianity and one year later, in 313, issued the Edict of Milan, granting religious freedom to the Christians of his domain. In 324, Constantine defeated Licinius, emperor of the East, and became sole ruler of the Roman Empire. The Edict of Milan now embraced all Christianity.

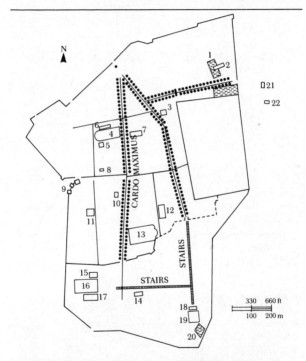

Fig. 5. *Jerusalem in the Byzantine Period, 330–638* A.D.

1. *Pool of Bethesda*
2. *Byzantine basilica, Mary Where She Was Born*
3. *Church of Our Lady of the Spasm*
4. *Church of the Holy Sepulchre*
5. *Baptistry*
6. *Patriarch's palace*
7. *Church of SS. Cosmas and Damian*
8. *Church of St. John the Baptist*
9. *David's Tower (the Citadel)*
10. *Syrian convent*
11. *Church of St. James*
12. *Church of St. Sophia*
13. *The Nea Church*
14. *St. Peter*
15. *Church of SS. Kyros and Johannes*
16. *Basilica of Hagia Sion*
17. *St. Stephen's Church*
18. *Eudocia's Church*
19. *Tetranympheum*
20. *Old pool*
21. *Tomb of the Virgin*
22. *Gethsemane*

Following the defeat of Licinius, Constantine moved the capital of the Roman Empire from Italy eastward to the shores of the Bosphorus. On the site of the Greek city of Byzantium he built a new capital named in his honor, Constantinople. While Christianity did not become the sole recognized religion of the Empire during Constantine's lifetime (this occurred in the reign of Theodosius, fifty years after Constantine's death), the intentions of the emperor were clear. In the new capital, inaugurated in 330 A.D., the performance of pagan rites was prohibited. Christianity was not to be simply a tolerated or even highly favored religion for long. The change brought by Constantine was felt almost immediately in Jerusalem, where the newly bestowed political and financial backing of the imperial family expressed itself in an upsurge of Christian building activity. Eventually this activity expanded beyond the city's Roman wall, especially in the south and the Mt. Zion area, around which a new wall was added that followed the one which had existed in the Second Temple period.

At some point it is important to explore the four main roads that have existed since Roman and Byzantine times and are still, to this day, the city's principal arteries. Three of these have already been mentioned (the Cardo Maximus, the Decumanus, and the Tyropoeon Valley road). A fourth road also existed in Roman times. It began in the area of today's Lions' Gate and ran westward to join up with the city's two main north-south roads. This is the route known today as the Via Dolorosa, which passed through the city's eastern marketplace, built by Hadrian. Once these four routes have been mastered and the relation between them understood, it becomes possible to walk anywhere within the Old City, and even venture into its maze of secondary roads and side streets without getting lost. This knowledge will also prove

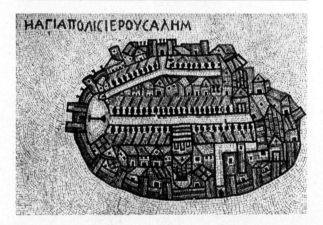

The sixth century Madaba Map of Jerusalem.

invaluable when you visit many of the city's churches. The validity or nonvalidity of the association of certain sites with particular events in the life of Jesus, or with ancient pilgrimage routes established in Byzantine times, is dependent upon this understanding and gives the visitor a basis for discriminating among the often contradictory theories and claims that are made here.

One important source concerning the city's internal layout, and the location of its most important Christian monuments during the Byzantine period, is the sixth-century mosaic map that was found in a church in the town of Madaba in Jordan and is known today as the Madaba Map. At the extreme left of the map is the city's northern gate. You can see that just inside the gate there was a circular plaza which contained a column on which the statue of Hadrian once stood. Today the northern (Damascus) gate is still called, in Arabic, Bab al-Amud, the Gate of the Pillar. Running north-south in the center of the map (here seen as right-left) is the Cardo, with columns flanking it on either side. (Above this is the colonnaded road that ran along the Tyropoeon Valley.)

Halfway down the Cardo, and leading directly from it, is one particularly large structure. This is the Church of the Holy Sepulchre, built by the emperor Constantine and dedicated in 335 A.D. If you walk southward from the Damascus Gate along the Suq you will find, on your right, the staircase that leads up to the ninth station on the Way of the Cross. This is approximately the point indicated on the map where the Cardo met the entranceway to the Church of the Holy Sepulchre. Today's church is not as large as the one built by Constantine and does not extend as far as the road, but the

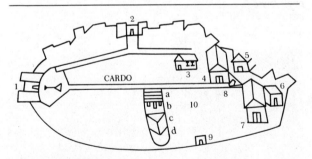

Fig. 6.   The Madaba Map.
Some important sites of Byzantine Jerusalem.

1. Northern Gate	*8. Southern gate*
2. Eastern gate	*9. Western gate*
3. Church of St. Sophia (the Praetorium)	*10. Church of the Holy Sepulchre*
4. The Nea Church	*(a) stairs*
5. St. Peter (house of Caiaphas)	*(b) entranceway*
6. Cenacle	*(c) basilica*
7. Hagia Sion	*(d) rotunda*

structure depicted in the mosaic is known to have been
the one that existed in Byzantine times. Here, furthest from
the road, we see a rotunda, followed by a rectangular building, the basilica. Following this were the three doors which
led into the complex, and then the stairs that led down to the
Cardo.

The Church of the Holy Sepulchre especially illustrates
the importance of possessing a thorough knowledge of the
city's history, ancient traditions, and geographical layout.
The freeing of the Jerusalem Church from its political con-
straints resulted in a flowering of new churches, new traditions, and sweeping changes in the liturgy and religious
practices. These changes were never made in a vacuum.
Almost always they were based on knowledge still available
at the time, and which the newly flowering Hellenistic
Church in Jerusalem made use of, but whose sources
(Judeo-Christian) they preferred to forget. It is this period,
then, that is vital in helping us to uncover what has been
lost, and to reach a new appreciation of Jerusalem's sacred
sites and their origins.

The amazing story of the Church of the Holy Sepulchre is
indicative of the period as a whole. In 325 A.D., five years
before Constantine inaugurated his new capital, Constantinople, he convened at Nicea, a town to the southeast of the
site of Byzantium, the first Ecumenical or General Council
of the Church. The council's lesser aim was to deal with the
physical organization of the Church, and to establish the
great sees and patriarchates. Its major aim was to establish
in this new "Christian Empire" a single orthodox faith.

For many of the Church Fathers present at this first Ecumenical Council, the greatest danger to a single unified
faith lay in the views of a priest from Alexandria named
Arius, who maintained that in the Holy Trinity the Son was
inferior to the Father. Arius had sought to preserve the transcendence and uniqueness of God by drawing a line between
the Creator and His creation. Jesus, he claimed, was a part
of creation—a superior creation, to be sure, but a creation
nevertheless. His opponents argued that man's salvation depended upon his union with God, and that only God could
open this way for man. Jesus, by his sacrifice, had cleansed
man of his original sin, but man's long sojourn in the realm
of darkness had so weakened him that he was incapable of
returning to the light unaided. The bridge between God and
man was the incarnate Christ, who, though begotten, was
one in essence with the Father.

The Council of Nicea declared Arianism a heresy. But by
singling out Arianism for special attention and condemnation, the council effectively obscured the very real differences that existed among Christian communities in the early
fourth century. For three hundred years, Christianity had
been a persecuted religion, establishing itself where it could.
Spread over the vastness of the Roman Empire, its communities were to a large measure independent and often

guarded traditions and beliefs which were part of their individual organic growth and development. Most significant, however, was that many of the most basic beliefs held by these communities came from two different and increasingly incompatible sources: the Christian Church of the Jews, and the Christian Church of the Gentiles.

The Christian Church of the Jews found its direct source in the Mother Church of Jerusalem. Its members, like the apostles before them, were Jews who adhered to Mosaic law. By the time of the Council of Nicea the Judeo-Christian Church was no longer a single entity. During the three hundred years of its history it had founded numerous independent communities and directly or indirectly influenced many others. Many of the most basic beliefs of these communities, whose sources lay in the first days of Christianity, differed radically from those of Gentile Christians, who had originally converted from paganism, did not observe Mosaic law, and were the heirs of a very different culture and religious mentality. It was these Judeo-Christian beliefs, especially those concerning the nature of Jesus, that found their way into the ideas of Arius, and that the Council of Nicea sought so desperately to suppress.

Among the delegates to the first Ecumenical Council was Macarius, bishop of Jerusalem. Macarius was not a Judeo-Christian, nor was the Church of the Jews invited to be represented at the council. But Macarius brought with him to Nicea something belonging to the Judeo-Christians even more significant than their theological beliefs. He brought their tradition concerning the exact location of the tomb of Jesus.

This tradition did not exist in isolation but arose out of a more general Judeo-Christian belief concerning the sacredness of certain caves and grottoes. These were called "mystic," "lucid," or "well-lighted" grottoes. "Well-lighted" meant not a natural or even artificial light but a place illumined by the Divine Presence. The concept had its beginning in Bethlehem, at the Grotto of the Nativity. The apocryphal Gospel of St. James describes the presence of a great light at the birth of Jesus—the divine light that came into the world to illuminate the darkness.

Mystic grottoes were not limited to the birthplace of Jesus. Other places sanctified by the presence of God also became "well-lighted" grottoes. Three were held to be especially sacred: the Grotto of the Nativity in Bethlehem, the grotto on the Mount of Olives where Jesus prayed and revealed the mysteries of the world to his disciples, and the grotto that served as his tomb.

The first ten bishops of Jerusalem had all been Judeo-Christians. In the middle of the second century, leadership of the Church of Jerusalem passed into the hands of the Hellenistic Christians, that is, to those of Gentile origin. Mutual hostility between the two groups, especially regarding the practice of Mosaic law, made their integration impossible. Well before the Council of Nicea the Judeo-Christians of Jerusalem had formed an independent community, jealously guarding their own traditions and beliefs. One of these traditions concerned the performance of religious devotions at the sites of "well-lighted" grottoes to commemorate the mysteries that had originally taken place there.

Even before the time of Constantine, the Fathers of the Hellenistic Church were bitterly opposed to these practices and in their writings accused the Judeo-Christians of carrying out in these grottoes secret rites which were unacceptable to the Church. It was thus through the Church's long and bitter opposition to these practices and its inability to stop them that Macarius knew the location of these sacred places so well. It is clear that Macarius was absolutely convinced of the authenticity of these sites, and successfully communicated this conviction to the emperor at Nicea.

Macarius's information concerning the tomb of Jesus must have been very convincing indeed for him to have insisted on a location that was surely as problematic in his own time as it has been throughout the ensuing ages. Jewish law prohibits burial within the walls of Jerusalem. The Gospels state quite clearly that the place of the Crucifixion and the tomb of Jesus lay outside the city walls. Visitors and pilgrims to the Church of the Holy Sepulchre have always been disturbed to find it in the heart of the city. It is only today that we know with reasonable certainty that at the time of the Crucifixion the site of the present church did lie outside the city walls. But only just outside. It is important to realize that for nearly all of its sixteen-hundred-year history the authenticity of the church's location was upheld by tradition alone.

The Madaba Map confirms that the Church of the Holy Sepulchre lay just to the west of the Cardo, and modern archeological research has now established that the Cardo was built along the line once occupied by the Second Wall. When we see how close Calvary and the tomb were to this Second Wall, and understand that even when the church was built the identity of this wall with the Cardo was unknown, we can appreciate how controversial the site has always been. A difference of only a hundred yards would have put it within the city walls at the time of Jesus, invalidating the site. We can thus see how very accurate and reliable the ancient Judeo-Christian traditions were. And it was these very traditions, and their sources, that the Hellenistic Church was so determined to suppress at Nicea, and eventually did so.

If you continue southward along the Suq, you will eventually come to the point where it crosses David Street. This is where the Cardo met the Decumanus. The latter still existed in the Byzantine period, though it is not shown in the Madaba Map. There are two reasons for this: First, the map is primarily a plan of Christian holy sites that lay in proximity to the city's main routes; since no such sites lay along the

Decumanus, it was not included. Secondly, the Decumanus was the main road leading from the west to the Temple Mount. In Roman times, when a temple to Jupiter existed on the Mount, the road was still an important artery. The Byzantines, however, chose not to emphasize this route which led to the place they believed had been abandoned by God, and whose ruins provided living proof of Jesus's prophecy concerning the destruction of the Temple.

Crossing over David Street, you can see before you the entranceway to a reconstructed section of the Byzantine Cardo. One of the more interesting side tours of Jerusalem is the one of the Jewish Quarter that begins here. A specially marked route with thirty-six sites of historical and archeological interest has been set up by the Ministry of Housing and the Company for the Reconstruction and Development of the Jewish Quarter in the Old City of Jerusalem Ltd. They have also put out a small booklet called *Quartertour* which has good maps, gives a short history of the quarter and a description of the sites of interest, and shows how to get from one to the next.

The Reconstructed Byzantine Cardo

There is no evidence that the section of the Cardo running from David Street southward existed before the sixth century. Its construction seems to have been related to a number of important churches that lay along its route in the Mt. Zion area. Especially important was the Nea Church, also built in the sixth century. The discovery of the latter during the excavations of the Jewish Quarter was significant for defining Christianity's early pilgrimage routes. The Nea is known to have lain close by the Church of St. Sophia, which commemorated the site where Jesus was judged by Pilate and from which he set out on his way to Calvary. So we know that the route used by the Byzantines to commemorate the Passion of Jesus was the one that ran from St. Sophia, along the Cardo, to the Church of the Holy Sepulchre. (Remains of the Nea Church can be seen on the tour of the Jewish Quarter.) In 614 the Persians captured Jerusalem and destroyed many of its churches, including the Nea and the Church of St. Sophia. Fourteen years later the city was retaken by the Byzantines, only to fall to the Muslims in 638. Under Muslim rule shops began to be built alongside the route, and in time it became a bazaar similar to the present one. The Crusaders preserved the bazaar, and there is evidence that it was still active in the sixteenth century, though by the eighteenth century it had disappeared from the city's maps, and was forgotten.

As you enter the Cardo, to your right you can see excavated remains of the First Wall. Two glass-covered observation pits permit you to look down to the base of the walls where the level of the city originally stood. This part of the Cardo is a reconstruction of the Crusaders' bazaar. Further on, a second section re-creates the Cardo as it must have

appeared in Byzantine times. A further section of the Byzantine Cardo has been rebuilt in the open. Another 656 feet
(200 meters) of Cardo lies buried under the present city
streets, and culminates at an ancient gate some 394 feet
(120 meters) east of today's Zion Gate.

Synagogues

If you are already in the Jewish Quarter, and have decided
not to take the tour mentioned above, do take the time to visit
at least two of the quarter's nearby, and better-known, synagogues, the Ramban and the Sephardic. Despite the Talmud's many rules and prescriptions concerning synagogues,
in practice a Jewish place of worship can be almost anywhere that ten men meet together to pray. Thus, synagogues
are not innately sacred places. Sometimes a congregation

*Fig. 7. The Land of Israel opposite the holy opening,
according to Rabbi Abraham Azulai, 1685.*

can form around a holy site such as the Western Wall or the
tomb of a saint, but these are exceptions.

Jewish traditions, however, do give special significance to
prayers offered in Jerusalem. One modern Talmudic scholar
has tried to explain this by using an analogy with geological
formations. Just as a fault can exist in the geological strata,
so too in Jerusalem (on the Temple Mount) there is a kind of
break in reality through which the divine flows into the
world. This idea is not a new one to Judaism. In the seventeenth century the Kabbalist rabbi Abraham Azulai described the various spheres or worlds that surround the
earth, separating it from the divine. He maintained that God
caused a gap to "pierce" these spheres so that His holiness
might pass through them. It was this gap, he claimed, which

hovered over the Hebrew tribes in their wanderings, and finally settled with them in the land of Israel, Jerusalem, and the Temple itself.

This idea of a gap which permits the divine to penetrate the world of the profane is one of the cornerstones of the many works of Mircea Eliade, especially his *The Sacred and the Profane*. Eliade calls the ordinary space that surrounds us everywhere, profane space. Its chief characteristics are its continuousness and homogeneity, which is Eliade's way of saying that all its parts belong to one level of reality. The sacred appears when there is a break in this undifferentiated vastness, and another level of reality becomes manifest. The resulting space is noncontinuous and nonhomogeneous. Instead of the relativity of all points that make up profane space, there now appears in its midst the absolute reality of the sacred, that is, a unique, fixed point to which all others can become oriented. This is often expressed in ancient creation myths where a mound or hillock suddenly rises out of the primordial waters (which represent continuous non-differentiated sameness, or chaos), and becomes the center from which the world of form and order is created. For Eliade, as for others, this point lies along a line which emanates from the heavenly world above, penetrates our own, and descends into the netherworld below. This is the *axis mundi*, or world axis, which joins the three normally separated cosmic levels of the universe, heaven, earth, and hell, and makes communication between them possible. The temple that invariably lies at the center of this area of absolute reality is the place on earth where the influence of the divine can radiate into the world, and which for man acts as a window or gateway to the world above.

The Mishnah (the first section of the Talmud, comprising oral interpretations of the Scriptures) states that as the influence of the divine penetrated and flowed into the world, sacred places were established. At the very center was the Holy of Holies in the Temple. Then, radiating out from this, in ever diminishing holiness, were the Sanctuary, the area between the Porch and the Altar, the Court of the Priests, the Court of the Israelites, the Court of the Women, the ramparts surrounding the inner courts of the Temple, the area within the walls of Jerusalem, other walled cities of Israel, and finally, the land of Israel itself. Today the Temple no longer exists, and the closest a man can approach to these inner spheres of holiness is the walls of the Temple Mount and the synagogues within the walls of Jerusalem. Here, it is believed, prayers are most effective because they rise directly through the window that opens onto the world above. According to Jewish tradition, God also prays, and it is in Jerusalem that his prayers fall directly onto the world below.

The Ramban Synagogue is of historical importance in that its founding can be said to mark the beginning of the Jewish Quarter. In 1267 the famous physician and head of the

Spanish rabbinate Rabbi Moshe ben Nachman or Nachma-nides, known (from the initials of his name) as the Ramban, emigrated from Spain to Jerusalem. This apparently had less to do with idealism than with the fact that he was fleeing for his life following a victory in a debate with rep-resentatives of the Catholic Church in the presence of King James I of Aragon. (The king is said to have remarked, "I have never seen a man defend with so much ability some-thing which is so wrong.") Once in Jerusalem, the Ramban aided the return of Jews to the city and built a synagogue, said to have been located on Mt. Zion, and around which the new community became established. Around the year 1400 the fear of Bedouin attacks prompted the Jewish com-munity to relocate itself within the city walls. Again it es-tablished itself around its new synagogue, which at some point began to be called by the name of the community's founder, the Ramban. The adjacent minaret is also a part of the synagogue's history. The property originally belonged to a Jew who, because of a disagreement with the Jewish community, converted to Islam and dedicated the site to the building of a mosque. The proximity of the two struc-tures led to numerous clashes between the two communi-ties, and the synagogue's subsequent history was a stormy one until it was finally closed by the Muslims in 1588. It was reopened only after the liberation of the Jewish Quarter by Israeli forces in 1967.

The RAMBAN SYNAGOGUE *(Hebrew: Beit HaKnesset HaRamban)* is open Sunday to Friday, 8 A.M.–4 P.M., and on Saturday for Sabbath services.

The Sephardic Synagogue Prior to the mid-nineteenth cen-tury and the liberalization of religious policies toward Jews and Christians, there were no really impressive synagogues in the Jewish Quarter. The laws promulgated by Omar fol-lowing the Muslim capture of the city in 638 forbade the building of any new non-Muslim places of worship (though existing ones could be repaired). Since all the synagogues within the city walls had long since been destroyed by the Byzantines, it effectively left the Jews in the same position they had been in before the conquest. Muslim policies to-ward Jews, however, were far more flexible than those of the Byzantines, and sites of Jewish worship were established at a number of places, such as the walls and gates of the Temple Mount. As noted above, around the year 1400 the Jews were permitted to build a central synagogue, which in time came to be associated with the Ramban, and which served Jews of all national origins. The closing of the Ramban Synagogue in 1588 signaled the end of a united Jewish worship and the establishment of synagogues that served individual congregations of particular origins and traditions—an arrangement which in large measure still pre-vails today. Near the end of the sixteenth century, the Se-phardim, or Jews of Spanish origin (who were the leading

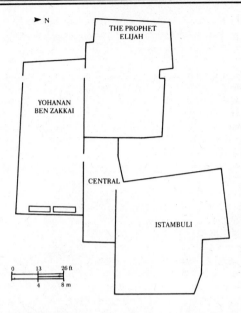

Fig. 8. The Sephardic Synagogues.
An unusual feature of the Rabban Yohanan Ben Zakkai Synagogue
is the double Holy Ark.

Jewish community of the time), built their own synagogue.
This was the Holy Congregation of Talmud Torah (a Talmud
Torah is an institute for religious studies). When the Talmud
Torah itself was transferred to a new location in the mid-
nineteenth century, the synagogue became known by its
present name, *The Prophet Elijah Synagogue.* According to
a legend, the Jewish community at one time consisted of
only nine men, and on the eve of Yom Kippur, the Day of
Atonement, the holiest day of the Jewish year, there was no
tenth man to complete the *minyan,* the quorum of ten men
required for public prayer. Suddenly an old man appeared at
the synagogue, and prayer began. At the end of the Day of
Atonement each of the nine turned to the old man to invite
him to supper, but he had disappeared. They then understood that it had been the prophet Elijah who had come to
complete their *minyan.* Note that the Prophet Elijah Synagogue, as well as the others making up the present Sephardic Synagogue, is built below ground level. The Talmud
states that synagogues must be built on the highest part of
the city, or at least exceed all other structures in height. But
Muslim law forbade them to be built above the level
of ordinary (Muslim) houses. In time their position below
ground level gave rise to the belief that this had been inten-
tional and was meant to recall the verse in Psalms, "Out of
the depths have I cried unto thee, O Lord" (Psalms 130:1).
Around 1615 a second Sephardic synagogue was estab-

lished here. This was the **Rabban Yohanan Ben Zakkai Synagogue**, originally known as the Great Holy Congregation. Rabban Yohanan Ben Zakkai was the last of the great sages to teach in Jerusalem before the destruction of the Temple, and it was believed that the present synagogue stood on the site of his academy. It was claimed that the synagogue once contained a jug of oil and a shofar (ram's horn) saved from the Temple. It was believed that just before the coming of the Messiah the prophet Elijah would use the oil to light the eternal flame and then blow the shofar to signal Israel's redemption. The present synagogue was rebuilt according to what is known of its original plan.

The Central Synagogue was originally a courtyard which served as the women's section of the Yohanan Ben Zakkai Synagogue. It was built as a separate place of worship in the mid-eighteenth century and called the Assembly of Zion.

The Istambuli Synagogue was the last of the four to be constructed (1764). Its name probably denotes that it was built by Jews who immigrated from Turkey, and over the years it has also served a number of non-Sephardic communities. In the mid-nineteenth century the four synagogues were rebuilt as the single complex we see today, and restored again after the Six Day War.

Shimon Ben-Eliezer's *Destruction and Renewal: The Synagogues of the Jewish Quarter*, a booklet published in Israel and available in most Jerusalem bookshops, provides additional information for those interested.

The SEPHARDIC SYNAGOGUE *(Hebrew: Beit HaKnesset HaSephardi)* is open Sunday to Thursday, 9 A.M.–3 P.M.; Friday, 9 A.M.–1 P.M.; and on Saturday for Sabbath services.

THE FIRST MUSLIM PERIOD, 638–1099

The mission of the prophet Muhammad and the rise of Islam in the late sixth to early seventh century cannot be explained in any normal, rational way. The spectacular spread of the new religion beyond the borders of Arabia at the expense of the older, larger, and more powerful world powers of the day (the Byzantine and Persian empires), within decades of the prophet's death, is a phenomenon unique in world history.

The conquest of Jerusalem by the forces of the caliph Omar Ibn al-Khattab took place in 638 and initiated a 450-year period of Muslim rule over the city. This first Muslim period came to an end with the establishment of the Latin Kingdom of Jerusalem by the Crusaders in 1099. In some respects the Muslim city differed little from the Byzantine one which had preceded it. Its walls followed exactly the same course. Its internal layout was the same. Many of its Christian inhabitants left the city and were replaced by Muslims of varied origins. But the Christian holy places were left untouched, and the city's religious life and daily life in general went on much as it had before.

Yet despite this seeming continuity, changes of a different order were initiated whose consequences were far greater than any of a purely physical nature. These were changes regarding the Temple Mount, which had been abandoned by the Christians and whose ruins had contrasted sharply with

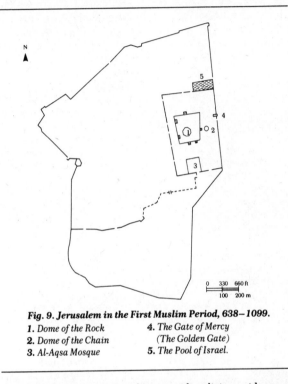

Fig. 9. Jerusalem in the First Muslim Period, 638–1099.
1. *Dome of the Rock*
2. *Dome of the Chain*
3. *Al-Aqsa Mosque*
4. *The Gate of Mercy*
   (The Golden Gate)
5. *The Pool of Israel.*

the city's magnificent churches, providing living evidence of God's abandonment of the old covenant and his establishment of the new. Christians of the time believed that God's abandonment of the old Israel had been a final one and that the Temple Mount would never be rebuilt. It made little difference to them that the Jews believed otherwise, and that for them the exile of the Chosen People and of the Divine Presence from Jerusalem were linked together in a mystically oriented eschatological history that would find its fulfillment in the redemption that would be initiated by the coming of the Messiah at the end of time. For Christians these Jewish hopes were a fairy tale, the visual proof of which could be seen in the abandoned Temple Mount. The Muslim conquest now threatened to change all this.

Muslims consider Jerusalem their third holiest city, ranking in sacredness only after Mecca and Medina. This is not a late political invention but goes back to the very foundation of Islam, and is reflected in a number of the city's names. Bayt al-Muqqadas or Bayt al-Maqdis is the Arabic form of the Hebrew name for the Temple (Beit HaMikdash), and was well known in Medina even before the rise of Islam. In the earliest days of the new religion it was the name used for both Solomon's Temple and the city itself. In time this ambiguity was resolved by calling the city Bayt al-Muqqadas and the Temple simply al-Bayt (the House). Later the city was also called al-Kuds (like the Hebrew HaKodesh, which means "the Holy"), or al-Kuds al-Sharifa, the Holy and Noble. In the first century of Islam it was regarded as one of the most sacred places in the world. It was believed to have been the first place blessed by God, and was the site of numerous divine revelations made to his prophets. It was the source of all sweet water springs and winds, and was associated with the gathering together of mankind and the final judgment at the end of the world. But, most important, it was the site of Solomon's Temple, which itself was the doorway that opened onto paradise and celestial Jerusalem. The most powerful and lasting expression of the latter was Muhammad's Night Journey to Jerusalem and his ascension from the Temple Mount to the throne of Allah. (*See* page 58.) These beliefs found expression in monumental building projects in the area of the Temple Mount, an activity which contrasted sharply with those of the preceding Christian period, and which reflected the vast differences in the theological outlooks of the two religions. It was clear from the very beginning, however, that the Muslim emphasis on the Temple Mount was not a mere return to Judaism or a repetition of Jewish thought. While Jews were again permitted to live in the city and establish places of worship at its holy sites, especially in the area of the Temple Mount, Muslim activity in the city was the product of a new, and for Muslims a final, revelation.

The four and a half centuries comprising this early Muslim period were far from uniform. Its flowering took place in its early years under the Umayyad dynasty, which ruled from Syria (661–750). This was the period that saw the reconstruction of the Temple Mount, and the building of the Dome of the Rock, the al-Aqsa Mosque, and the Gate of Mercy. Modern archeological excavations have also brought to light a royal complex surrounding the southern wall and southwest corner of the Temple Mount. Muslim concentration in this part of the city was also reflected in its occupation of today's nearby Jewish Quarter, which as a result was closed to Christian worship. The area included the sites that had been occupied by the Nea Church and the nearby Church of St. Sophia. The latter was especially important as the site of the Praetorium, from which for centuries the Easter processional had set out on its march to Calvary (northward along the Cardo Maximus). Muslim occupation of the area forced Christians to "relocate" the Praetorium on Mt. Zion, and to establish a new route for the Good Friday procession that cut across today's Armenian Quarter to present-day Christian Street and on to the Church of the Holy Sepulchre.

The House of Umayyad was succeeded by the Abbasid dynasty (750–969), which ruled from Baghdad in Iraq. This was also a flourishing period, but nothing like the one that had preceded it. Overall, the Abbasids in Jerusalem seem to have been more intent on discrediting the Umayyads than in making any real contribution of their own. In 969 Jerusalem fell under the Fatimid rulers of Egypt, and the city entered a period of neglect and decline which culminated with the reign of the mad caliph al-Hakim, who ordered the destruction of churches and synagogues throughout his empire. In 1071 Jerusalem came under the control of the Seljuk Turks, whose pillage of the city and terrible persecution of its Christians spurred the First Crusade.

This early Muslim period also saw the first division of the city into residential zones according to religious affiliation, the forerunners of today's Jewish, Armenian, Christian, and Muslim quarters. This division was not imposed on the city's inhabitants but apparently came about as a result of the desire of each religious group to live together in one general area. The Christians, Muslims, and Armenians even then occupied approximately the same quarters they do today. The Jews lived mainly in the area of the Dung Gate, though they apparently also occupied the northern portion of today's Muslim Quarter, which also came to be known as the Jewish Quarter.

THE CRUSADER PERIOD, 1099–1187

The southern wall of the city, the one that had surrounded the City of David and Mt. Zion in previous periods, was probably destroyed during the reign of al-Hakim and was never rebuilt. The Crusader city was thus similar in shape to Aelia Capitolina, and it was this shape that survived through all subsequent periods, and is the one we still see today. The period itself was one of an incredible flowering of Christian art and architecture such as had not been seen since the early Byzantine period. Most of the more ancient churches surviving in Jerusalem today were either built or reconstructed in this period. Despite the vigor of the Latin Kingdom (the kingdom of the Crusaders), its duration was relatively short. Jerusalem itself surrendered in 1187, some three months after the defeat of the Crusader armies by Salah a-Din (Saladin) at the battle of the Horns of Hittin, near the Sea of Galilee. Following the fall of Jerusalem the Crusaders retained a stronghold in the northern coastal area based at St. Jean d'Acre (today's city of Acco). In 1229 diplomacy again won them partial control of Jerusalem, but this lasted only some fifteen years. The last vestige of Christian rule in the north of the country came to an end in 1291.

Two events took place in Jerusalem during the Crusader period whose consequences in both time and space spread far beyond the narrow confines of the Latin Kingdom, and whose effect on the ordinary human being eventually far exceeded those of the so-called historical events of the day. The first of these seemed innocent enough in origin. It entailed the transfer of the Good Friday procession from its traditional Mt. Zion–Holy Sepulchre route to a new route which began just to the north of the Temple Mount and in time became stabilized in the form of today's Via Dolorosa. The real reason for this change is obscure, but it successfully disguised a subtle change in emphasis which was to bear fruit during the centuries that followed; it was a change, moreover, which could not have been effected on the old

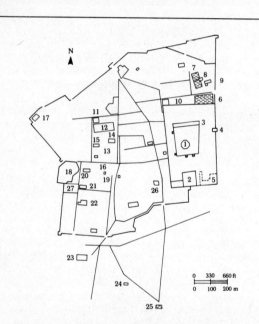

Fig. 10. Jerusalem in the Crusader Period, 1099–1187.

1. *Templum Domini*	**15.** *St. Mary la Grange*
2. *Templum Solomonis*	**16.** *St. John the Baptist*
3. *Temple Monastery*	**17.** *Tancred's Tower*
4. *The Golden Gate*	**18.** *David's Tower*
5. *Solomon's Stables*	**19.** *Syrian convent*
6. *Old pool*	**20.** *St. James*
7. *Old pool*	**21.** *St. Thomas*
8. *Crusader chapel*	**22.** *St. James Cathedral*
9. *Church and Convent of St. Anne*	**23.** *St. Mary on Mt. Zion*
10. *Church of the Repose*	**24.** *St. Peter in Gallicantu*
11. *Patriarch's palace*	**25.** *Pool of the Shiloah*
12. *Church of the Holy Sepulchre*	**26.** *St. Mary of the Germans*
13. *Muristan*	**27.** *Royal palace*
14. *St. Mary la Latine*	

route, where every step and gesture had long become frozen by tradition. The change concerned the inclusion in the new route of sites connected with various stages in the Passion of Christ. The emphasis on Christ's sufferings, which had been unknown in the old tradition (which focused on his victory), eventually found fertile ground in thirteenth- and four-teenth-century Europe and set in motion the cult of the Passion, which dramatically changed the direction of west-ern Christian religious thought and practice.—

The second event remains shrouded in mystery, and has throughout the ages often been the subject of wild and fanciful speculation. This is the appearance in the Latin Kingdom of the Order of Knights Templars. In the year 1099, Muslim Jerusalem fell to the forces of Christianity. Nineteen years later, in 1118, nine French knights pre-sented themselves to the Crusader king of Jerusalem, Bald-win II. The Crusaders had already broken preceding Christian tradition by establishing themselves on the Tem-ple Mount. The king's palace and court were situated on the site of the al-Aqsa Mosque. The nine knights revealed their purpose to Baldwin: They had come to Jerusalem with the aim of establishing a community which would protect Chris-tian pilgrims traveling on public roads. Their offer to form such a community was immediately accepted by Baldwin, who also made a wing of his palace available to them. The knights then presented themselves to the patriarch of Jeru-salem to apprise him of their mission and their desire to be considered soldiers of Christ and to live in semimonastic fashion. The patriarch, too, approved their mission, and the knights swore to disown all personal possessions and took vows of obedience and chastity. Following this meeting, the Canons of the Holy Sepulchre ceded their holdings on the Temple Mount in favor of the knights. Shortly after that, Baldwin vacated his palace and reestablished himself and his court at the Citadel, or David's Tower, at today's Jaffa Gate. The entire Temple Mount was now the sole possession of the nine knights, who, because of their association with the site of Solomon's Temple, came to be known in French as the Chevaliers du Temple, or Templiers. In English, "Templiers" became "Templars," while "Chevaliers du Tem-ple," whose precise meaning is "Knights of the Temple," became the Knights Templars. For nine years the group occupied the Temple Mount, their activities remaining se-cret and independent of all authority, both royal and reli-gious. Only once in this period was a new member permitted to join the group. This was Hugues, count of Champagne, who had abandoned his wife and children and what amounted to a kingdom in order to become a Templar. Their residence, the al-Aqsa Mosque, was named Templum Solo-monis (the Temple of Solomon), while the Dome of the Rock became their church and was named Templum Domini, the Temple of God.

Scholars investigating the Templars are forced to concede

that the stated aim of protecting Christian travelers in the Holy Land was nothing more than a cover, and that the Templars' true purpose lay elsewhere. The evidence is circumstantial, but nevertheless overwhelming. First of all, the role of protecting pilgrims was one of the responsibilities of another order, already established in Jerusalem, the Knights Hospitalers. Secondly, the deference shown the Templars by both king and clergy was out of all proportion to their modestly stated aims. Add to this the fact that the Templars were themselves neither Crusaders nor pilgrims, had taken part in no military engagements, and had sworn no oaths of fealty to either king or church, and it becomes clear that the two ruling bodies of the Latin Kingdom owed them no reciprocal obligations, nor was it likely that they would cede them their places of residence on the Temple Mount except for very good reasons.

No one believes that men of the standing of the count of Champagne, among others, were ready to renounce all in order to become the mere protectors of pilgrims. Further evidence of a different and much larger role lies in the incredible concessions granted the Templars by the papacy. They were declared to be free of all authority, both religious and secular, thus making them a state within a state. They were answerable to no one, and their activities could be kept secret. When the order later expanded, the oath of allegiance was to the order's Grand Master alone. They were also granted the status of a semimonastic order. Their rule was given to them by St. Bernard, who would seem to have been their guiding light from the beginning, and who was connected in one way or another with a number of the original knights of the order. The connection between St. Bernard, the Cistercian Order, the mission of the Knights Templars in Jerusalem, and the subsequent flowering of Gothic cathedrals in France and Europe seems to be unquestionable. The Templars, being free of all taxation, quickly became the richest order in the world; it is suspected by many, therefore, that they were financially responsible for this flowering—a state of affairs that continued until the destruction of the order by Philip the Fair of France.

It is said that for those who understand, the Gothic cathedrals can be read like books which contain great and hidden knowledge that has been passed down through esoteric schools throughout the ages. It is also said that the Templars were in Jerusalem to seek a great and hidden treasure. Unfortunately, it is at this point that writers begin to speculate that this treasure was physical rather than in the realm of knowledge and ideas. Thus, many claim that the Templars sought, and even found, the Ark of the Covenant, or other holy relics of Solomon's Temple, which themselves are claimed to have been sources of great power and knowledge. But it is highly unlikely that St. Bernard and the nine knights who went to Jerusalem would have undertaken such a speculative venture. Nor would such unproven speculation have been enough for all authorities to make them such enormous and continuous concessions from the very beginning. It is much more likely that the knights knew exactly what they were looking for and where it could be found, and that the object of this search was obvious to all to whom they made a part of their secret known.

Jerusalem's priceless treasure had been the Temple of Solomon. Its greatness lay not only in the mystery of its being the abode on earth of the One God, and in the sacred objects which it contained, but in the building itself. Its plan and dimensions had originated with God and had passed through Moses, Aaron, Joshua, and the prophets, to David and Solomon. It reflected God's celestial Temple and throne on high, and its manifestation was thus a revelation in our own world of truths of a higher divine order. Moreover, as with all sacred buildings, it had required men who could understand these truths and translate them into wood, stone, jewels, and fine metals. Little is known concerning these schools of builders. The Old Testament mentions King Hiram of Tyre and the families of Jewish priests. With the destruction of the First and then the Second Temple even this slim thread of connection comes to an end, and for the ensuing three hundred years of Roman rule we know nothing concerning them. The following three hundred years of the Byzantine period is also disappointing because of Christianity's rejection of the Temple Mount and the eternal value of Solomon's building. The final years of the Byzantine period came close to seeing the complete destruction of the Temple Mount and the severing of any possible remaining links with schools of builders whose traditions guarded the last vestiges of the Temple's inner meaning. Only the Muslim capture of Jerusalem prevented the final destruction, and the subsequent building of the Dome of the Rock insured that a portion of this divine knowledge was preserved. For four hundred years the Temple Mount and the knowledge preserved here remained unappreciated and inaccessible to the Christian West. St. Bernard's contacts with sources of information or schools with links to the knowledge contained on the Temple Mount, and in the Dome of the Rock in particular, remain unknown. It is clear that St. Bernard recognized that European civilization was being given only a short period to decipher the secrets that were there and bring them to the West. This was most probably the task undertaken by the Knights Templars. The subsequent Gothic period insured that a part of this knowledge would be preserved in the West. In 1187 Christian Jerusalem once again fell to the Muslims. During the period of Christian rule the Dome of the Rock had been preserved from destruction by the Knights Templars. Restored to Muslim protection, it could remain safe until a more tolerant and understanding world could appreciate its true value.

THE LATER MUSLIM PERIOD,
AYYUBID AND MAMELUKE (1187–1517)

Christian rule in Jerusalem came to an end with its capture by Salah a-Din (Saladin), the Ayyubid, in 1187. In all, the Latin Kingdom of Jerusalem had lasted only eighty-eight years. Following its reconquest, the city was ruled by the Ayyubids, though the Crusader presence in Israel was still a factor to be reckoned with. While Jerusalem and most of the inland towns were Muslim, the coastal cities were still mainly Christian. In 1219 the Muslim ruler al-Malik al-Mu'athin, fearing that the Christians might recapture Jerusalem and entrench themselves behind its formidable walls and towers, ordered the city's defenses destroyed. In 1229, by diplomacy, an agreement was reached with the Muslims which permitted the Christians to reenter Jerusalem. But this time their control of the city was not complete. While they ruled the city itself, the Temple Mount remained in Muslim hands. Fifteen years later, in 1244, even this partial hold was lost and the Crusaders were forced to leave Jerusalem, this time never to return. In 1260 the city came under the rule of the Mamelukes, who had originally served as royal guards to the Ayyubids, but who eventually overthrew them and ruled in their place until defeated by the Ottoman Turks in 1517.

During the later Mameluke era the city underwent a period of neglect and decline. This was in sharp contrast to its earlier years, which had witnessed some of Jerusalem's finest achievements in Islamic architecture and learning. The latter impulse had already begun under the rule of Salah a-Din and the Ayyubids, which can be seen as a reaction by Islam to the many years of foreign, Christian rule of a holy city. While the sacredness of Jerusalem to Islam had never been in question, following the days of the Umayyads it had found less and less external expression. Jerusalem's capture by Christianity on religious grounds forced the Muslims to counter with a forceful and explicit expression of their own religious claims to the city. The flowering during this period of so many institutes of Islamic law as well as Dervish and Sufi schools leads one to believe, however, that the motivation behind this was not wholly political reaction. The great knowledge that lay behind the building of places such as the Dome of the Rock had largely been lost during the more than 350 years of early Muslim rule of the city. It may well have been the Christians' own interest in these subjects and the discoveries they made on the Temple Mount that stimulated a renewed Muslim preoccupation with the city's theological basis.

THE TURKISH PERIOD, 1517–1917

In 1517 the Ottoman Turk Selim I defeated the Mamelukes of Egypt and Syria, and Jerusalem became part of the Turkish Empire. Three names are especially associated with the Turkish period. The first is that of the sixteenth-century sultan Suleiman the Magnificent, who rebuilt the city's defenses for the first time in over three hundred years, following the line of the previous city wall. Suleiman's wall is essentially the one we still see today. The only minor changes made by Suleiman were the shifting of the Zion Gate westward in order to give direct access to Mt. Zion and the Tomb of David, and the sealing of three of the gates of the Temple Mount—the Triple Gate, the Single Gate, and the Golden Gate (the Gate of Mercy).

As mentioned earlier, the main roads encountered today within the Old City of Jerusalem are the same ones that have existed in all times and ages. We can now add to this the integrity of the city's walls, in terms of both their position and the location of their gates, which open onto these internal roads of access. For the modern tourist these facts may seem to be of little consequence. City walls, especially, seem at best little more than a colorful and delightful anachronism. But pilgrims of all ages have understood that these barriers and openings, and the routes which they dictate, form an integral part of their pilgrimage.

The separation between secular and religious events is a relatively recent phenomenon. For the men who built and rebuilt Jerusalem's walls, no such division existed. These walls were indeed the city's defenses, protecting the inhabitants and sacred sites from attack. But for their builders these massive stone bulwarks were also the physical manifestation of a far more significant history.

Jerusalem is a sacred place, a center from which the creative spirit descends into the world. But it is also a center to which the pilgrim can ascend out of spiritual darkness. As Jerusalem represents the sacred, so its walls represent the boundary between the sacred and the profane. This division exists in all ancient traditions. And it is here that takes place the never-ending struggle between order and chaos. A breach in the walls in time of war not only threatened the destruction of the city by human forces but permitted the inflowing of the forces of chaos whose ends these attacking armies served.

Doors which open onto the sacred hold a special place in all ancient traditions. Usually these are associated with temple or church doors, or doors which open onto sanctuaries. But Jerusalem itself is a holy place, and here it is the city's gates which act as points of passage between the profane and the sacred.

Within the city these gates defined certain definite routes leading to sacred sites and to the Temple itself. Pilgrims have always known that not all roads lead to the divine, but that "strait is the gate, and narrow is the way, which leadeth unto life" (Matthew 7:14). These routes in turn led to other walls and gates surrounding various sanctuaries and eventually to the Temple itself. And at the Temple Mount each of the many gates had its function, each gate played its specific role. In his long ascent out of spiritual chaos and darkness the pilgrim passed through each of these gates of passage, retracing the path of the Creative Spirit's descent into the world. Yet of all these it was the gates of the city itself, the first great barrier, that were of special significance.

Today, except for Jerusalem, it is difficult to find a sacred city whose walls and gates are the ones that have existed from the beginning. This indicates that the struggle at these places between the sacred and the profane, between good and evil, between order and chaos, has come to an end. The stubbornness with which Jerusalem has rebuilt and maintained its walls and gates and roads in all ages indicates that the struggle here is still an active one. More important, it indicates that the Divine Presence has not deserted the place of its choosing, and though it hides its face, it has never ceased to join with men in writing here a history of the sacred.

Today you can take the Ramparts Walk along the top of the city's wall and get a view of the city and its residential areas which otherwise cannot be attained. The walk can be begun at the Jaffa, Zion, Lions', or Damascus gates. There are two places where it is worthwhile to come down from the walls and visit sites of historical importance. The first is at the site of the Citadel, or David's Tower, near the Jaffa Gate. The second is at the Damascus Gate. Here, below the present gate, are the remains of one of the Roman emperor Hadrian's four victory gates, an adjacent Roman guardroom, and the large paving stones marking the beginning of the Cardo Maximus. The walk along the ramparts from the Damascus Gate to the Stork Tower in the northeast corner of the wall is also of special interest. From here you can clearly see the topographical layout of the city. Note that the road leading from the area of the Damascus Gate southward marks the lowest part of the city. This is the Tyropoeon Valley, mentioned earlier. Today it is no longer as deep as it once was, but you can still see how it must have originally divided the western and eastern parts of the city. Looking southward into the distance you can also see the mountains and valleys that surround Jerusalem on three sides. As you walk southward along the eastern wall this will become more and more apparent. When you reach the southern wall of the city you will be able to see again the area comprising the old City of David and appreciate that the City of David was situated on the lowest of Jerusalem's hills, surrounded on the three sides, while towering above it to the north was the Temple Mount.

The other names of importance in the Turkish period were the nineteenth-century Egyptian rulers Ibrahim Pasha and Muhammad Ali. It was during their reigns that foreign consulates were first opened in Jerusalem, and economic concessions made to various European powers. This marked not only the beginning of the modernization of Jerusalem but the beginning of a religious liberalization as well. Jews and Christians had always been present in Jerusalem during the Muslim period, but it effectively remained a Muslim city where the rights and privileges of other religions were strictly curtailed and limited. The concessions made by Ibrahim Pasha and Muhammad Ali led to the building of new churches and synagogues within the city, which had been forbidden for over a thousand years under the laws originally laid down by Omar in the seventh century. This new development led to ever-increasing demands for further liberalization and rights of access to holy places. Especially significant in this respect were the demands of the Jews to rights of prayer at the Western Wall of the Temple Mount. The steps of this liberalization are difficult to follow, but an overall pattern is clear. Starting with the era of Ibrahim Pasha and Muhammad Ali, the almost hermetically sealed Muslim Jerusalem gradually began to open. This movement culminated at the close of the Six Day War in 1967, when, under Israeli control, the city and its holy places were at last, for the first time in history, opened to all.

An invaluable source of information of all kinds for visitors to Jerusalem is the *Israel Government Tourist Information Office*, which has two locations: Rehov HaMelech George 24 (24 King George St.), tel. 241281/2; and just inside the Jaffa Gate, tel. 282295/6. (If calling from outside the city, first dial the Jerusalem area code, 02.) Among its many other services, the Information Office provides free maps of the city.

2

THE TEMPLE MOUNT

The Temple Mount is a huge enclosed platform built on the summit of the hill called Mt. Moriah. As its name suggests, it was an artificial mountain built as a setting for the perfect jewel that once stood at its center, the Jewish Temple. In Hebrew it is called Har HaBayit, meaning the Mountain of the House (God's House, i.e., the Temple). In Arabic it is Haram es-Sharif, the Noble Sanctuary. For both Jew and Muslim this site is the very heart of the city, and without it there would have been no sacred place called Jerusalem. The present structure (trapezoidal in shape and covering an area of some 1,500,000 square feet, or 144,000 square meters) is essentially the one built by Herod the Great in the late first century B.C. Little is known concerning the exact dimensions of the original Temple Mount built by King Solomon in the tenth century B.C., though it is generally believed to have covered only about half the area of the enclosure we see today.

While the building of the Temple is associated with King Solomon, the choice of the site of Mt. Moriah is generally attributed to his father, King David. The immediate cause of this selection is related in II Samuel 24. Here we are told that David committed a great sin against God by deciding to take a census of the people. As punishment, God unleashed a plague upon the land which took the lives of some seventy thousand Israelites. But "when the angel stretched out his hand upon Jerusalem to destroy it, the Lord repented him of the evil, and said to the angel that destroyed the people, It is enough: stay now thine hand. And the angel of the Lord was by the threshing-place of Araunah the Jebusite" on the summit of Mt. Moriah. David was then commanded by the prophet Gad to build an altar on the site of the threshing floor. "So the Lord was intreated for the land, and the plague was stayed from Israel." We are never told why David's act of counting the people was considered to be such a great sin. Some contend that the answer can be found in God's promise to Abraham that his descendants would be as numerous as the stars in the sky, which was a biblical way of expressing God's infinite bounty to Israel. By counting the people, David had shown a lack of faith in God's promise. By repenting of his action and building an altar at the place shown to him, David reestablished Abraham's original covenant with God, which once again permitted His infinite bounty to flow into the world. It was at the site of this renewal that David instructed Solomon to build the Temple.

Muslim tradition also emphasizes the relationship between David and the site of the future Temple on Mt. Moriah. It is believed that it was here that David prayed for deliverance from the plague, and when his prayer was answered he saw angels ascending a golden ladder from the threshing floor to the sky, sheathing their swords as they went. From this, David understood that the summit of the hill was the point of access to heaven and the place where the Temple must be built.

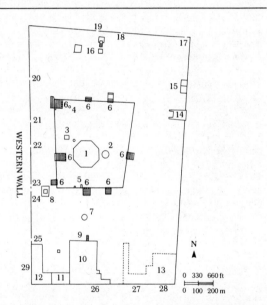

Fig. 11. The Temple Mount today.

 1. *Dome of the Rock*
 2. *Dome of the Chain*
 3. *Dome of the Ascension*
 4. *Dome of the Spirits*
 5. *Summer Pulpit*
 6. *The Scales*
 7. *Al-Kas Fountain*
 8. *Dome of Moses*
 9. *Stairs leading to ancient entranceway to Temple Mount*
10. *Al-Aqsa Mosque*
11. *Women's Mosque*
12. *Islamic Museum*
13. *Solomon's Stables*
14. *Gates of Mercy (the Golden Gate)*
15. *Solomon's Throne*
16. *Dome of Solomon*
17. *Gate of the Tribes*
18. *Gate of Forgiveness*
19. *Gate of Darkness*
20. *Prison Gate*
21. *Iron Gate*
22. *Gate of the Cotton Merchants*
23. *Gate of Peace*
24. *Gate of the Chain*
25. *Gate of the Moroccans*
26. *The Double Gate*
27. *The Triple Gate*
28. *The Single Gate*
29. *Robinson's Arch*

In 586 B.C. the Babylonian king Nebuchadnezzar captured Jerusalem, destroyed the Temple built by Solomon,
and forced the Jews into exile. Shortly afterward, however,
the Babylonians were defeated by the Persians, whose liberal
policies allowed the Jews to return to their homeland and
rebuild the holy sanctuary. This was the Second Temple,
and the Mount it stood on was most likely the one that had
existed in Solomon's day. The only really substantial change
in the Temple Mount took place in the reign of Herod the
Great, five centuries later. Herod is known to have been one
of the wealthiest men of his day, and much of his fortune
was dedicated to financing monumental building projects
such as Herodium, Masada, and Caesarea Maritime. In Jerusalem he turned his hand to building the Antonia Fortress
to the north of the Temple Mount; the Citadel, at today's
Jaffa Gate; and a royal palace that ran from the Citadel
southward to today's Armenian Quarter. But at Mt. Moriah,
the most prestigious site of all, he ran into trouble. The
dimensions of the Temple had been set by law. Its plan had
been given by God to Moses, by Moses to Joshua, by Joshua
to the prophets, by the prophets to David, and by David to
Solomon. This restriction did not fit in with Herod's ambi-
tions and plans to build here the greatest of all his monuments. To overcome the difficulty and secure the permission
of the nation to begin the work, he claimed, apparently with
some justification, that the height of the Second Temple was
different from that of the one built by Solomon. But while the
changes Herod could make regarding the Temple itself were
limited to greater height and perhaps more magnificent decoration, there were no legal restrictions regarding the size of
the Temple Mount. It was here, therefore, that he expended
the greater part of his energy, enlarging the Mount beyond
all recognition.

It is important for our story to note that not all of Herod's
Temple Mount was considered sacred. The southern extension—where today's al-Aqsa Mosque is located—
contained a huge royal stoa which served as the commercial
center of the city (and at times also the judicial). This open-
sided roofed structure was separated from the Temple courts
by a wall with signs forbidding entry to non-Jews. There was
no direct access between the stoa, which was open to all
people, and the Temple courts, which were open only to
Jews. To reach the Temple from the stoa, one had to leave
the Temple Mount and reenter it by the appropriate doorway. A memory of the royal stoa and its function is recorded
in the Gospel story of Jesus overturning the tables of the
moneychangers on the Temple Mount. It is clear that by the
time the Gospel was written it had already been forgotten
that this part of the Temple Mount was not regarded as
sacred, and that financial transactions carried out here were
not considered to be religiously offensive.

Herod's Temple was destroyed, and the Jews exiled from
the city, in the year 70 A.D., at the culmination of the rebel-

lion against Rome known as the First Jewish War. For centuries it was believed that the destruction had been total, and that none of the monuments built by Herod had been left standing. Extensive excavations at the Temple Mount have shown that this was not so. While the Temple itself was indeed destroyed, many of the other structures, including the royal stoa, remained basically intact. Except for a period when the Romans established a temple of Jupiter on the Temple Mount, the site remained largely as it had been following 70 A.D. In the early fourth century, with the triumph of Christianity under the emperor Constantine (effectively the first Byzantine emperor), vast new building projects were undertaken in Jerusalem. But the area of the Temple Mount was left untouched. This was no oversight. The destroyed and abandoned Temple Mount was meant to contrast with the magnificent new Christian structures, such as the Church of the Holy Sepulchre, and provide living proof that God had abandoned the old covenant with Israel, and established the new. Its ruins verified Jesus's prophecy regarding the Temple that "there shall not be left here one stone upon another, that shall not be thrown down" (Matthew 24:2).

In the sixth century there began a series of events whose consequences cannot be evaluated in any ordinary way. The emperor Justinian decided to build a new church in Jerusalem, a church of gigantic proportions to be called the Nea, or New, Church (the New Church of Mary). A Christian historian of the time, Procopius, recorded that the builders had been unable to find a source of marble necessary for making the columns of the church, but that God had suddenly and miraculously revealed one to them. Today it is known that these were marble columns taken from the remains of the royal stoa that stood on the southern part of the Temple Mount. By that time the Jews, like the writers of the Gospels before them, had completely forgotten that the southern part of the Temple Mount was not a sacred site, and considered the act one of sacrilege. It was neither forgotten nor forgiven.

In 614, Byzantium suffered a defeat in its perpetual war with the Persian Empire, and the Persians occupied Jerusalem. The chief victims of the invasion were the city's churches. There can be no doubt that much of this destruction was due to Jewish elements in the Persian forces who saw the event as an opportunity for revenge and entertained the hope that, after nearly six hundred years of subjugation and exile, the Persians would return control of the city to them and allow them to rebuild the Temple as they had permitted their ancestors to do a thousand years earlier. But in 628 the Byzantines retook Jerusalem, and now it was their turn to wreak vengeance on the Jews—most strikingly in regard to the Temple Mount. Whereas Christians had till then been content to let it stand as a reminder of God's abandonment of Israel, now they began systematically to dismantle and destroy it so that it would never again serve as a rallying point for Jewish nationalism. You can clearly see that the platform on which the Dome of the Rock stands is some 9.8 feet (3 meters) higher than the southern and western part of the enclosure. In Herod's time the entire Mount was this height, and its lowering is the result of the dismantling that was begun in 628. That the Temple Mount still exists today can be laid solely to the credit of Islam. Only the unexpected and phenomenally rapid rise and spread of the new faith, and the Muslim capture of Jerusalem in 638, prevented the Byzantines from carrying their plan to completion.

THE DOME OF THE ROCK
(*Arabic: Kubbat as-Sakhrah; Hebrew: Kipat HaSela*)

The Dome of the Rock is a Muslim monument—not a mosque—built round the bare rock of the summit of Mt. Moriah. It is sometimes erroneously called the Mosque of Omar, referring to the second caliph, Omar Ibn al-Khattab, who negotiated the surrender of Jerusalem in 638. One of Omar's stated aims when visiting Jerusalem was to pray at the Mihrab Dawud, the Sanctuary of David, the name given by Muslims to the site of the Temple. The patriarch of Jerusalem, sensing that such an action would lead to a renewal of activity on the Temple Mount, in contradiction of Christian belief, first led the caliph to the Church of the Holy Sepulchre, then to the church on Mt. Zion, claiming each in turn to be the desired spot. But Omar was not to be fooled, stating that the prophet Muhammad himself had described to him the sacred place. Eventually the caliph was brought

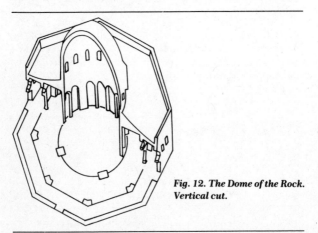

Fig. 12. *The Dome of the Rock. Vertical cut.*

to the Temple Mount, where the summit of Mt. Moriah was discovered under mounds of refuse after centuries of neglect. While no building was erected here during Omar's

lifetime, the patriarch's fears eventually proved to be justi-
fied. Some fifty-five years later, in 692, the caliph Abd
al-Malik built the Dome of the Rock on the spot where Omar
had prayed. Many reasons have been given for the building
of this monument. All but one contain some fragment of
truth necessary for understanding the building's true and
hidden meaning.

Reason 1: As an alternative to Mecca This is the reason most
often heard or read about, and it is the only one that has no
basis whatever in fact.

The first four caliphs had been elected, and ruled from
Mecca. Following these, Omar's general in Syria, Mu'awiya,
set up a dynastic caliphate. This was the Umayyad dynasty,
which ruled from Damascus, and was the house to which
Abd al-Malik belonged. In 750 the House of Umayyad fell
(though it continued to rule in Spain and the west), and was
succeeded by the Abbasids, who ruled from Baghdad, in

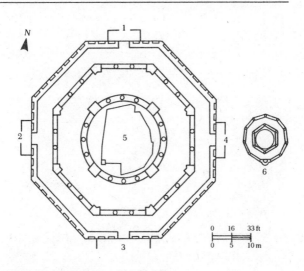

Fig. 13. Plan of the Dome of the Rock.

1. *Gate of Paradise*
2. *Gate of David*
3. *Gate of Prayer*
4. *Western Gate, today's main entrance*
5. *The sacred rock*
6. *Dome of the Chain*

Iraq. The Abbasids tried to justify the change in dynasty by
showing the Umayyads to be unbelievers and unworthy of
the caliphate. One such attempt was an account written by
the Iraqi historian Ya'qubi concerning Abd al-Malik's reasons for building the Dome of the Rock. In al-Malik's time a
rival caliph, Ibn al-Zubayr, was in possession of Mecca. Ya'-
qubi asserted that al-Malik had sought to divert pilgrims
from Mecca by setting up Jerusalem as a rival religious
center (for fear that pilgrims from Syria would fall under

al-Zubayr's influence). Ya'qubi further claimed that the
design of the Dome of the Rock, with its two circumam-
bulatories around the rock, stemmed from the ritual require-
ments of the *tawaf,* the circumambulation of the Ka'bah.
These claims, it is clear, were politically motivated to show
that al-Malik and the House of Umayyad had abrogated one
of the five pillars of Islam (the pilgrimage to Mecca) only a
generation after the prophet's death. It is now known beyond
doubt that pilgrimage from Syria to Mecca did not cease
during al-Malik's reign. Nor is there any evidence to support
the allegation that the Kubbat as-Sakhrah in Jerusalem was
ever used to replace the Ka'bah in Mecca.

Reason 2: Its Relation to Solomon's Temple Muslim legends
regarding the building of the Temple (largely derived from
Jewish sources) tend to emphasize its miraculous nature,
and Solomon's control and use of demons during its construction. The latter fits well with the idea that for the divine
to manifest itself in the world or in man (in this case in the
form of the Temple), the lower forces of chaos must be
controlled and made to serve that which is higher. The Dome

Jeweled plant from the Dome of the Rock.

of the Rock was indeed intended to express the essence of
Solomon's Temple as a reflection of paradise. This tradition
is preserved in the mosaic decorations of the columns and
piers of the octagonal zone, and to some extent the dome of
the building. Here we see trees with multicolored trunks,
some inlaid with jewels, bearing magnificent foliage and
clusters of fruit. Other trees bear quite naturalistic fruit but
grow out of jeweled bases bearing collars of precious stones
and gold. There are acanthus leaves with stems encrusted
with jewels and crowns, and still other plants bearing blos-

soms and fruit which rise from jeweled pedestals laden with crowns and ornaments. Early commentaries on the Qur'ān state that demons collected precious stones and metals for the construction of the Temple, and when the building was complete it shone in the darkness like the full moon. More important, however, are traditions regarding Solomon's gardens. It was believed that trees grew spontaneously in the Temple during its construction. Each day Solomon would inquire of the trees what special qualities they possessed, record the information, and transplant them in a magnificent garden that surrounded the structure. One tradition relates that the garden consisted of artificial trees which were made of gold and jewels but bore real fruit. (A Jewish legend records that the golden trees will lose their fruit if the Temple is destroyed but will bloom again when the Temple is rebuilt at the time of the Messiah.) Most significant, however, is the variety of mosaic trees and fruits, many of which are associated with different and even mutually exclusive climates. Yet here they all grow together in an earthly paradise which reflects the real paradise to which the building opens.

Plants with royal insignias from the Dome of the Rock.

Reason 3: As a Representation of the Victory of Islam, the Final Revelation An additional interpretation has been given to some of the jewel-studded mosaics, especially those of the dome. Here rising out of amphorae are crowns surmounted by wings, diadems encrusted with hangings of precious stones, breastplates, necklaces, and earrings. They are partly insignias of Persian rulers, and partly the ornaments worn by Christ, the Virgin, and the saints in Byzantine art: symbols of holiness, wealth, and power, which represent here the opponents of Islam. The motifs surround and face the center of the monument, which is Islam, the final revelation. The juxtaposition of the two elements represents the final victory of Islam over the unbelievers and the bringing of the Christians and Zoroastrians into the fold of the new religion.

Reason 4: Its Relation to Other Architectural Structures
The tenth-century Jerusalem historian al-Mukaddasi wrote that the Dome of the Rock was constructed in order to offset the influence of the beautiful Christian monuments of the city, especially the Church of the Holy Sepulchre. Leaving the question of religious competition aside, later writers have emphasized the similarity of the two buildings, in regard to both the size of their domes and the overall layout of the circular areas beneath them. Some investigators have taken the question even farther by showing a whole line of architectural evolution leading from the earliest circular Roman mausoleums to the present Muslim monument. Four structures are generally regarded as landmarks in this evolution. The first is the rotunda of the Church of the Holy Sepulchre (early fourth century), whose antecedents are said to lie in the great mausoleums of Rome. Second is the Church of the Ascension on the Mount of Olives (late fourth century), with an outer octagon derived from an inner circle by the same method later used in the Dome of the Rock. The third is the cathedral at Bosra, in Syria (early sixth century), which extends the system by including a double ambulatory and an intermediate octagon. And finally, the Dome of the Rock itself.

What is curious about this evolution—which many see as merely one of architectural style—is that it so dramatically cuts across religious and cultural boundaries. At the time the Dome of the Rock was built, there was as yet no school of Muslim art and architecture per se, and the builders were largely Byzantines and Persians from Syria. How was it possible, then, for these builders to construct a monument which from its beginning has been regarded as expressing something so typically Muslim? What is expressed in the Dome of the Rock that could find a common thread in pagan Rome, Christian Byzantium, Zoroastrian Persia, and the new religion of Islam? The answer seems to lie in the schools of builders themselves. We shall later see that the Dome of the Rock is not merely the culmination of an architectural style but the repository of great knowledge whose possessors had, perhaps for untold centuries, cultivated and refined it, seeking for it the ultimate form of its revelation.

Reason 5: To Commemorate the Night Journey of the Prophet Muhammad Of all the traditions associated with the Dome of the Rock, the one best known today is connected with the Night Journey (*isra'*) and the ascension to heaven (*mi'raj*) of the prophet Muhammad. The inner meaning of this journey and its relevance to Jerusalem and the Temple Mount will be discussed later, when we visit the al-Aqsa

Mosque. Despite its present importance, it is clear that at the time of Omar and even that of al-Malik it played no pronounced role here. It would seem that it was only during the reign of al-Malik's son, al-Walid (builder of the al-Aqsa Mosque), that the theme began to gain in significance until it achieved the primacy it has today.

According to tradition, Muhammad was sleeping near the Ka'bah when he was suddenly commanded to depart Mecca on a winged steed called al-Buraq ("the Lightning"). Accompanied by the angel Gabriel, he was carried first to Sinai, then to Bethlehem, and finally to the gate of the Temple Mount. Here he dismounted, tied al-Buraq to a ring (which some say was also used by former prophets), and went up to the sacred rock which had stood in the center of Solomon's Temple. There he met Abraham, Moses, Jesus, and other apostles of God and led them in prayer. Then, accompanied by Gabriel, he ascended a ladder of light into heaven. Passing through the seven heavens and witnessing the delights of paradise, he finally stood in the presence of Allah, who bestowed upon him the gift of the five daily prayers his followers were to perform. He then descended to the sacred rock and returned to Mecca astride al-Buraq, arriving before the night was through.

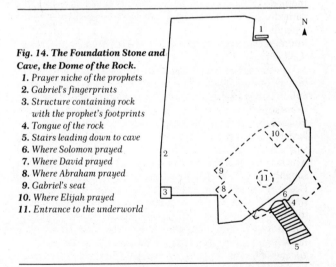

Fig. 14. The Foundation Stone and Cave, the Dome of the Rock.
1. *Prayer niche of the prophets*
2. *Gabriel's fingerprints*
3. *Structure containing rock with the prophet's footprints*
4. *Tongue of the rock*
5. *Stairs leading down to cave*
6. *Where Solomon prayed*
7. *Where David prayed*
8. *Where Abraham prayed*
9. *Gabriel's seat*
10. *Where Elijah prayed*
11. *Entrance to the underworld*

We have already seen that the summit of Mt. Moriah, the sacred rock around which the Kubbat as-Sakhrah was built, was considered by Muslims at a very early period to be the point of access to heaven. This is confirmed not only by the overall story of Muhammad's ascension here but also by numerous lesser details of the tradition. At the northwest corner of the rock is a prayer niche where it is believed Muhammad led the prophets and apostles of the older faiths in prayer. This belief is generally viewed as serving to demonstrate symbolically the superiority of Islam over the older religions. But while this is certainly the intention, the place of prayer is also important—on the rock that stood directly below paradise and the celestial Temple. Prayers recited here were believed to be the most effective, since they rose directly to the world above. At the northeast corner of the rock is a protuberance called the tongue of the rock (*lison es-Sakhrah*). One legend relates that when Muhammad arrived in Jerusalem on his Night Journey he greeted the rock with the words *"Salem aleik ya sakhrat Allah"* ("Peace be unto you, rock of Allah"). To which the rock replied, *"Salem aleik ya rassul Allah"* ("Peace be unto you, messenger of Allah"). Then Muhammad stood on the rock and began his ascent to heaven. The rock itself began to ascend with him and had to be restored to its place by the angel Gabriel. On the southern edge of the rock visitors are still shown the depression caused by the angel's fingers. Muslims believe that the rock from which the prophet ascended was one of the rocks from the Garden of Eden. Jews believe it to be the rock that was plucked from beneath the throne of God and thrown into the void, and from which the entire world was created. The legend of the rock's ascent expresses its desire to return to its heavenly origin, and its ability to do so at the point of contact between heaven and earth. More significant, however, is that it does so only when the prophet ascends. The rock, like man, is in exile, and will not return to its source until all things are perfected and return to their origin. The ascent of the prophet, who is perfect before God, fools the rock into thinking that the time has come, and it has to be held down by heavenly forces lest it return to its home, which would bring the world to an end before the appointed time. The tradition of the angel's fingerprints imbedded in the stone is also important. The fact that the heavenly can penetrate the earthly at the place believed to be the point of contact between heaven and earth, is meant to demonstrate that the contact is real. You will also notice that on the part of the rock that forms the ceiling to the cave below there is an opening. The piece removed to make the opening is now housed in the lower part of the small structure at the southeast corner, and is believed to contain the impression of the footprints made by the prophet when he stood on the sacred rock. (Muslims place their hands through the small opening and touch it for luck. In the upper part of the structure there is a silver box said to contain three hairs from the prophet's beard.)

THE SACRED ARCHITECTURE OF THE DOME OF THE ROCK

Now that we have considered the various reasons put forth for the building of the Dome of the Rock, let us turn to the evidence of the architecture itself and see how it was built and what each step was meant to represent.

The Horizontal Aspect of the Plan

1. The first step taken by the builders was to inscribe the smallest possible circle around the sacred rock. In reality the starting point is not the circle but the point at its center. This represents the absolute, the point of unity, the one primordial and eternal source of all potential and creation. This point has no measurable dimensions. The

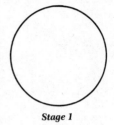

Stage 1

circle is in effect an enlargement of this point, a kind of photographic blowup, which permits all that lies within to be magnified and made visible.

2. Next the builders inscribed within the circle two interlocking squares. The absolute contains within itself all worlds and levels, from the very fine to the very coarse. The builders wished to show what took place within the absolute, but it was impossible to represent so many worlds and levels in such a restricted two-dimensional space. They therefore chose one level that would be capable of representing all levels. The choice fell on our own world, the lowest and coarsest (or most solid and material) of all. The choice was a suitable one for two reasons. First, implicit in this level are all the intervening stages and transformations which must be passed through in order to reach it. And second, it was precisely by not representing the higher levels that the

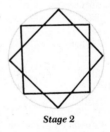

Stage 2

builders made clear that these were finer worlds whose materiality remained invisible to our eyes. In many traditions the material earthly world is expressed by a square, which represents the stability of matter and its ability to resist external forces from all directions. It also represents the four winds, the four directions of the compass or four corners of the world, and most importantly the four elements—earth, air, fire, and water. The builders of the Dome of the Rock knew, however, that in addition to the four elements there are four qualities or natures (hot, cold, dry, and humid), which combine in pairs with each of the elements to form all phenomena. (Fire is hot and dry; water, humid and cold; air, humid and hot; and earth, cold and dry.) Thus the full potential of the absolute is symbolized in the material world not by the number 4 (the square), but by the number 8, or two groups of four (two interlocking squares).

3. (a) The next step was to extend the lines of the two squares until they met at points outside the circle. (b) These points were then joined to form an octagon, which corresponds to the inner octagon of the Dome of the Rock. The sides of the octagon are the same lengths as the sides of the squares within the circle. This represents the manifestation outside the circle of the absolute of the four elements and four qualities making up our world.

Before creation, all the elements making up the absolute existed in perfect unity and constituted a world of infinite time and space. It was the view of the builders of the Dome of the Rock that the creation meant the destruction of this primordial harmony. Creation was the formation of a finite earthly world through the separation of the elements composing it from the greater whole to which they originally belonged.

The creation of a world outside the bounds of the absolute seems to carry with it a contradiction. By definition the absolute should contain all, including the manifestation of its own potential. In reality this is the case. Nothing really exists outside the absolute. Its extension beyond the circle is simply meant to symbolize the partiality of man, who sees only his own level and is no longer capable of seeing the whole. In his fallen state he feels separated from the greater inner worlds to which he really belongs.

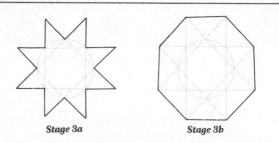

Stage 3a   Stage 3b

4. It was at this stage that the builders presented a unique idea. The story of the fall, or man's separation from his source, exists in some form in all traditions; and in each, "the fall" is followed by "the return" which constitutes the path of man's salvation and redemption. This is invariably a return to the center, and the state of pristine unity which existed at the beginning of time. However, instead of returning to the center the builders extended the sides of the figure representing the earthly world outward (a). These met at points outside the octagon which, when joined, formed two interlocking squares similar to the ones that had existed in the circle of the absolute before creation. (b) This figure was then enclosed within a circle.

The idea presented here was revolutionary. Unity was not achieved by returning to the center. Rather, at the very nadir of man's fall (the inner octagon), there existed something, a seed of possibility, which permitted the earthly world to expand outward. And it was this seed that also permitted the center to expand, englobe the world of the fall, and create a new, larger world of the absolute. The implications were clear. It was not only man, the microcosm, who was evolving but also the macrocosm, the absolute itself. And it was man's role in this drama (and his actions at the lowest point of his fall) that made this evolution possible.

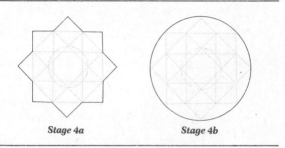

Stage 4a   *Stage 4b*

5. (*a*) The path of man's fall (dotted lines) was then extended to the limits of the new circle of the absolute. (*b*) These points were then joined to form a second octagon (corresponding to the outer octagon of the Dome of the Rock). This represented the formation of a second but different earthly world—a world that was not separated from the greater whole but rather lay entirely within it.

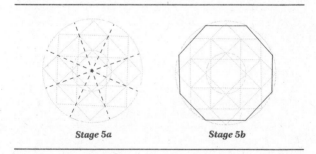

Stage 5a   *Stage 5b*

The Vertical Aspect of the Plan

The Inner Circular Area While the horizontal plan of the building reveals the stages in the inner evolution of man and of the world from an unknown period when all still lay in uncreated potential until the establishment of a divine kingdom on earth, its vertical aspect tells quite a different story. Here the world is presented as it is. Not as it is in a profane sense, but as it is in its present relation to that which is higher (and, by the same token, to that which is lower). What is presented, in other words, is a detailed picture of the hierarchy of forces or influences presently acting in our world.

The story begins at the tallest part of the building, the structure's inner circle. The single point of unity is located in the center of the dome. This point contains within itself all worlds. But here, as with the central point of the horizontal plan, these worlds remain unseen and unknown. The "photographic blowup" of this point is contained in the volume enclosed by the dome above and the rock below. As with the horizontal plan, only the lowest and most solid of worlds is materially represented here. This is the sacred rock. All intervening worlds, whose existence and transformations take place in the invisible, are understood to exist in the volume above. While these worlds indeed remain invisible, some attempt has been made to portray their essence, however minimally. This is to be found in the decorations of the dome and the drum on which it sits. The highest of these worlds are far too fine to comprehend, and permit no ordinary concepts of form. They are thus represented by geometrical designs (arabesques) whose wavy lines simply convey a sense of movement between worlds. Below these are representations of the worlds of form. At first glance these forms seem familiar. But if you look again and recall what has been said before, you will see that they are forms belonging to a more paradisal world. Here are all kinds of fantastic jeweled plants, and royal insignias that denote man's state before the fall. These same forms are found also in other parts of the building, but here alone they are made entirely of golden-colored mosaics. This color, which so dominates the central part of the structure, portrays the golden light of the absolute when everything still lay in potential and perfect repose at the dawn of creation. On the first day God said, "Let there be light!" but He created the sun, moon, and stars only on the fourth day. Thus it is the original and perfect light of God that burst forth from the Creator Himself that bathes all here in gold.

The presence of this light is made possible by the perfect relation that existed among all things at the beginning. In order to portray the nature of this relationship, the builders chose one world that would demonstrate the interaction possible between the absolute and creation. Once again they chose the most material level—the world of man, represented here by the sacred rock. This might appear to be a strange choice, yet rocks have certain remarkable qualities. During the day they absorb the sun's radiation that falls upon them, but at night they return the energy they have received. This exemplifies the harmony between God and His creation. The true light of the world is the breath of God, by whose "compassion and mercy" all is made. When God breathes out, His creation breathes in, and the world is filled with His light. But when God breathes in, the world must breathe out and return what it has received so that there will be no night and day but a universe bathed in the continuous light of the eternal. This is the partnership that takes place between the dome above and the rock below, and the result is the light in the golden mosaics.

Another related idea is that of charity, one of the five pillars of Islam. The Qur'ān tells us that all men are poor, and that all they have comes from God. As God gives to them, so are they enjoined to give to others. Thus the relation between the dome and the rock can also be seen as the flow of God's compassion and its reflection in perfect charity. The most interesting theme, however, is that of sacrifice. The flow of light and life into the world can be seen as a result of a sacrifice made above by God of a part of His own essence. Its return from below is the sacrifice made by man.

The Outer Ambulatories (*the Octagonal Areas*) As you move outward from the perfect world of the center in the direction of the two octagonal ambulatories, you enter worlds of increasing imperfection, associated with the life of man on earth. Yet these are not the worlds of ordinary daily life.

The first important factor is the height of the roof, which starts much lower down than at the building's center, and continues to slope downward until it meets the outer wall. The two octagonal worlds represented here are thus no longer in direct vertical contact with the life that comes from above. The use of columns and piers throughout the structure creates an open plan which defines the relation between the three levels (the center and the two ambulatories). The octagonal worlds still have a certain vision or knowledge of the world of the center, but it is limited and partial, and decreases as one moves toward the periphery. The ideal relation between God above and man below, which gave birth to the perfect golden light of the center, cannot exist here. This is already evident from the mosaics of the inner octagon. Here there are more scenes of paradise, but dominated by shades of green, a more earthly and natural color. The decreasing influence of the center is even more pronounced in the outer octagon. Here plants are still green, but lie more in shadow, and their fantastic jeweled aspect tends to disappear. The decoration as a whole remains beautiful. The marble of the piers and the outer wall is perfectly cut, like the leaves of a book, but the color is dark, and it is clear that we are reaching the limits of the light.

Despite their differences, the three worlds represented in the Dome of the Rock are privileged worlds and represent three inner levels of humanity. At the center is the world of the perfect man. The first octagon is the world of the man on his way to perfection, and the influences which direct his life come directly from the center. The outer octagon is the world of the man who is no longer influenced by the chaos of the exterior world (outside the walls of the structure). The influences which guide his life come from the world of the first octagon, but he can already see beyond it and knows their true source. The doors of the Dome of the Rock represent an intermediary world. They open to the four cardinal points, and by extension to the four corners of the world. Here the influence of the inner worlds seeps into the world outside and calls to those who can hear. Outside the walls is the world of spiritual chaos and darkness where the inner light of the absolute does not reach. This is represented here (as it is in many sacred buildings) by the stained-glass windows. When viewed from outside, the windows appear black. When viewed from within the building, they are seen to contain magnificent designs and colors. This demonstrates how the ordinary light of the world which surrounds us everywhere has no power to reflect the inner world of man. It is in effect the light of spiritual darkness. Only the light that comes from within can reveal the magnificence of man's hidden possibilities.

THE FOUNDATION STONE

The rock in the center of the structure is called in Hebrew Even HaShetiyah, the Foundation Stone. Jewish tradition tells that when God created the world He took a great stone from beneath His throne of glory and threw it into the abyss. One end sank into the depths, while the other end stood above it. This is the point that stands in the center of the world. The great rock was called the Foundation Stone because here was planted the spirit of creation that was to spread in all directions. The first expansion of this spirit was the Temple and all the city of Jerusalem within the walls. The second was the Holy Land. The third was the rest of the world. And the great ocean surrounded them all.

It is said that Adam's body was formed from the dust of the rock so that in his wanderings he would always carry with him the memory of the place of his origin, and the desire to return there. Other legends call it the dust from the place of Adam's atonement. This is, of course, related to the belief that in the end of days all mankind—Adam's children—will assemble here to seek repentance, forgiveness, and salvation. Most significant, however, is the legend according to which Adam offered a sacrifice here after his creation. Adam's sacrifice was followed by others. It is said that this is the place where Cain and Abel made their offerings to God, as did Noah after the flood. Here Jacob had his vision of a ladder stretching between heaven and earth on which angels were ascending and descending. Then "Jacob awaked out of his sleep, and he said . . . this is none other but the house of God, and this is the gate of heaven. And Jacob rose up early in the morning, and took the stone that he had put for his pillows, and set it up for a pillar, and poured oil upon the top of it" (Genesis 28:16–18), in other words, dedicated an altar of sacrifice. This is the very place where Abraham built an altar and bound Isaac ("the land of Moriah"—Genesis 23:2). By being willing in his heart to return, or sacrifice, in perfect love and obedience God's most precious

gift, Abraham earned for his descendants the right to become a nation of priests, charged with maintaining the perfect sacrifice on God's altar at this the center of the world.

The role assigned to Abraham and his children became a
permanent one with the establishment of the Temple. The
Jewish Temple was not like the synagogue, church, or
mosque of today. It was not a place where people congre-
gated to worship. It was a house built as a dwelling place for
God on earth, and only priests were permitted to enter it. As
such it presented a mystery that was never better expressed
than by King Solomon himself at the Temple's dedication
ceremony. After having offered up his prayers he asked, "But
will God in very deed dwell with men on the earth? behold,
heaven, and the heaven of heavens cannot contain thee;
how much less this house which I have built!" (II Chronicles
6:18).

The answer is given by the sages who call Jerusalem and
the Temple God's footstool. The answer is significant when
we remember that in origin the Foundation Stone lay beneath the throne of God. This picture of God above, with his
feet resting on the rock below, fits in well with the image of
Universal Man. The Universal Man, or Perfect Man, stands
at the center of the universe (whose image he is), with feet
firmly planted in the world below, and with head reaching to
the heavens. He is the macrocosm to man's microcosm because in him flow the same forces connecting heaven and
earth that are possible in man. He integrates all the levels of
the universe in perfect harmony by joining what is above
with what is below in a single unified body. This is Jacob's
ladder with angels of light constantly ascending and descending, whose never-ending movements bear the perfect
sacrifices that illuminate the world.

The Two Temples The integration between heaven and earth
is also reflected in the idea of the two temples, the two places
of sacrifice. As mentioned earlier, the name usually given to
Jerusalem in the Old Testament is Yerushalem, the singular
form. In time, however, it came to be known by its plural
form, Yerushalayim. This reflected the idea of the two Jerusalems and the two Temples, the one in heaven and the one
on earth. It is difficult to say exactly when the idea of a
heavenly and an earthly Temple began to take shape. Already in the Psalms of David we read that "Jerusalem is
builded as a city that is compact [or joined] together" (Psalms
122:3). According to Jewish belief, this joining was not
one-sided. When the earthly Temple was destroyed and the
Shechinah (the Divine Presence) forced to leave it, God
swore that He would not enter into His Temple on high until
the earthly one had been rebuilt. We can now better understand the meaning behind this. Without the lower Temple
and its perfect sacrifice, all the efforts on high come to
nothing. When the sacrifice below ceases, all the worlds
above are forced into exile. In the time of the Second Temple

Jesus, as well as other prophets, had predicted its destruction. One Jewish sect, the Essenes, had already abandoned it, claiming it to be defiled and the sacrifice impure. Everywhere there were predictions of a new Temple that would not be built by the unclean hands of man but by the hands of God. This Temple became associated with the eschatological Temple, the one that would appear at the end of days. This was the Temple and Jerusalem of Ezekiel's vision, and the new heaven and new earth of the Revelation of St. John. It was the Temple of the Jerusalem belonging to the second earthly kingdom represented in the outer octagon of the Dome of the Rock. It belongs to a time when man will realize the potential of his evolution and succeed in expanding his inner horizons beyond the confines and exile of the first octagon. Then the truly perfect sacrifice will be established, and "The sun shall be no more thy light by day; neither for brightness shall the moon give light unto thee: but the Lord shall be unto thee an everlasting light, and thy God thy glory. Thy sun shall no more go down; neither shall thy moon withdraw itself: for the Lord shall be thine everlasting light, and the days of thy mourning shall be ended" (Isaiah 60:19–20).

The Cave Below the Rock
Crypts and caves have been associated with sacred places from the most ancient of times. Their role and meaning will be discussed at length when we visit the Christian churches of the city, especially the Church of the Holy Sepulchre. For the present, it is sufficient to recall the legend that when God threw the Foundation Stone into the abyss one end of it sank into the depths. One legend relates that King David incautiously removed a stone which plugged the abyss, nearly causing Jerusalem to disappear beneath the primordial waters of the deep.

Prayer niche dedicated to Solomon in the cave below the Foundation Stone, in the Dome of the Rock. Possibly the oldest surviving prayer niche in the world.

The cave originally extended much further in a southeasterly direction, but had to be closed to create support for one of the piers of the inner circle above. It contains numerous prayer niches and points of interest. The most important, historically, is the *mihrab* (prayer niche) dedicated to Solomon, or marking where he prayed. It is flat instead of concave and may well date from the time of Abd al-Malik (concave prayer niches did not come into use until 709 A.D., well after al-Malik's time). If so, this is the oldest surviving prayer niche in the world. Another point of interest is the marble slab at the center of the floor, which is believed by Muslims to cover the entranceway to the underworld. As you leave the cave, notice the entrance at the top of the stairs, which is from the Crusader period. This was the only time when there was a Christian presence (the Knights Templars) on the Temple Mount. The Dome of the Rock was converted into a church called Templum Domini, the Temple of God, and an altar set up on the rock above. Before leaving the building, take a look at the ceilings of the porches of the eastern and western entranceways. Here you can see the mosaics that once covered the entire exterior of the building before they were replaced with tiles.

The DOME OF THE ROCK is open every day except Friday and Muslim holy days, 8 A.M.–12 noon and 1–3 P.M.; during Ramadan, 8–11 A.M. only.

THE AL-AQSA MOSQUE (*Arabic: Al Masjid Al-Aqsa; Hebrew: Misgad al-Aqsa*)

Christian sources indicate that shortly after the Arab conquest of Jerusalem a rather primitive and simple Muslim place of prayer was established on the Temple Mount. (Simple as it may have been, it was reportedly capable of accommodating three thousand people.) It was built on the southern part of the mount and was apparently made by roofing over the ruins of Herod's royal stoa. The first al-Aqsa Mosque itself was built in 705 A.D., and is usually attributed to al-Walid, son of the caliph Abd al-Malik.

Both the Dome of the Rock and the al-Aqsa Mosque have suffered from numerous earthquakes and had to be rebuilt. But whereas the Dome of the Rock has always remained faithful to its original pattern and plan, the size and shape of the al-Aqsa Mosque have varied greatly over the centuries. The mosque we see today is a mixture (and often a reproduction) of styles from different periods, although the overall effect is one of simple beauty and grandeur. A major reconstruction was undertaken in the present century, and many of the original pieces can be seen in the adjoining museum.

Today the name al-Aqsa is generally associated with the mosque alone. This was not always the case; originally it applied to the whole of the Haram area. The word *masjid*—which we translate as "mosque" and associate with a partic-

ular building as we do with a synagogue or a church—
actually means in Arabic "a place of prostration (in prayer)."
In their classical form the great mosques consisted of an
open courtyard along whose four walls ran colonnades which
gave shelter to the worshippers. At the side of the enclosure
facing Mecca (the direction of prayer) the colonnade was
widened to form the place of assembly where worshippers
stood and knelt during prayer. This was called the covered
part or forepart of the mosque, and contained a niche
(*mihrab*) denoting the *qibla,* the direction of Mecca. The
colonnade on the opposite side of the courtyard was considered the back of the mosque. The enclosed courtyard itself
contained other buildings such as tombs or chapels. Often a
major structure stood at its center, with minor ones spread
over the area. This description also fits the Haram es-Sharif,
with al-Aqsa playing the role of the covered part of the
mosque.

The name given to the entire area, al Masjid al-Aqsa,
comes from sura (section) 17 of the Qur'ān, which mentions,
in a single sentence, the prophet's Night Journey: "Praise be
to Him who made His servant travel by night from the
Masjid al-Haram to the Masjid al-Aqsa." There has never
been any controversy regarding the Masjid al-Haram (the
Sacred Mosque), which was identified as the sanctuary of
the Kā'bah, in Mecca. But the Masjid al-Aqsa (the Further,
or Outer, Mosque) has always presented a problem. One
early tradition connected it with a small sanctuary on the
outskirts of Mecca. A second, more important, tradition
claimed that it did not refer to an actual earthly sanctuary
but to a heavenly one. This latter tradition brought into
question the very nature of the event. Was it a dream, a
vision, a trip made in the flesh, or a spiritual voyage?

Despite the many controversies regarding the mosque's
location, by the time of al-Walid and the building of al-Aqsa
the belief that it referred to the mosque in Jerusalem had
become the accepted one in the Muslim world. There is
considerable evidence to support the conviction that this was
not just another alternative which had won the day, but
rather what had been intended by the Qur'ān all along.

The first piece of evidence lies in some of the earliest
biographies of the prophet. In these it is told that when
Muhammad related his experience to the citizens of Mecca
he was met with hostility and derision by the aristocracy. He
was then asked by one of his closest companions, Abu Bakr,
to describe the place he had been to. And it was Abu Bakr
who recognized it as the Temple area of Jerusalem. We may
also recall here Omar's stubbornness regarding the location
of "David's Sanctuary," claiming that the prophet himself
had described the place to him.

The second piece of evidence concerns the importance of
Jerusalem in the environment which nurtured the first Muslim community—the city of Medina. According to Muslim

histories Medina's large population of Jews, who formed its leading community, had moved there after the destruction of Bayt al Mukaddas, or the Temple. Little can be said with certainty concerning the influence of these Jews on the prophet Muhammad and the earliest followers of Islam. There can be no doubt, however, that their traditions and beliefs played a role, since Islam did not pretend to be a new religion, but rather the final revelation of what had gone before. Like the Jews and Christians before them the Muslims were descended from Abraham, whom the Qur'ān describes as neither Jew nor Christian but a *hanif*. The term is untranslatable but refers to a holy man who has surrendered completely to God—in other words, a Muslim, since "Islam" means "submission" or "surrender" (to God). While the Qur'ān regarded the destruction of Solomon's Temple as a punishment for disobeying God, Muslims from the very beginning recognized the intrinsic sanctity of Jerusalem and the Temple area. It is known that at first the *qibla*, or direction in which the prophet prayed, was toward Jerusalem. The replacement of Jerusalem by the Kā'bah in Mecca came suddenly. Muhammad was at a place of prayer outside Medina and had just made the second prostration toward Jerusalem when he was divinely inspired to pray in future toward Mecca, and he immediately recited the revelation regarding this event as recorded in the second sura of the Qur'ān. He then turned south toward Mecca, and the whole congregation of believers turned with him.

The third piece of evidence is the inner meaning of the term "al-Aqsa." Attempts to locate the "furthest mosque" by geographical means must be subjective and doomed to failure. What is furthest from Mecca is relative and can mean almost anything. To understand the true significance one must look elsewhere for an objective point from which to measure it. And this point may have no direct relation to Mecca as is generally assumed, since the only truly objective starting point is not a geographical one but an inner spiritual one.

As we have seen in the Dome of the Rock, the inner circle of the absolute contains all possibilities and contradictions in a realm of perfect unity, where man is said to have existed before the fall. He is never really separated from the absolute which encompasses all. His illusory distance from the center, his partiality and exile, can be measured only by his inability or unwillingness to comprehend all the possibilities and contradictions of his own inner unity. The points forming the first octagon of the Dome of the Rock represent the furthest limit of this separation and fall, where a man awakens to the hopelessness of his partial life, and reorients himself to the path of return. This is the first step in renewing the harmony that existed within the circle of the absolute in the beginning. The point where this takes place is called Jerusalem, symbolized by the rebuilding of the Temple and the reestablishment of the perfect sacrifice. The city's Temple is called al-Aqsa, the furthest sanctuary, situated at the outer limit of man's fall, which is also the point of his return.

AL-AQSA is open at the same hours as the Dome of the Rock. See page 69.

THE GOLDEN GATE
(Hebrew: Sha'ar HaRachamim)

This rather large gatehouse, which once served as the eastern entranceway to the Temple Mount, is steeped in a vast body of legends and tradition linking it to events that will take place here at the end of days. The great doors of the structure's eastern facade (facing the Mount of Olives) were removed during the reign of the Turkish sultan Suleiman the Magnificent (sixteenth century), and the entranceway was sealed with stone blocks. The fact that it has remained sealed ever since has only enhanced the gate's eschatological importance, and fostered the belief that it will reopen only when the Messiah appears.

The Christian Tradition: The Golden Gate
The name Golden Gate seems to be a misnomer. In the days of the Temple the gate of the outer court of the Temple was called in Hebrew Sha'ar HaYafeh, the Beautiful Gate. In Greek "beautiful" is *horea,* which sounds like the Latin *aurea* (gold). In the fifth century, when Christians were identifying and naming the sacred sites of Jerusalem, the Temple had long since been destroyed and the Beautiful Gate no longer existed. However, there was still an eastern entranceway to the Temple Mount, and this was mistakenly identified as the Golden Gate.

Christians believe that it was by way of the Golden Gate that Jesus entered the Temple Mount after his descent from the Mount of Olives. The event is still celebrated on Palm Sunday, though the procession enters Jerusalem through the Lions' Gate. In 628, the Byzantine emperor Heraclius arrived in Jerusalem after defeating the Persians and recovering the "true cross" they had taken fourteen years earlier during the sacking of the Church of the Holy Sepulchre. When the emperor appeared on the Mount of Olives, the Christians of the city went out to meet him with palm leaves and olive branches, and in festive mood accompanied him to Jerusalem's eastern wall. (The description is reminiscent of Jesus's own triumphal entry.) But as Heraclius approached the Golden Gate, legend holds that the stones joined together and blocked his way. A cross was seen in the sky and an angel appeared admonishing him for entering in such splendor where Jesus had entered in such humility. Heraclius humbled himself and the stones removed themselves and let him enter.

The site is also a favorite subject of Christian iconography, which depicts it as the place where Joachim and Anne met after they had received a revelation concerning the birth of their daughter Mary. The association here is a double one. First of all, it is the gate through which the Messiah (Mary's son, Jesus) would pass. Second, Mary herself is the Golden Gate through which Jesus (the new Temple) will appear in the world.

The Jewish Tradition: Sha'ar HaRachamim— The Gate of Mercy

During the centuries following the destruction of the Temple, four places became focal points of Jewish prayer. Within Jerusalem were the Temple Mount and the Western Wall, while outside were the Mount of Olives and the Gate of Mercy. At the start of the Muslim period, Jews were permitted to approach the two sites inside the city walls. By the ninth century, access to the Temple Mount was forbidden to them while prayer at the Western Wall became increasingly difficult. As conditions worsened within the city, the two places outside it gained in importance. By the Middle Ages the Gate of Mercy had become a principal site of Jewish devotion. The gate's importance declined only toward the end of the Middle Ages, when the establishment of a Muslim cemetery here made access to it impossible. According to tradition, through this gate the Shechinah, the Divine Presence, abandoned Jerusalem after the destruction of the Temple, and through this gate it will one day return. At that time the Messiah will appear on the Mount of Olives. He will pass through the Valley of Jehoshaphat, setting in motion the resurrection of the dead, and enter Jerusalem through the Gate of Mercy.

The Muslim Tradition: Bab e-Tauba and Bab e-Rahma— The Gate of Repentance and the Gate of Mercy

Muslim tradition assigns each of the two doors of the gate a separate name. When the Qur'ān speaks of the last days and the Day of Judgment, it mentions no specific place where these events are to take place. However, traditionally it is Jerusalem. At that time, we are told, "There will arise a wall and within it a gate. Within the wall will be mercy, while outside it affliction." By the tenth century, this prophecy had been linked to these gates. Hence their names, the Gate of Repentance and the Gate of Mercy. According to legend, the angel Gabriel will blow on the ram's horn three times to signal the Resurrection and all mankind will assemble on the Mount of Olives. Abraham, Moses, Jesus, and Muhammad will stand beside the scales of justice. The gates of paradise and hell will be opened, and all men will be judged. From the Mount of Olives to a point near these gates there will be a bridge as thin as a single hair, as sharp as a sword, and as black as the darkest night, and over it the just will pass safely to eternal life.

As David prayed here and God forgave his sins, so too did generations of Muslims come to these gates to receive God's mercy. Many people chose to be buried here because they believed that they would be the first to be resurrected and enter paradise.

Who Built the Gate?

During the Six Day War a cannon shell exploding near the Golden Gate exposed below it an older, buried section of the Temple Mount's eastern wall and the upper part of an arch. The presence of the Muslim cemetery adjacent to the gate has prevented scientific excavations from taking place here. We therefore do not know whether the gate is indeed built on the foundations of a still earlier one whose entranceway may have been as much as 39 feet (12 meters) below present ground level.

On the basis of its architectural and artistic features the gate has generally been assumed to be Byzantine, with assorted additions and repairs carried out later. Today, a convincing alternate theory has been proposed (by Meir Ben-Dov, the Israeli archeologist responsible for the excavations at the Temple Mount) which assigns its original construction to the Umayyad rulers of Jerusalem who also built the Dome of the Rock and the al-Aqsa Mosque. The idea that such an elaborate structure was Byzantine should always have been suspect, given the then-prevailing Christian attitude toward the Temple Mount. Only the reliance on recognizable styles has kept the "Byzantine" theory alive.

In the Israel of the Byzantine period there was a rich flowering of local art. This lasted until long after the Arab conquest and was responsible for many of Jerusalem's finest Christian as well as Muslim monuments. A thorough investigation of the gate has shown it to be utterly free of Christian signs or symbols, thus opening the way to a possible Muslim dating. A great many architectural projects were undertaken in the Temple Mount area during the Umayyad period, and the only question remaining is why the gate was built. Medieval sources say that at one time the steps leading eastward from the Dome of the Rock were called the al-Buraq steps. Other sources of the same period confirm the connection between al-Buraq and the eastern side of the Temple. So the gates must have been built to commemorate Muhammad's arrival in Jerusalem and the place where he tied his steed, al-Buraq. It is no accident that this echoes Jesus' triumphal entry at the same place while seated upon an ass. Both events prefigure what is to come at the end of days. (The association between the Golden Gate and Muhammad's arrival in Jerusalem is no longer made today. The tradition of al-Buraq was transferred to the Temple Mount's western wall earlier this century when Jewish nationalism began to be associated with that site and Arab nationalism sought to refute Jewish claims to it.)

THE MINOR MONUMENTS

There are about a hundred minor monuments scattered over the Haram area. These include domes, porticoes, religious schools, arcades, praying platforms, minarets, drinking fountains, and gates. The best known are:

The Scales
At various points surrounding the Dome of the Rock you can see arcades consisting of long free-standing pillars supporting arches. These are called the "balances" or the "scales." It is believed that on the Day of Judgment the scales for weighing each man's good and evil deeds will be hung here.

The Scales leading to the Dome of the Rock.

The Dome of the Chain
Just outside the eastern entranceway to the Dome of the Rock is a relatively large domed monument called the Tribunal of the Prophet David, or, more popularly, the Dome of the Chain. It stands right in the center of the Haram area, just where one would expect to find the Dome of the Rock. Its original purpose is unknown, but its similarity to the Dome of the Rock is striking. It is said that in King David's time a chain was suspended from the dome. Parties to a dispute had to hold the chain while taking an oath or giving evidence. If a lie was told, a link would fall from the chain, and the king was able to determine the honesty of those who came before him in judgment. This tradition is also reflected in the name given to the eastern door of the Dome of the Rock, the Gate of David.

However, this legend bears no relation to the facts. At the time of David there were no structures here, and the domed monument itself dates only from the time of Abd al-Malik and the period following the Muslim conquest. However, remembering all we have seen in the Dome of the Rock (which was constructed in the same period, and probably by the same builders), we will realize that the legend does preserve the ideas the builders of both monuments wished to express. As in the Dome of the Rock, the vertical line from the center of the dome above to the floor below represents the chain of all the worlds that exist in the absolute. The last to hold on to this chain is man. But his hold is tenuous. As long as he continues to serve that which is higher (represented in the legend by the truth) the chain remains intact, but when he serves what is lower (represented by the lie) the link is severed.

A second tradition holds that the structure was used as the treasury for the Muslims of the city. The open plan made it impossible to enter the building without being seen, while the treasure itself was kept on a second floor, which could be reached only by a ladder.

The Dome of the Ascension
This is a thirteenth-century octagonal structure dedicated to the place where Muhammad prayed before his ascension to heaven. This event is usually commemorated inside the Dome of the Rock. There are traditions which also link it with the cave beneath the rock, but there are no reasons given to support these traditions.

The Dome of the Ascension. Note the similarity to the Church of the Ascension on the Mount of Olives. (See page 211.)

The Gate of the Cotton Merchants, the Temple Mount.

The Gates

There is an enormous number of gates to the Temple Mount, which is unusual in a structure that could easily be used as a fortress in times of emergency (and, indeed, has often been so used). Herod also built his enclosure with more entranceways than were necessary. Gateways are the least defensible part of a structure, and Herod wished to convince Rome that his intentions were religious rather than military.

The Arabic word for gate is *bab*, which also refers to the chapter of a book. Both represent the beginning or the end of a journey. As you walk through Jerusalem, notice the different doors and gateways which open onto sacred places or onto the city itself. These entranceways serve more than just a practical purpose. Their often elegant form and design acts as a striking point of separation between the world inside and the world outside (i.e., between the worlds of the sacred and the profane). (*See* page 47.)

THE OPHEL ARCHEOLOGICAL GARDEN

This is not a sacred site, but is of great significance because so much of Jerusalem's history has been uncovered here. The archeological garden was opened to the public in 1986 following fifteen years of excavations at the foot of the Temple Mount. It is perhaps the most important excavation ever to take place in Jerusalem. The archeologists have uncovered twenty-five levels of occupation ranging from the time of Solomon, who first settled the Ophel in the tenth century B.C., to the sixteenth-century Ottoman sultan Suleiman the Magnificent, who was the last to repair and rebuild the city's walls.

There is a well-signposted route to guide you through the garden. Each of the eighteen stations contains an explanation, in English, of what you can see. The descriptions are necessarily short and cannot convey the fullness of the flow of history. A far more rewarding experience is to take the tour given by one of the archeologists who worked on the site. The tour begins in the afternoon (every day except Friday and Saturday) at the entranceway to the site. You do not have to sign up ahead of time, the price is minimal, the groups are usually very small, and the commentary is given in English. The tour takes about an hour and a half. It is informative, extremely interesting, and highly recommended. (It is best to pass by here beforehand and check the exact time the tour is being given.)

THE STATIONS

1. *The Entranceway to the Site* Located just inside the Dung Gate.

2. *The Southwest Corner of Herod's Temple Mount* This is the beginning of the western retaining wall of Herod's Temple Mount. It runs northward for 1,590 feet (485 meters), of which you see here only 230 feet (70 meters). All four retaining walls were built on bedrock. Because it was built on a hill, the wall's foundations were laid anywhere between 6.5 and 65.5 feet (2–20 meters) below ground level. Today it rises only 75 feet (23 meters) above the ground, and of these only 46 feet (14 meters) are of the original 105-foot (32-meter) Herodian masonry. The Herodian blocks are easily distinguished from the later ones by their enormous size and dressed margins. The smallest weigh 2 to 5 tons, and at the corners are some over 50 tons. (During the excavation one block was found weighing 400 tons, surely the largest in the ancient world.)

Blocks weighing 50–100 tons, at the southwest corner of the Temple Mount.

3. *Robinson's Arch* Further on, you can see above you the remains of an arch jutting out of the western wall. This is all that is left of what must have been the largest overpass in the world, joining the esplanade below with the royal stoa above.

Hebrew inscription on a typical Herodian stone with dressed margins. "And when ye see this, your heart shall rejoice, and your bones shall flourish like an herb..." (Isaiah 66:14).

4. *A Hebrew Inscription* On one of the blocks below Robinson's Arch, etched in Hebrew letters are the words of Isaiah, "And when ye see this, your heart shall rejoice, and your bones shall flourish like an herb ..." (Isaiah 66:14). In Isaiah the line continues, "and the hand of the Lord shall be known toward his servants, and his indignation toward his enemies." From the fourth century on, this was interpreted as a prophecy concerning the end of days. The inscription was probably made by a hopeful Jew at a period when the rebuilding of the Temple and the fulfillment of the prophecy seemed imminent, most likely at the end of the fourth century during the reign of "the apostate" emperor Julian, who considered Constantine's alliance with the Christian Church to be an error. When, in 361, Julian became the ruler of the Roman Empire, he determined to strip Christianity of its preferred status. One of his moves was to ally himself with the Jews, and allow them to rebuild the Temple. However, he was killed two years later, before the plan could be implemented.

5. *A Paved Road* This is a section of the 33-foot-wide (10 meters) paved road that ran along the western wall of the Temple Mount in the days of Herod. It was the city's most important thoroughfare and marketplace. Where the road meets the wall a section has been exposed which permits you to see well below ground level. Here you can see a part of the wall's foundations as well as those of small shops that ran all along the eastern side of the road.

6. *The Pier of Robinson's Arch* These are the remains of the support for Robinson's Arch on the western side of the paved road. It was 49 feet (15 meters) long and 12 feet (3.7 meters) wide. The weight of the arch it carried is estimated at 1,000 tons. There were four shops located in the base of the pier. The arches of their doors helped support the tremendous weight above.

7. *The Courtyard of the Umayyad Palace* Returning to the southwest corner of the Temple Mount, you can also see here the corners of three other buildings originally built in Umayyad times. Station 7 itself is located in the courtyard of the building that served as the Umayyad palace. This was one of the most important finds of the excavation. As mentioned earlier, the Abbasid caliphs and their historians tried to downplay the importance, and as much as possible obliterate the memory, of anything Umayyad. Prior to the recent excavations the presence of a royal complex here was not even suspected. These buildings, together with the structures on the Temple Mount, clearly show the important place Jerusalem held in early Muslim thought. With the rise of the Abbasid dynasty this importance began to wane. The royal buildings either collapsed or were purposely destroyed, and Jerusalem entered a period of neglect and decline.

8. *The Observation Point Above the Excavations* Here you can get an excellent view of the Ophel excavations, beyond it the City of David, and the mountains and deep valleys that enclosed it. You are now atop the remains of a fortified tower that lies at about the midpoint of the southern wall of the Temple Mount (the al-Aqsa Mosque is just behind us). The present-day city wall begins here, runs south to the limit of the excavation, and then turns westward. To the east of the north-south wall you can see the continuation of the excavations. Before the eleventh century the city wall included all the excavated area. The tower and present north-south wall were first built in the latter part of the eleventh century as a fortification against the impending Crusader attack. It was at this time that the various southern entranceways to the Temple Mount were blocked up.

9. *A Byzantine Residence* While the Temple Mount itself lay in ruins in the Byzantine period, the area directly to the south became a densely populated residential district, especially in the later Byzantine period of the sixth to seventh centuries. Here you can see a number of rooms from one of these multistoried dwellings, including a basement that was used as a storeroom.

10. *A Building of the Herodian* (*Second Temple*) *Period* The building was destroyed at the time of the Jewish War. Further damage was caused by subsequent building in the area. The original building has been partly reconstructed. At the time of the Temple there were three Jewish festivals when every man was required to make a pilgrimage to the Temple and offer sacrifice. To enter the Temple Mount one had to show proof of being ritually clean. The building contains a number of ritual baths, far too many for the needs of a single family. It is either a public dormitory for pilgrims or a private house whose owner offered people the service of ritual bathing just before they entered the sacred precinct.

11. Cistern A cistern cut in the bedrock of the Herodian house for storing rainwater to be used in the ritual baths.

12. The Acra Pool It is rare to find a structure from before the time of Herod close by the present southern wall of the Temple Mount. As we recall, Herod greatly extended the Temple Mount. Today a seam, or joint between two walls, can still be seen in its eastern wall 105 feet (32 meters) north of its southeast corner. This is where the Herodian extension southward joined the wall of the previous period. Herod laid the foundations of the Temple Mount and the esplanade fronting it (on the south) on bedrock. Thus any earlier buildings almost certainly have been demolished.

After the Jews returned from exile in Babylon in the sixth century B.C. and rebuilt the Temple, they enjoyed two centuries of peace and religious freedom under Persian rule. This era came to an end in the mid-fourth century B.C. with Alexander the Great's conquest of the east. This was by no means a revolution, and the earlier Hellenistic period, under Alexander's successors, was still one of relative religious tolerance. Gradually, however, the spread of Greek culture began to take its toll on Jerusalem. The struggle between Jewish traditionalists and Hellenists often reached such dimensions that the rulers of the country had to intervene. In the mid-second century B.C. the ruler was the Seleucid emperor Antiochus IV (Antiochus Epiphanes, who ruled from Syria), who decided to settle the argument once and for all in favor of Hellenism.

It was Antiochus' excesses in carrying out this policy that eventually sparked the successful rebellion led by the Hasmonean family (the Maccabees). He massacred the population of Jerusalem; defiled the Temple by setting up his own image in the Temple court and halting the sacrifices; and to be sure he was obeyed, he constructed the Acra fortress to overlook the Temple Mount from the south. The fortress was eventually destroyed by Simon the Hasmonean. After this, houses with ritual baths and cisterns were built on the site (as you saw in stations 10 and 11). Finally the area was appropriated by Herod for paving the street and square facing the main entranceways to the Temple Mount. Today we see the plastered pool that formed a part of the Acra.

13. Umayyad Buildings Along both sides of the path are remains of Byzantine houses. Such intensive building, with house nearly touching house, is usually indicative of the later Byzantine period (fifth–sixth centuries). Adjoining the southern wall is the remains of a large Umayyad structure. Note the wall which surrounded the entire Ophel area before the new lines of defense were drawn in the late eleventh century.

14. A Public Building from the First Temple Period Again, a very rare find, and not easy to see. Under the corners of the Umayyad structure it is possible to distinguish the margins of a government building from the First Temple period (tenth–sixth centuries B.C.). In the very early days of Jewish Jerusalem the geographical separation between functions was an interesting one. Below was the City of David, where the general population lived. Above this was the Ophel, with the royal administration. And highest of all was the Temple. This vertical hierarchy of people, king, God typified the Jewish kingdom.

15. A Byzantine Neighborhood A continuation of the Byzantine neighborhood. These were once two-story houses consisting of several rooms built around a central courtyard. At the moment it is not possible to enter the area.

16. The Triple Gate—The Eastern Hulda Gate This area— the partially restored stairway leading to the Temple Mount and its entranceways—is perhaps the most exciting part of

The Triple Gate—The Eastern Hulda Gate.
Entranceway to Herod's Temple Mount.

the tour. For the first time in untold centuries you can feel what it must have been like to approach the most magnificent temple and sacred precinct in the ancient world. The entranceways and gates used today by visitors to the Temple Mount give you a sense of leaving the outside world and entering a fortress or monastery. Here, looking south to the approaches to the Mount, we can appreciate the words of Jeremiah, "Arise ye, and let us go up to Zion unto the Lord our God" (Jeremiah 31:6). The pilgrim not only had to make the steep ascent to these gates, but once here he was faced with a structure that towered majestically above him.

The Mishnah is quite explicit on this matter: "There were five gates to the Temple Mount." These included "the two Hulda gates to the south that served for coming in and going out" (Mishnah, Midot Tractate 1:3). Today these two main entranceways to the sacred enclosure are known as the Triple Gate (the eastern Hulda Gate where you are now) and the Double Gate (the western Hulda Gate at station 17, 230 feet [70 meters] further west). The name Hulda has two possible derivations. The first relates it to the prophetess Hulda, who is reputed to have sat here to deliver her prophecies in the First Temple period. Some also claim that she was buried here. The second possibility relates it to the sloping vaulted tunnel that joined the gates to the esplanade of the sacred enclosure 46 feet (14 meters) above. *Hulda* is the Hebrew word for "rat," and the pilgrim's passage through the tunnel and exit above was likened to the way a rodent emerges from its underground burrow.

The three sealed arched gates are products of the rebuilding of the areas of the Temple Mount undertaken by the Umayyads. In the Second Temple period they were rectangular, with one high central door and two lower flanking ones, which were for entrance only. Visitors entered here, walked around the Temple, and left by the western Hulda Gate. The only exception to this rule was those who had suffered some sort of tragedy during the previous year: they entered through the western gate and exited through the eastern one. Thus, anyone seen going in the opposite direction was immediately known to be a mourner, and even perfect strangers would say, "May he that dwelleth in this house give thee comfort" (Midot 2:2).

17. *The Double Gate—The Western Hulda Gate* Almost all of the Double Gate, as well as a good part of the staircase facing it, is blocked by the fortified tower built in the eleventh century. Notice the irregular pattern in which the steps are built. People have a natural tendency to speed up while descending steps, and this pattern forced visitors to continue to walk in a slow and dignified manner. The staircase here was three times as wide as the one facing the Triple Gate. Even today, people attending a religious service arrive at different times, but at the end they all leave at once. Thus, a wider exit area was required.

Before leaving the area, look to the east of the Triple Gate, where you will see the remains of yet another sealed gate. This is called the Single Gate. You have already had a close look at the massive retaining walls built by Herod. In order to construct the Temple esplanade on one level, the area between the walls (in the southern part of the Mount at least) was not filled in with rubble as one might expect. Instead, Herod used layers of high-domed vaults resting on stone pillars. There were technical reasons for this, but more important were the religious ones. For Jews, any contact with the dead makes one ritually unclean, and to this day members of priestly families are forbidden to enter cemeteries. Assuring the ritual purity of the priests officiating at the Temple was vital. Since it could not be known what graves might be hidden in the depths of the earth below the Temple Mount, Jewish law prescribed that the void formed by building a vault over a grave neutralized its inherent ritual impurity. A stone floor built over such vaults could then be walked on without fear of contamination. These vaults were partly destroyed or damaged in the Byzantine period, but rebuilt and repaired in the early Muslim period. In the Crusader period the Knights Templars used these vaulted halls for stabling their horses, giving them the name Solomon's Stables (though the Temple did not extend this far south in Solomon's time). The entrance to these stables seems to have been from inside the Temple Mount through the tunnel that led down to the Triple Gate. Near the base of this tunnel an entranceway was broken through to the vaulted area. At a certain point during the Crusader period, the Single Gate was constructed to permit direct access from the southern wall.

18. Gate Made by Excavators The tour ends at the gate made by the excavators in the existing Old City wall in order to join the two parts of the Ophel Archeological Garden. From here you can see the exit at station 1.

The OPHEL ARCHEOLOGICAL GARDEN is open Sunday to Thursday, 9 A.M.–5 P.M.; Friday, 9 A.M.–3 P.M. Closed Saturday.

THE WESTERN WALL *(Hebrew: HaKotel HaMa'aravi)*

One of Judaism's most sacred sites is the Western Wall, sometimes called the Wailing Wall—a 197-foot (60-meter) stretch of the 1,590-foot-long (485 meters) western retaining wall of the Temple Mount. Looking at the point where the Western Wall Plaza meets the wall we can distinguish, from the base upward, seven layers of massive Herodian stone blocks with their typically worked margins. Above these are four or five layers of large stones, without margins, dating from the Umayyad reconstruction of the Temple Mount. And higher still, rows of smaller stones dating from various subsequent periods. Below the level of the plaza are a further eight levels of Herodian stone blocks which reach down to the Second Temple period paved road we saw before. Below these lie nine more Herodian levels which act as the wall's foundations. These latter have never been fully uncovered, but some impression of their depth can be gained from the exposed shaft alongside the continuation of the wall under Wilson's Arch.

The Western Wall Plaza is divided into separate prayer areas for men and women (the northern two-thirds for men, the southern third for women). At the extreme righthand corner of the women's area, adjacent to the vaulted room used by them in bad weather, you can see part of one enormous stone block, beneath which there is a section filled in with much smaller ones. This is the remains of Coponius' Gate, today called Barclay's Gate after its nineteenth-century discoverer. It is the only complete gate to have survived from the period of the Second Temple. Except for the central eastern Hulda Gate, all the gates to the Temple Mount were the same size. Their openings were in the ratio of 2:1, measuring 36 feet (11 meters) by 18 feet (5.6 meters).

The Jewish attitude toward the Western Wall represents perhaps the clearest answer we shall find in Jerusalem to the question, What is a sacred place? The story of Mt. Moriah begins with the Foundation Stone from which the world was created. Its sanctity is not dependent upon man, and cannot be abrogated by earthly events. Even the destruction of its most significant material representation, the Temple, cannot affect the site's inherent holiness since it lies opposite the gates of heaven, which never close.

As we have seen, the Temple was not built as a place of assembly and prayer but as a sanctuary to house the Shechinah, the Divine Presence on earth. This sanctuary was especially associated with the Temple's innermost sanctum, the Holy of Holies, entered only once a year by the high priest on the Day of Atonement. In the First Temple the Divine Presence was believed to sit upon the Ark of the Covenant, which was set against the western wall of the Temple itself. In Herod's Temple there was no ark (it had disappeared during the destruction of the First Temple), but the association of the Shechinah with the western wall of the Temple continued. There is a tradition that when Herod's Temple was itself destroyed (on the ninth day of the month of Av, the same date as the destruction of the First Temple), only its western wall survived. This reflected the belief that the Shechinah's presence at the place of contact between heaven and earth was a permanent one. God's promise to Solomon that "I have chosen and sanctified this house, that my name may be there for ever: and mine eyes and mine heart shall be there perpetually" (II Chronicles 7:16) came to be understood to mean that the Divine Presence would never leave the western wall. Even when God's sanctuary was physically destroyed, it remained God's sanctuary invisibly.

The Temple's destruction did not diminish Jewish devotion to the sacred site, though access to it was limited and depended on the ruling power of the day. During the Roman and Byzantine periods, when Jews were officially banned from the city, the closest available approach was on the Mount of Olives, which became a center for Jewish prayer and a place of mourning for the ruined Temple. With the Arab conquest, Jews were again permitted to live in the city and places of prayer were established at the Temple Mount's eastern and western walls, as well as at its gates, especially the newly reconstructed Hulda Gates in the south. In the early Arab period there was even some limited access to the Temple Mount itself. By the eleventh century a sizable Jewish Quarter had grown up to the southwest of the Temple Mount, enjoying easy access to the Western Wall. And it was perhaps this accessibility that led to its becoming a favored place of prayer. During the five hundred years that followed, the place underwent a gradual yet very definite transformation in the consciousness of the Jewish people. The ancient tradition concerning the Divine Presence somehow began to detach itself from the western wall of the Temple itself, and reattach itself to the more visible western wall of the Temple Mount.

This phenomenon is often found in Jerusalem. The traditions themselves remain, but sometimes change their setting or become overlaid with new elements that change their original emphasis. The tradition regarding the western wall of the Temple Mount is only some eight hundred years old—but the tradition underlying it, the tradition regarding the permanent sanctuary of the Divine Presence, is much older. Understanding this does not destroy what is there, and what visitors to the site feel. On the contrary, it intensifies this feeling by permitting us to see beyond the material walls before us, and refocus our vision on the invisible. As we approach the Western Wall, something opens in us, revealing feelings and emotions we did not even know were there or had long forgotten. It is easy to say that it is the heart that opens, but what is the heart if not an inner reflection of the true, unseen, divine sanctuary before which we are standing?

There is access to the WESTERN WALL 24 hours a day, 365 days a year.

3

THE CHURCH OF THE HOLY SEPULCHRE

The Church of the Holy Sepulchre is the most important Christian monument in the city of Jerusalem. It enshrines Christianity's two most revered sites: the hill of Calvary, where Jesus was crucified, and the tomb where he was buried and resurrected. The great mysteries that took place here marked significant points in the development of man's spiritual possibilities. Some of the lessons of these mysteries can still be deciphered in the building and in the ancient legends and traditions that surround it.

Today's church is hidden behind a maze of shops, dwelling places, and holy sites that line the narrow streets of the Old City. The result is that the building itself is not visible until you are actually facing it across the courtyard in front of the entranceway. The first impression is deceptive, because even here only a very small part of the structure is visible. This relatively modest and not very well preserved Crusader facade gives absolutely no hint as to what actually lies within. Certainly nobody coming upon it unawares would ever guess that this was the place where two of the greatest events in Christian history took place.

Before you begin a more detailed study of the church, it is a good idea to enter and have a quick look around. It does not matter much what direction you take. What is important is to see as much as possible and get a good feel for the place.

The impression of vastness is completely unexpected. More important, however, is the apparent lack of internal unity. The church seems to be made up of numerous independent elements almost glued together. There are large open spaces, confined spaces, small chapels, large chapels, modern chapels, and chapels whose state of decay and disrepair seems beyond belief. There are rows of columns that seem to go nowhere and be related to nothing. Modern reconstructed altars of the Latin rite lie right alongside altars, icons, and hanging lamps of the Eastern rite. There is also a very unusual element here: a vertical vastness unrelated to height. You will feel this when you go up to Calvary and again when you descend first the long staircase to the crypt, and then another set of stairs to the cave below. And throughout it all there is an atmosphere of semigloom and darkness.

It is certainly not the classic picture of a holy place, and at first glance there seems to be little here to inspire anyone but the most fervent believer. Yet the Church of the Holy Sepulchre, more than any other Christian monument in Jerusalem, contains all the elements that make up a truly sacred site.

A SHORT HISTORY OF THE CHURCH

The Church of the Holy Sepulchre has been destroyed and rebuilt several times. The present building is essentially the one modified by the Crusaders in the twelfth century. But to let it go at that would be misleading, for it is an aggregate of chapels, monasteries, and living quarters, dating from different periods, some reaching back to the original fourth-century Constantinian structure. It is the contrast between the unity of the exterior structure and the individuality still maintained by many of its interior parts that makes it so difficult to understand. To cut through this difficulty one needs to grasp at least in broad outline the history of the church and the stages of its construction.

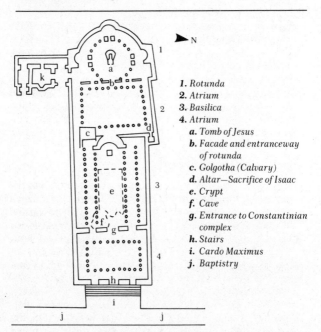

N

1. Rotunda
2. Atrium
3. Basilica
4. Atrium
    a. Tomb of Jesus
    b. Facade and entranceway of rotunda
    c. Golgotha (Calvary)
    d. Altar—Sacrifice of Isaac
    e. Crypt
    f. Cave
    g. Entrance to Constantinian complex
    h. Stairs
    i. Cardo Maximus
    j. Baptistry

Fig. 15. Constantine's Church of the Holy Sepulchre, fourth century.

THE CHURCH OF CONSTANTINE

Much of the information we have concerning the church built by Constantine and dedicated in 335 A.D. (and, indeed, for much of fourth-century Jerusalem) comes from three sources: Bishop Eusebius of Caesarea, who was an eyewitness to the building of the church, and recorded the events in his *Life of Constantine*; the account of the anonymous Pilgrim of Bordeaux, who visited the Holy Land in 333; and Egeria, a Spanish nun who spent three years in Jerusalem and the Holy Land in the latter part of the fourth century. Unlike today's church, Constantine's was a group of independent structures joined together by covered colonnades and open yards, and included:

A Rotunda A round structure built in the form of a mausoleum with three apses in its outer wall. It was called, in Greek, the *Anastasis*, or Resurrection. In the center of the rotunda stood the tomb of Jesus.

An Atrium An inner courtyard lying between the facade of the rotunda and the basilica. This was open to the sky and surrounded on three sides by covered colonnades. In the southeast corner of the atrium lay the hill of Calvary. In the northeast corner there was an altar commemorating the sacrifice of Isaac.

The Basilica of Constantine Beneath the basilica there were a crypt (which in the Crusader period became the Chapel of St. Helen) and a cave (which in the Crusader period became the Chapel of the Finding of the Cross).

Another Atrium A second courtyard surrounded by covered colonnades stood before the entrance to the basilica. At the eastern side of the atrium three doors led into the Constantinian complex. Beyond the doors a staircase led down to the Cardo Maximus.

THE CHURCH OF MODESTUS

In 614 A.D. the Persians captured Jerusalem, set fire to the Holy Sepulchre, and carried off the True Cross, on which Jesus had been crucified. Repairs to the church were carried out by Modestus, abbot of the monastery of St. Theodosius near Bethlehem (Modestus later became patriarch of Jerusalem). The fire badly damaged the church but did not destroy it, and no major change was made in its overall structure and design. One important addition made by Modestus was a chapel dedicated to Adam at the foot of Calvary. In 628 the Byzantine emperor Heraclius defeated the Persians and retook the True Cross. The dedication of the church repaired by Modestus coincided with the triumphal entry of Heraclius and the cross into Jerusalem.

THE MUSLIM CAPTURE OF THE CITY

The weakening of both the Byzantine and Persian empires by constant warfare, combined with the zeal of the new religion of Islam, led to the capture of Jerusalem in 638 by the forces of the Caliph Omar. Omar visited the Church of the Holy Sepulchre together with the patriarch of Jerusalem. While they were seated in the atrium between the rotunda and the basilica, the muezzin called the faithful to prayer. The patriarch immediately prepared a place for Omar in the basilica and invited him to pray there. But the caliph refused and left the basilica by the eastern door, crossed the atrium, and prayed on the steps. Afterward Omar explained his action to the patriarch: "If I had prayed in the church, it would have been lost to you forever. The faithful [Muslims] would have taken it for themselves, saying 'Omar prayed here.' " In 935, in confirmation of the caliph's words, the Muslim rulers of Jerusalem closed the eastern entrance to the Holy Sepulchre and built there a small mosque because Omar had prayed there 250 years earlier.

Following the Arab conquest there were several changes of dynasty among the Muslim rulers of the city. In the mid-tenth century power fell to the Fatimid rulers of Egypt, and under their rule the Church of the Holy Sepulchre suffered its greatest calamity. In 1009, on the orders of the Fatimid caliph Hakim, the edifice built by Constantine and repaired by Modestus was completely destroyed.

THE CHURCH OF CONSTANTINE MONOMACHUS

In 1020 Christians were permitted to pray in the ruins of the church. Shortly afterward, the Muslim authorities permitted its rebuilding with funds provided by the Byzantine emperor

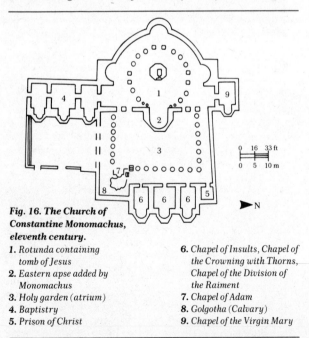

**Fig. 16. The Church of
Constantine Monomachus,
eleventh century.**

1. *Rotunda containing
   tomb of Jesus*
2. *Eastern apse added by
   Monomachus*
3. *Holy garden (atrium)*
4. *Baptistry*
5. *Prison of Christ*

6. *Chapel of Insults, Chapel of
   the Crowning with Thorns,
   Chapel of the Division of
   the Raiment*
7. *Chapel of Adam*
8. *Golgotha (Calvary)*
9. *Chapel of the Virgin Mary*

Constantine Monomachus. The church built by Monomachus, and inaugurated in 1048, was constructed on a much
smaller scale. The basilica and eastern atrium were not rebuilt, and prayers were now held in the rotunda. An eastern
apse was added to the original design of the building. This
gave it the form of a Greek cross and provided the additional
space needed to accommodate the much reduced Christian
community. In front of the rotunda the old courtyard was
reconstructed and was now called the Holy Garden. To the
east of the courtyard three new chapels were added commemorating events from the Passion of Jesus. These were
the Chapel of Insults, the Chapel of the Crowning with
Thorns, and the Chapel of the Division of the Raiment. On
Calvary a Chapel of the Nailing to the Cross was added
alongside the site of the Crucifixion, while around the Holy
Garden, galleries were added above the colonnade.

THE CRUSADER CHURCH

Until the Crusader conquest of Jerusalem in 1099, the
Church of the Holy Sepulchre had been a group of separate
structures. The biggest change made by the Crusaders was
to enclose all these separate parts under one roof in the form

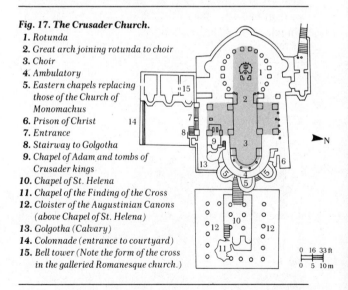

Fig. 17. The Crusader Church.
1. *Rotunda*
2. *Great arch joining rotunda to choir*
3. *Choir*
4. *Ambulatory*
5. *Eastern chapels replacing those of the Church of Monomachus*
6. *Prison of Christ*
7. *Entrance*
8. *Stairway to Golgotha*
9. *Chapel of Adam and tombs of Crusader kings*
10. *Chapel of St. Helena*
11. *Chapel of the Finding of the Cross*
12. *Cloister of the Augustinian Canons (above Chapel of St. Helena)*
13. *Golgotha (Calvary)*
14. *Colonnade (entrance to courtyard)*
15. *Bell tower (Note the form of the cross in the galleried Romanesque church.)*

of a galleried Romanesque church. It took fifty years to
complete and was dedicated in 1149.
   Where the Holy Garden had been, the Crusaders built the
choir of their church, joining it to the rotunda (which now
became the nave of the church) by removing the eastern
apse added by Monomachus. Around the choir there was a
semicircular ambulatory with three new chapels replacing

those of Monomachus. Calvary was enlarged westward, and a new entranceway was built in the south. Under the ruins of the Constantine basilica the former crypt and cave became respectively the Chapel of St. Helena and the Chapel of the Finding of the Cross.

Although the Church of the Holy Sepulchre has seen many changes in the past eight hundred years, its overall plan remains what it became in the twelfth century. In 1808 a fire damaged the church and many hurried and improvised repairs were carried out. Since 1961 the three main groups represented at the Holy Sepulchre (Greek Orthodox, Franciscans—representing the Roman Catholics—and Armenians) have been carrying out work to return the church to its original Crusader character.

THE STATUS QUO

Part of the problem in carrying out these repairs to the church stems from the so-called law of the status quo, or more precisely just the status quo.

Over the centuries the many schisms in the Christian world produced intense rivalries between the different churches over the custodianship of Jerusalem's holy sites. During the relatively short periods of Christian domination of the Holy Land, when political and religious authority were combined, rivalries were kept in hand by the dominant military power of the day. Thus in the Byzantine period, and in the early Arab epoch when Byzantine influence was still strong, the Orthodox Church was dominant, while in the Crusader period authority fell to the Latin Church.

Following the fall of the Latin Kingdom and the reassertion of Arab power, the rivalries began again in earnest. The Arabs saw themselves as the legal owners of all the holy places but were willing, for a price (most often a very high one), to grant Christians "exclusive" rights of worship at shrines that held no religious interest for Muslims. The result was a long history of bribery and intrigue. Holy sites changed hands with incredible frequency, while churches and congregations of limited financial means were often forced to relinquish their traditional holdings. This state of affairs persisted after the Holy Land came under the control of the Ottoman Turks in 1517.

In 1757 the Turkish government—perhaps in despair of ever finding a solution in the face of the conflicting pressures being brought to bear upon it by various Christian groups and governments—effectively froze the status quo at a number of Jerusalem's most problematic holy places, foremost among them the Church of the Holy Sepulchre. This decision was confirmed in 1852 and subsequently guaranteed by a conference of European powers in 1878. The minutiae of the status quo were registered by the British in 1929, and they are still in effect today. The status quo is not a solution to the problem of the ownership of Jerusalem's holy sites, but no one today wishes to envisage what would take place should its restrictions be lifted.

As far as the Church of the Holy Sepulchre is concerned, the status quo confirmed the Greek Orthodox, the Franciscans, and the Armenians as the three major guardians of the various sites within the church. Some of the areas are administered jointly while others are held as "exclusive possessions." Some very minor rights are granted to the Copts, the Ethiopians, and the Syrian Orthodox. The status quo effectively ended all changes within the church, both liturgical and physical. During the British Mandate, changes were forced upon the three major groups when it was feared that the whole building was in danger of collapsing. Under Israeli influence a modus vivendi of sorts has been reached that permits each of the groups to undertake changes in the areas under their control. But changes are slow. Agreement is difficult to reach. Rights are jealously guarded and rivalries are in some ways as strong today as ever.

THE HOLY SEPULCHRE TODAY

Now let us return to the courtyard and begin to take a closer look at the elements making up the church.

Although the Church of the Holy Sepulchre is Christianity's most important sacred site, it is perhaps the least understood edifice in the city of Jerusalem. This is due to the reasons mentioned above coupled with the enormous complexity of today's structure, which contains some forty chapels, altars, and sites of historical interest. Tours of the church are invariably disappointing, and leave the visitor with the feeling that he has missed something essential. The following guide seeks to help fill a growing need to understand a building which reflects so much of the city's history and has been instrumental in the development of Christian belief and thought.

Stairway (*1*) The western entrance to the courtyard leads down from Christian Street. All religious processions to the Church of the Holy Sepulchre pass through here.

Minaret and Mosque of Omar (*2*) To the south of the stairway is the thirteenth-century mosque dedicated to the place where Omar prayed when he visited the Holy Sepulchre in 638 A.D. This is not the site of the actual event which took place on the stairs to the east of Constantine's church.

Greek Orthodox Monastery of the Virgin Mary (*3*) During the Crusader period this was the site of the palace of the grand master of the Knights Hospitalers (Knights of St. John), who inhabited the area of the Muristan just to the west of the Church of the Holy Sepulchre. More recently it served as the residence of the Greek Orthodox superior of the Tomb of the Virgin Mary.

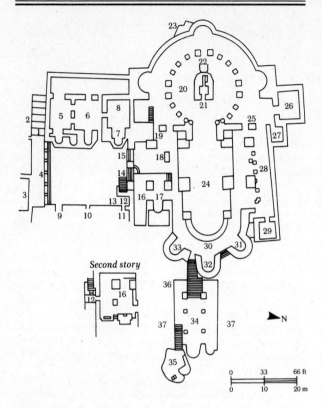

Fig. 18. The Church of the Holy Sepulchre today.

1. Stairway
2. Minaret and Mosque of Omar
3. Monastery of the Virgin Mary
4. Colonnade
5. Chapel of St. James
6. Chapel of St. John
7. Chapel of the Forty Martyrs
8. Bell tower
9. Monastery of Abraham
10. Chapel of St. John the Evangelist
11. Chapel of St. Michael
12. Chapel of the Franks
13. Chapel of St. Mary of Egypt
14. Facade
15. Entrance
16. Golgotha (Calvary)
17. Chapel of Adam
18. Stone of Anointing
19. Holy Women
20. Rotunda
21. The Tomb of Jesus (Edicule)
22. Chapel of the Copts
23. Syrian Orthodox Chapel
24. Katholicon
25. Altar of Mary Magdalene
26. Chapel of the Virgin Mary
27. Franciscan sacristy
28. Arches of the Virgin
29. Prison of Christ
30. Ambulatory
31. Chapel of St. Longinus
32. Chapel of the Division of the Raiment
33. Chapel of the Mocking
34. Chapel of St. Helena
35. Chapel of the Finding of the Cross
36. Chapel of the Four Beasts (entrance through 11)
37. Deir es-Sultan (entrance through 36)

Colonnade (4) The Crusader courtyard was bordered on the south by a portico of seven columns resting on a short flight of steps. The bases of the columns are still visible. At the western end you can see the only remaining column (with a Byzantine capital of basket design) and part of an arch.

Greek Orthodox Chapel of St. James (5), Greek Orthodox Chapel of St. John (6), and Armenian Chapel of the Forty Martyrs (7) Three chapels border the western side of the courtyard. The Pilgrim of Bordeaux reported seeing a baptistry here in 333 A.D. even before the church was completed. The candidate would have entered the vestibule of the baptistry, and facing west would have renounced Satan and disrobed. He would then have been led to the baptistry proper, where he entered the water facing east. He was then led to a third room, where he received the white robe of stainless birth.

The early fourth-century baptismal rites carried out here symbolized a number of important ideas existing in the Church at that time. The candidate, who had been lost in the world of darkness and sin, entered the first room, which represented the lower world into which he had fallen, and faced the west. This was the direction of the setting sun, the direction of night and death. It was the realm of the master of darkness, Satan, whom the candidate had served until now. He faced his old master and renounced him. Then he removed his clothes, which symbolized the garments of corruption and sin which God had woven for Adam, and stood naked, in the state of pristine innocence that had preceded the fall.

The candidate then entered a second room which represented the intermediate world of transition and transformation. Here he faced the east, the direction of the morning sun, for his own soul had lain in darkness and was about to emerge. Immersion and coming out of the water was the act by which the soul would be reborn into the light. In the third room, which represented the higher world from which man had fallen, he was dressed in a white robe symbolizing the sinless body with which man had been created at the beginning of time.

The theme of rebirth through water is very ancient and is particularly emphasized in mythologies dealing with the cycle of the sun. Most ancient traditions viewed the world as being surrounded by a vast primeval ocean. Each evening the sun, the source of all light and life, descended into the waters of the west, into the land of darkness and death. Yet each morning the sun emerged newborn from the waters of the east. This symbolism was not lost on early Church fathers such as St. John Chrysostom, who saw baptism as representing death, burial in the darkness of the deep, and resurrection to new life.

On an even deeper level, the function of baptism is to lead to the birth of the higher from the lower, the fine from the coarse, or as the alchemists stated it, the creation of gold from base metals. For this special transformation to take place the waters had to have a special quality. Water is the ultimate symbol of the world of primordial formlessness and chaos, not because it is inherently evil, but because its powers of dissolution and constant movement abolish all forms and prevent their stable reintegration. Thus, all that enters its depths is resolved into its component parts and becomes the germ of potential life it had been before the creation. But the waters of baptism had an even more valuable property: to purify, to dissolve the coarse, and, in short, to wash away sin. To achieve this the waters had to receive a special sanctification that would give them the powers of healing, both physically and spiritually. Some traditions hold that it was by Christ's own baptism and descent into the Jordan River that all waters were thus sanctified.

There are claims that the fourth-century baptistry was built on the site of a Roman bath. In the Crusader period three chapels replaced the ancient baptistry. Today's Chapel of St. James is the parish church of the Greek Orthodox Arab community in Jerusalem. The Greek Orthodox Chapel of St. John lies on the site of the actual baptistry. The Armenian Chapel of the Forty Martyrs was originally dedicated by Monomachus in the eleventh century to the apostle John, who was present at the Crucifixion. Today it commemorates second-century martyrs of the Armenian Church—the Forty Martyrs of Sebastia—who died for the faith by being drowned in a freezing lake.

Bell Tower (8) The use of church bells was forbidden by the Muslim authorities. After the Crusader conquest, a five-story bell tower was built over the Chapel of the Forty Martyrs. The upper two stories of the bell tower were destroyed by an earthquake in 1545.

Greek Orthodox Monastery of Abraham (9) This is the present residence of the Greek Orthodox superior of the Church of the Holy Sepulchre. In pre-Christian times a stone quarry reached here. The floor of the quarry was 15 feet (4.6 meters) below present ground level. As a means of both raising the level of the courtyard and collecting rainwater, Constantine's architects built here a cistern consisting of two rows of eighteen massive arched pillars. Permission to see the cistern, which is very impressive, must be obtained from the Greek Orthodox Patriarchate, located in the Old City on Greek Orthodox Patriarchate Road, just to the west of the Church of the Holy Sepulchre.

Armenian Chapel of St. John the Evangelist (10) This is a curious chapel which is rarely open to visitors. It consists solely of an apse and an altar. In work carried out here by the Armenians a set of ancient steps was discovered leading up to the altar. There is speculation that this is all that is left of a former church or chapel which the Crusaders demolished when building the present courtyard.

Ethiopian Chapel of St. Michael (*11*) This entrance leads to a small chapel dedicated to St. Michael, and then up a set of stairs to the Chapel of the Four Beasts, and the Ethiopian monastic quarters of Deir es-Sultan. (*See* p. 124.)

Latin Chapel of the Franks (*12*) To the right of the entrance to the Holy Sepulchre is a staircase leading up to a small Franciscan oratory dedicated to Our Lady of Sorrows and St. John. It is popularly called the Chapel of the Franks. It was built by the Crusaders as an open portico giving direct access to Calvary. This entrance was sealed off by Salah a-Din (Saladin) at the end of the Crusader period. Remnants of a mosaic that typified much of the artwork of the Crusader church can be seen above the sealed passageway leading to Calvary. The floral design on a golden background is reminiscent of work seen in the Dome of the Rock. One tradition holds that this is the place to which Mary withdrew while preparations were being made for the Crucifixion.

Greek Orthodox Chapel of St. Mary of Egypt (*13*) This chapel is dedicated to a woman of Egypt who, after seeing a painting of the Virgin Mary while visiting the Holy Sepulchre, was miraculously converted to Christianity. The chapel is used only once a year and is closed at all other times.

Facade (*14*) The use of pointed arches in the doors and windows of the facade is an adoption of eastern architectural features by the Crusaders at a time when rounded arches were still being used in the West. The capitals of the columns upon which these arches rest are said to be so typically Corinthian that some feel they may come from a Roman building (Crusader architects made extensive use of materials from destroyed buildings and monuments). Some of the capitals of the smaller columns have leaves plaited horizontally—a Byzantine imitation of the Corinthian style. The cornices (the lower one continuing to the Chapel of the Franks) contain floral designs in the Roman style of the second and third centuries, and may well have been taken from a Roman temple. The gables above the doors were once decorated in mosaics, while the doors themselves were covered with bands of worked bronze. Nothing of this has survived. The lintels, containing floral designs and scenes from the last journey of Jesus to Jerusalem are today in the Rockefeller Museum. The right door was sealed by Salah a-Din at the close of the Crusader period.

Entrance (*15*) As we enter the Church of the Holy Sepulchre, we must recall that up to the time of Monomachus the complex of separate structures was quite evident to the eye. The Crusaders obscured this by including everything within one overall structure, that of a galleried Romanesque church in the form of a cross. As you enter, you find yourself in the transept—the arms of the cross (*see* Fig. 17). The choir lies to the east in the present Greek Orthodox Katholicon. In the west, where we would expect to find the nave, there is the rotunda. Around the apse of the Katholicon there is an ambulatory containing a number of chapels. The wall in front of us as we enter is one of the stone walls which were added to the Katholicon after the fire of 1808, and have ever since obscured the nature of the overall design.

To build the southern transept of the church the Crusaders made a breach in the two-storied portico of the Holy Garden at approximately the point where we are now standing. An exterior facade (the present entrance) was erected that would have the same shape as the transept. An extra thickness was given to the facade until it joined with the beginning of the transept. The transept then cut across the choir, passing under the dome, continuing on the other side, and finished by abutting the columns of the northern portico remaining from the church of Monomachus. This plan will become evident as you proceed through the church.

Calvary (16) A staircase to the right of the entrance leads up to Calvary (Golgotha). Earliest records show that the place of the Crucifixion did not hold the same importance in the time of Constantine as it does today. The church was built mainly to enshrine the tomb of Jesus and commemorate the triumph of the Resurrection rather than the defeat of the cross. In the time of Constantine, Calvary was an unadorned rock surmounted by a simple cross and was probably venerated from the basilica.

In the early fifth century, an altar was constructed on Calvary and the rock was surmounted by a golden jeweled cross said to contain a small piece of the True Cross. A hundred years later a small chapel was built on the summit of the hill to protect it from weathering. By the seventh century the entire hill was enclosed in a modest independent structure. In the eleventh century Monomachus added, alongside the Chapel of the Crucifixion, a chapel commemorating the nailing of Jesus to the cross.

The Crusaders were the first to integrate Calvary fully into the general structure of the church. The old walls containing the hill were torn down, the two chapels were extended westward, and two new staircases were built. One staircase led directly to Calvary from the outside (the staircase leading to today's Chapel of the Franks). The second led directly down from the Chapel of the Crucifixion to the Crusader choir (today's Katholicon). The present stairs were built after the fire of 1808.

The Sacred Mountain The hill of Calvary is an example par excellence of the sacred mountain, which symbolizes the meeting place of the three cosmic levels of the universe: heaven, earth, and the underworld. All ancient traditions speak of a universal axis, or *axis mundi,* which connects these three worlds, and makes communication between them possible. Mountains have always been particularly suitable to this imagery since their bases are rooted in the depths while their summits soar above the ordinary. While even for ancient man the mountain was only an image, the axis which it symbolized, and which he believed ran through it, was very real. Since it was only through this axis that influences could pass from one world to another, it was always at the site of its earthly image that the great events of our own world took shape.

The three cosmic levels of the universe represented by the hill of Calvary are symbolically incorporated into the structure of the church. In the upper level, where you are now, is the summit of the hill, where heaven and earth met. Here the invisible which descended from the divine world manifested as it entered our own earthly world. The form it took was that of the crucified Christ, whose cross with its horizontal and vertical elements again symbolized the meeting place between worlds where the divine life became flesh. It is at first difficult to understand why the divine should appear in our world in the form of death. As we proceed through the church, we shall see that the life which came from above was not intended to stop at the summit of the hill but to descend the axis to its very depths. The symbolic form taken for this descent was the living blood of Christ, which, having been spilled on the cross, seeped down through the rock to bring salvation and life to those lost in the darkness of the worlds below. This emphasizes one of the themes in the Dome of the Rock—that all life in the lower world is initiated by divine sacrifice from above.

Latin Chapel of the Nailing to the Cross Calvary today is divided into two naves, as it was in the Crusader period. The

Abraham's sacrifice of Isaac. Mosaic from the Chapel of the Nailing to the Cross, Calvary.

southern nave, containing the present Latin chapel, was first constructed by Monomachus in 1048, and houses the tenth and eleventh stations on the Way of the Cross. Most of the decoration in this chapel was renewed in 1926. Three large mosaics adorn the walls. Above the altar, Jesus is seen nailed to the cross. His mother stands above him while Mary Magdalene is on her knees with her face pressed to the ground. At the head of the cross is the executioner. On the southern wall the mosaic to the left portrays the apostle John and the three Marys who were present at the execution (Mary, the mother of Jesus; her sister, Mary, wife of Cleophas; and Mary Magdalene). The mosaic on the right shows Abraham about to sacrifice Isaac—a forerunner of God's willingness to sacrifice His own beloved Son. On the vaults of the ceiling are mosaics in the style of ancient Christian basilicas. The vault near the altar contains a mosaic of Christ ascending to heaven, which is all that remains of the Crusader mosaics which once filled the church. The floor was retiled to resemble the floor of the Crusader period. The Latin altar of silver on bronze, the only piece of Renaissance art in Jerusalem,

The nailing of Jesus to the cross. God's sacrifice of His own beloved Son. Mosaic from the Chapel of the Nailing to the Cross, Calvary.

was a gift of Cardinal Ferdinand de Medici in 1588. The grillwork surrounding the altar contains six panels depicting scenes from the Passion of Jesus.

The Greek Orthodox Chapel of the Crucifixion This is located in the northern nave, and is the Twelfth Station of the Cross. An opening under the altar indicates the exact spot of the Crucifixion. To the right of the altar a rectangular opening reveals the rift in the rock of Calvary which is said to have been made by an earthquake that took place at the moment of Jesus's death. Behind the altar is a representation of Jesus on the cross. To his right is his mother, Mary, and on the left the apostle John. The wall behind the altar is divided into panels with scenes from the Passion worked in silver. The chapel is decorated in eastern style with hanging lamps and candles. The eastern vault depicts a starry sky with heads of angels, while the western one contains scenes from the Passion. Recently major reconstruction work was undertaken to make the rock of Calvary more visible.

Latin Altar to Our Lady of Sorrows Between the Latin and Greek Orthodox chapels is a small altar belonging to the Franciscans. It commemorates the taking down of Jesus from the cross and is dedicated to Our Lady of Sorrows. It is the thirteenth Station of the Cross. The statue of Mary was a gift from the Queen of Portugal in 1778. The sword piercing the heart represents the prophecy made to Mary in Luke 2:34–35: "And Simeon blessed them, and said unto Mary his mother, Behold, this child is set for the fall and rising again of many in Israel; and for a sign which shall be spoken against; (Yea, a sword shall pierce through thy own soul also,) that the thoughts of many hearts may be revealed." Beneath the altar is a grille on which can be seen the instruments of the Passion as well as the last words of Christ.

The True Cross The cross upon which Jesus was crucified, or the True Cross, holds a special place in Christian thought. The facts we have concerning it are both confusing and contradictory. Egeria's account of the Church of Constantine includes a reference to the existence of a small chapel at the foot of Calvary called "Behind the Cross." Here, she tells us, the remains of the holy wood of the cross were kept in a gold and silver box and venerated on the Friday before Easter. There seems to have been no connection between the "holy wood" mentioned by Egeria and the simple cross that stood above Calvary at the same time. In the fifth century the emperor Theodosius replaced the simple cross with a jeweled golden one which reportedly contained a small piece of the "holy wood." In 614 the Persians captured Jerusalem, set fire to the Church of the Holy Sepulchre, and, we are told, carried off the True Cross. But there are no references to indicate whether this refers to the gold and silver box containing its remains, the golden cross which contained a small piece of the "holy wood," or both, or something else altogether. History further states that in 628 the Byzantine emperor Heraclius recaptured the True Cross and returned it to Jerusalem. But in 633, overwhelmed by the Arab invasion, Heraclius relinquished Syria (including the Holy Land) and took the True Cross to Constantinople. In the Crusader period the True Cross reputedly reappeared in the Church of the Holy Sepulchre, where it was kept in the Chapel of Mary Magdalene and carried by the Crusaders into battle.

The Chapel of Adam (*17*) The Chapel of Adam, which lies directly beneath the Chapel of the Crucifixion, was originally consecrated in 628 by Modestus during reconstructions carried out after the Persian invasion. Today it is in an appalling state, and all that remains is a small window through which we can see a section of the rock of Calvary as it appears on the ground level of the church. What is important here is the fissure that runs through the rock, the same one glimpsed on the summit of the hill. According to tradition, this is the fissure through which the blood of Christ flowed to the worlds below.

The name of Adam was given to the chapel because early Christians believed that the bones of Adam, who had led mankind into error, had been placed beneath this hill to await the redemption brought by Christ, the new Adam. According to tradition, when Jesus died, an earthquake caused the hill to split and the blood of Christ dripped down the crack onto the skull of Adam, redeeming him, and through him all mankind. This theme is depicted in eastern iconography, where a skull is often portrayed at the foot of the cross. This was why the Crusader kings of Jerusalem located their places of burial just to the west of this chapel. The last of these tombs were removed in the repairs carried out after the fire of 1808, when the present staircases were built.

Over the centuries the traditions associated with this site also gave rise to a great deal of speculation concerning the name of the hill. In the time of Jesus, it was called in Aramaic—the language then spoken by the Jews of Palestine—Goghalta, meaning "skull." (The cognate Hebrew word is *goolgolet*.) From this came the modern usage Golgotha. In Latin, the word for "skull" is *calvaria*, from which we derive the name Calvary. Today both Golgotha and Calvary are used to denote the hill where Jesus was crucified. The association of this hill with a name meaning "skull" is certainly pre-Christian in date, and its origins are unknown. But in time this association, coupled with the legends regarding the skull of Adam, proved too tempting for some, and even such great figures as St. Jerome began to describe Calvary as a rounded rock in the shape of a skull. Today many guides still tell visitors to the church that this is called the Chapel of Adam because the rock here is in the shape of Adam's skull.

While the traditions and legends surrounding this chapel are interesting and informative, they are largely superficial. The true story of Adam's redemption lies not here but in the depths of the church, and in the story of Christ's descent to the underworld.

The real symbolism expressed by this chapel is an interesting one. This is the part of the sacred mountain that belongs to the level of the earth. It is located on the ground floor of the church and on the level of the surrounding streets where men go about their daily business. We can see the fissure through which the divine flows from the heavenly world above to the underworld below, but from here it is impossible to see the summit of the hill where the divine enters our world. Nor is it possible to see the depths where the divine is destined to flow and carry out its work. Many traditions describe mankind and the earth as an intermediate world. What we see here confirms this view. The *axis mundi* is anchored in the heavens above and in the underworld below, while on the level of the earth we are mere witnesses to the flow of forces between them. This situation is not just metaphorical but the actual condition of man. The sources of the great forces at play in the world are beyond man's earthly vision and beyond his grasp. But when someone chooses to leave the street outside and approach the sacred on the level of the earth, he sees that his role is to be an open channel for the accomplishment of the divine plan. Only if he surrenders himself in this way can higher influences penetrate his earthly body and flow to the darkest depths of his being, enabling what is heaviest and coarsest in him and lies in the greatest darkness to be transformed and rise up to the light.

The Stone of Anointing (*18*) The Jewish Sabbath begins on Friday evening. According to Jewish law, no one may be buried on the Sabbath. Jesus was crucified on a Friday, and, with sundown approaching, his body could not be taken far from the place of crucifixion but had to be prepared close by and buried quickly. On the wall that encloses the Katholicon are paintings depicting the events that took place here: Jesus being taken down from the cross and his embalming. In the late Byzantine period (ninth to eleventh century) the "preparation of the body" was commemorated in this area in an oratory dedicated to Mary. When the Crusaders constructed the present entrance, the oratory was removed. In the thirteenth century a simple stone of anointing was placed here. The stone has been replaced on various occasions, and the present rectangular stone slab dates from 1810 and is owned jointly by all the denominations. The lamps above the stone belong to the different communities represented in the Holy Sepulchre. Ownership by the various groups is regulated by the law of the status quo.

The Holy Women (*19*) A small circular stone slab surrounded by an iron cage commemorates the place where the three Marys stood and watched the Crucifixion. It belongs to the Armenians and commemorates the event though not the actual place, whose exact location is unknown. Some traditions claim that this is the place to which the mother of Jesus withdrew while preparations for the Crucifixion were taking place. On the wall behind is a mosaic of the Crucifixion copied from an ancient Armenian manuscript. To the left is the Armenian sacristy and a staircase leading to living quarters and an oratory belonging to the Armenian community.

This upper level is usually closed to the public, but can be visited by getting permission from the Armenian patriarchate. It is well worth the effort; it contains many interesting (even if often reproduced) examples of Armenian religious art and architecture throughout the ages.

The Rotunda (20)

Constantine ordered the building of two structures: a monument that would glorify the tomb of the Savior, and a basilica that would be the major church of Jerusalem. While the church as a whole was dedicated in 335 A.D., the rotunda itself was only completed many years later. First the builders had to disengage the tomb from the rocky hill in which it lay, and level around it a circular space 105 feet (35 meters) in diameter. It is estimated that 135,000 cubic feet (5,000 cubic meters) of stone was removed in the operation. This took the form of dressed blocks, which were used in the building of the basilica.

The fire set by the Persians in 614 caused no serious damage to the rotunda, and after repairs made by Modestus in 628 it remained essentially the same building constructed in the fourth century. The destruction caused by the caliph Hakim in 1009 was a different story, but while the greater part of the Church of the Holy Sepulchre was indeed "destroyed to its foundations," the pillars of the outer western wall of the rotunda survived and provided the basis for its restoration by Monomachus in 1048.

It is known today that the form of the exterior of the envelope of the present rotunda is the same as that of the original monument. Although the interior layout has been destroyed and reconstructed many times, the columns and pillars of the interior circular colonnade stand on the same foundations as those of the original Byzantine church. The rotunda is thus the only part of the Constantinian monument that remains relatively intact, at least on ground level.

With the destruction of the basilica by Hakim and the decision not to rebuild it (due to lack of funds, and the presence of a mosque at its entrance), Monomachus had to take into consideration that the rotunda would become the central place of worship. To this end, he enlarged the building by reconstructing it in the same basic form as before, but adding in the east an apse symmetrical with those in the north, west, and south. This gave it the overall shape of a Greek cross, and added the space necessary to accommodate the Christian community of Jerusalem. Monomachus also added an upper floor, which was later incorporated into the Crusader design of a galleried church.

It is still possible to get an impression of the rotunda as a separate building, as it was in the time of Monomachus and before. If you retrace your steps to the Stone of Anointing and look toward the rotunda, you see that to arrive there you have to pass under an arch. The wall containing this arch was part of the facade and entranceway to the rotunda, while you are standing in what was the courtyard that stood before it. Exactly the same can be seen in the north.

The three original apses of the rotunda still exist. The western one is visible and is the site of the Syrian Orthodox Chapel of Joseph of Arimathea (who buried Jesus). The southern and northern apses are obscured by monastic lodgings and storerooms now occupying the space between the interior circular colonnade and the outer fourth-century walls. Until relatively recent times there was an open semicircular ambulatory here.

Fifty years after Monomachus, the Crusaders enclosed all the separate buildings, including the rotunda, within a single overall structure. The choir of the Romanesque church (the present Katholicon) was built in the Holy Garden. The eastern apse of the rotunda, added by Monomachus, was removed and in its place a large arch was constructed joining the rotunda to the choir, the rotunda now serving as the nave of the church. Galleries constructed around the choir by the Crusaders were placed on the same level as those of the rotunda, forming one continuous floor, thus completing the construction of a galleried Romanesque church.

The Shape of the Rotunda Scholars have remarked that the shape of the rotunda drew its inspiration from a number of great Roman mausoleums of the time. Ancient peoples have always used the circle to designate the whole, the heavenly perfection, or completeness, of life. In the early Christian period it became the symbol for God, in whom all realities are united in one Being. Thus the Holy Trinity was often indicated by drawing three concentric circles. As Christianity spread, death came to be seen as a liberation from earthly limitations and a reintegration into the primordial wholeness of life. It was natural, then, that the shape of the building entombing the dead should itself symbolize the greater reality to which the departed now belonged. But while the rounded walls of the rotunda denote that the horizontal earthly plane of life and death is surrounded by a greater wholeness and reality, they cannot be viewed in isolation from the rotunda's great rounded dome of heaven above, nor from the tomb below, with its entranceway to the underworld. The greater wholeness of the earthly world depends for its very existence on its harmonious integration with the worlds both above and below. The symbol of this integration—the symbol behind all symbols—is the cycle of the sun, whose movement traces a great vertical cosmic circle which englobes all worlds.

From very early times man saw the analogy between the cycle of the sun and his own earthly predicament of birth, life, and death. He often used human terms to describe the sun's daily or yearly journey. Thus there was the newborn sun, full of youthful vigor, rising to full maturity, manhood, and strength in the highest vaults of heaven. From there his powers steadily weakened as he declined into old age, and died, and sank beneath the earth. The analogy between great cosmic events and the human condition was natural to ancient man, whose traditions and teachings told him that he was a microcosm of the All, the "image of God"; that the same laws that governed the universe governed him. Thus, man saw in the rebirth of the sun an analogy to his own possible rebirth and salvation, and reintegration into the great cycle of the One. The secret of rebirth lay in the darkness beneath the earth, where the old sun of night and coldest winter lay locked in the body of the great monster of the deep, unable to go on. Yet each day, each new year, the sun was liberated from this prison of death. Who had set him free? Who had set in motion the cycle that had come to an end? Man, too, sought this great liberator.

The theme played out at the Holy Sepulchre is one of mankind's greatest and most ancient teachings: the cycle of life, not on its earthly level, but in its cosmic meaning. Mythologically it is the story of the fall of man—the bearer of the divine spark—through the levels of the universe, and his redemption and return to the source. This lesson could only be taught at the tomb. Modern man occasionally seeks the higher but often wishes to ignore what is lower. Ancient peoples, however, understood that it was the descent into the lower world that was all-important. It was there that the great secrets were revealed, and transformation, redemption, and salvation made possible. Thus in earliest Christian times, centuries before the rotunda was built, the tomb of Jesus became the site where the Judeo-Christians reenacted the great mysteries that had taken place here. (*See* p. 110.)

The Tomb of Jesus (The Edicule or Sepulchre) (21)

This is the fourteenth, and final, Station of the Cross. Although it is the site of Christ's Resurrection as well as his tomb, the station itself commemorates only the burial. Today a number of Jerusalem's Christian communities feel that much of the meaning of the Passion of Christ has been lost by placing too great an emphasis on its tragic aspects. This is especially pronounced at the five stations located inside the Church of the Holy Sepulchre, all of which are devoted to defeat and death.

Later, when you visit the Via Dolorosa and the other Stations of the Cross, you will see that the emphasis on tragedy is a relatively recent phenomenon. Originally, the rotunda containing the tomb was called the Anastasis, or Resurrection, and it was to commemorate this event that in the fourth century Constantine undertook such a vast, complicated, and even politically questionable project. (It will be remembered that at the time of his decision a Temple of Venus stood on the site and the majority of the city's inhabitants were still pagans.) The emperor's intentions and the views of contemporary Christians were clearly recorded by Eusebius, bishop of Caesarea, in his *Life of Constantine*: Constantine "deemed it necessary to bring to life in Jerusalem the blessed place of the resurrection of the savior." He "commanded that there shall be erected round the Grotto of Salvation a sanctuary of magnificence. . . . At once the work was carried out, and as layer after layer of subsoil was stripped away, the most holy memorial of the savior's resurrection, beyond all our hopes, came into view. The Holy of Holies, the cave was, like our savior, restored to life. . . . And over the true memorial of salvation was built the New Jerusalem, facing the far-famed one of old."

These words of Eusebius confirm not only the emphasis on the Resurrection, but also the importance of the physical

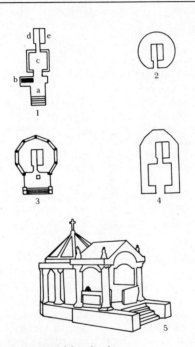

Fig. 19. Formation of the edicule.
1. *The tomb of Jesus before excavation by Constantine.*
    a. Stairs leading down to entranceway
    b. Stone for sealing entrance
    c. Antechamber with benches along sides
    d. Burial chamber
    e. Bench on which body lay
2. *Tomb was disengaged from the hill containing it, and the entranceway and antechamber were cut away.*
3. *Burial chamber was then formed into a small building (edicule). A new entranceway and antechamber were added and the whole structure "adorned with columns and much ornament."*
4. *The edicule today.*
5. *Educated guess regarding the appearance of the original Constantinian edicule.*

site where the event took place. This has always been seen as a radical departure from Christianity's accepted theological views regarding sacred places. The new Christian Temple was a spiritual one, the body of the Church united in Christ. Eusebius's description of the cave as the Holy of Holies, combined with the name New Jerusalem, however, emphasized its physical aspect by contrasting the new architectural creation with the ruins of the Jewish Temple to the east.

But Eusebius's view is not as radical as one might think. The holiness of the Jewish Temple had been based on the presence there of the spirit of God, but according even to Jewish tradition this spirit had abandoned the Temple and the city. The *axis mundi* which had run through the Temple's Holy of Holies, where the spirit of God became manifest on earth, had been withdrawn. For Eusebius the axis had returned to Jerusalem with Jesus, whose journey through the three cosmic worlds had established it at the site of the Holy Sepulchre.

The first task of the builders of the Church of the Holy Sepulcfre was to disengage the tomb, consisting of a burial chamber, anteroom, and sealing stone, from the rocky slope containing it. Once the tomb was free, the anteroom was carved away and the burial chamber shaped to the form of a small building (*edicule* = "little house"). A new anteroom was added and the whole structure "adorned with columns and much ornament." At the time of the dedication of the basilica the edicule was venerated in a large open area of leveled rock, while around it the construction of the rotunda continued. Indirect evidence has led to an educated guess regarding the appearance of the structure.

The Arab chronicler Yahia records that in 1009 the Egyptian caliph Hakim gave orders to destroy the Church of the Holy Sepulchre "until all traces of it have disappeared, and to endeavor to uproot its foundations." The rock of the holy grotto was "broken by pickaxe, and indeed most of it was hewed out and carried off." Though the account suggests that a small part of the original rock of the tomb may have escaped destruction, it would seem that on the 18th of October, 1009, the sacred grotto ceased to exist.

After the destruction by Hakim, the edicule was rebuilt by Monomachus in 1048. The first functional change in its design was made by the Crusaders in 1119. The antechamber was elongated and given two additional openings in the north and south to facilitate the flow of pilgrims. The antechamber, by then called the Chapel of the Angel, was covered in mosaics and contained a small altar with remnants of the stone which it was claimed had covered the entrance. After the Crusader period the northern and southern openings were sealed.

While the outer form of the edicule has seen many changes, both before and after the Crusader period, its inner content has remained basically the same: an anteroom and a burial chamber resembling a type of cave tomb from the Second Temple period.

The nearness of the tomb to the place of crucifixion conforms with the demands of Jewish law regarding burial and with the account related in the Gospels. "Now in the place where he was crucified there was a garden; and in the garden a new sepulchre, wherein was never man yet laid" (according to tradition, the tomb belonged to Joseph of Arimathea, who had built it for his own use). "There laid they Jesus therefore because of the Jews' preparation day" (just before the Sabbath); "for the sepulchre was nigh at hand" (John 19:41–42).

The present edicule was rebuilt after the fire of 1808 and dedicated in 1810. Eyewitnesses to the rebuilding claimed that very little of the original rock remained. Almost all the core behind the marble of the edicule is masonry.

The Ornamentation of the Face This is divided among the three major groups represented at the Holy Sepulchre and conforms to the dictates of the status quo. Of the four rows of lamps, the uppermost belongs to the Franciscans, the two middle ones to the Greek Orthodox, and the lower one to the Armenians. Corresponding to these, behind the lamps, are three pictures of the Resurrection. The twelve very large candlesticks are divided among the three communities.

Chapel of the Angel This name given to the antechamber relates to events mentioned in the Gospel of St. Mark 16: 1–6. "And when the sabbath was past, Mary Magdalene, and Mary the mother of James, and Salome, had bought sweet spices, that they might come and anoint him. And very early in the morning the first day of the week, they came unto the sepulchre at the rising of the sun. And they said among themselves, Who shall roll us away the stone from the door of the sepulchre? And when they looked, they saw that the stone was rolled away: for it was very great. And entering into the sepulchre, they saw a young man sitting on the right side, clothed in a long white garment; and they were affrighted. And he saith unto them, Be not affrighted: Ye seek Jesus of Nazareth, which was crucified: he is risen; he is not here: behold the place where they laid him." In the center of the antechamber a short glass-covered pillar contains a piece of the rock said to have covered the entrance to the cave.

Inner Chamber Here a marble slab, which represents the place where the body of Jesus was laid, covers what little may remain of the original rock of the cave. Over the slab are three representations of the Crucifixion—the one on the left belonging to the Franciscans, the middle one to the Greek Orthodox, and the one on the right to the Armenians. The ornamentation here and that in the antechamber are again in compliance with the status quo.

The Holy Fire

There are no detailed records of the rites carried out at the tomb of Jesus by the very earliest Christians. However, we do know that this was one of the "mystic" caves of the Judeo-Christians associated with the life of Jesus, where the divine light miraculously appeared in the world. This symbolizes the passing of the divine from one world to another. In the late fourth century the Spanish pilgrim Egeria described a ceremony carried out at the tomb which formed a regular part of the service. The bishop would enter the darkened cave and emerge bearing a fire whose source reportedly came neither from inside nor from outside the tomb itself. In the mid-ninth century Bernard the Wise (a monk from Mont-St.-Michel) was the first to record a ceremony called the Holy Fire which took place at the tomb at Easter. This unforgettable ceremony is still practiced today by the Eastern Church on the Saturday preceding the Eastern Orthodox Easter Sunday (which does not always fall on the same date as the Easter of the Western Churches). Thousands upon thousands of people crush into the area of the rotunda until there is literally no place to move. The crowd waits for hours under unbearable conditions. As the hour of the Holy Fire approaches (about midday) a number of processions around the rotunda take place, at first in an orderly manner, then becoming more and more chaotic as the screaming and shouting reverberates around the church. Suddenly all the lights go out, and the church is plunged into darkness. Absolute silence falls upon the crowd, which appears now as so many phantom shadows. Everything is still, and it seems as if all life has been suspended. Then all at once through a circular opening in its southern wall, a flaming bundle of thirty-three tapers (one for each year of the life of Jesus) is thrust from the tomb to the waiting crowd outside. The fire is passed from one person to another as each lights his own bundle of thirty-three candles. In moments the rotunda is ablaze with light. The bells begin to ring and the crowd cheers, screams, and claps with joy. Before the shouting has had time to die down the different denominations begin their processions around the tomb with singing and prayers. In former times the ceremony was considered so important by Russian pilgrims that many did not wait in Jerusalem for Easter Sunday but left the church immediately to return to Russia bearing the Holy Fire, where it was passed quickly throughout the country.

The ceremony itself is very old, though no doubt certain details have changed with time. Its meaning has been largely lost even for those who practice it. Vague references are made to the victory of Christ, or the descent of the Holy Fire from heaven, but that is all. It is clear that the profound effect it has on all who see it does not stem from known ideas or preconceived beliefs. Rather, it seems to come from something far deeper in man which instinctively recognizes the great truths being taught.

The Lesson of the Tomb

To understand the lesson of the tomb, which symbolizes the mystery of death and resurrection, it is important to remember that the great vertical circle which contains all three cosmic worlds is never completely visible to our eyes. The sun is seen only in its daytime course. In our world the place of transition between the light of the visible world of the living above and the darkness of the unseen world of the dead below, is marked by the periphery of a horizontal circular plane whose outer limit forms the horizon. This plane is represented by the floor of the rotunda, at whose center lies the tomb. This center, we shall see, is all-important.

It now becomes easier to understand why the rounded walls of the rotunda, which represent the horizon itself, represented the encircling of our earthly world by a world of a greater reality. Because the horizon is visible to us, its distance appears measurable. At some finite point the world of the horizon seems to join our own, but this is an illusion. The true distance to the horizon can be measured only by our own vain efforts to attain it, yet no matter how quickly we move or how far we travel, the horizon remains equally distant from our grasp—a world eternally removed from the one we know.

The setting and rising of the sun take place at the horizon. It is the meeting place and door between the worlds. The rotunda's great dome of heaven flowing down to meet the church's circular walls at the horizon indicates that the movement and interaction between all cosmic forces takes place beyond the world of man.

But at the center of this vast outer world that surrounds us lies the inner world of the microcosm. This is symbolized by the cave-tomb where the great events that took place beyond the horizon became manifest in the world of man. The death and miraculous rebirth of the divine light of the sun is paralleled here in the burial and resurrection of Jesus. The true microcosm, of course, is man himself, and all traditions have taught that it is at the deepest center of man's being that the great cosmic events are played out. The use of the cave-tomb to symbolize the place of this drama says a great deal concerning the nature and construction of man's inner world.

For many ancient peoples, as well as the early Judeo-Christians, the cave was the site where the rites of the great mysteries of death and rebirth were carried out. The cave, hidden within the earth and far from the rays of the sun, was the land of the dead. The door to this land was the door to the tomb. For man too, the cave-tomb represented the darkest of hidden places within himself where the spirit of the divine did not penetrate. The door to this place represented the voluntary inner death spoken of by all mystics, the death that takes place in life.

The man who succeeds in reaching this secret, hidden place is the cosmic hero. He opens, and keeps open, the door between worlds, and enters into the darkness below to liberate the life that has become trapped there. The great cosmic cycle which began from above and which came to an end in the land of death must be renewed so that the divine spark lost in the darkness can return to the source.

The adventures of the cosmic or divine hero are described in the myths and legends of all traditions. In Christianity it is epitomized in the story of St. George and the dragon. This legend is very ancient, well predating Christianity itself. The name of the hero derives from the Syriac, signifying "he who comes from afar." It relates to one who travels the long way to the underworld, and says a great deal concerning his origins. The dragon or great serpent, an even more ancient symbol, is the great monster of chaos and death that lies in the depths of the world below and swallows all that enters its domain. Its great adversary is the sun. Each day the sun is devoured by this monster, and life, light, and order come to an end. For life to continue, the sun must be released from its prison of death. This is the task of the hero. St. George kills the dragon with his spear.

The renewal of life through the slaying of the monster of the deep was a favorite theme in the ancient world. In Mesopotamia, creation began with the divine hero cutting the dragon's body in two, and then using the pieces to build the world. The meaning of this act is made clear by the account in Genesis. In the beginning, below the heavens lay the waters of chaos. Creation began when God separated the waters. Divine life is eternal and everywhere, but becomes hidden and lost when chaos is permitted to reign. By the killing of the monster, by the cutting of its body in two, by the separation of the waters, chaos is rendered powerless, its realm pushed back, and the light and order obscured by darkness are set free and reappear.

All creation myths thus symbolized the renewal of life. But not all life shared equally by this act. For the earth and all that belonged to it, it was a renewal of all that was—a re-creation. For the divine light, it was a new creation. The first creation had sent the light downward along an inevitable path which came to an end in the darkness below. Now the light, set free from its prison, was sent upward along a completely new path. It was this light that appeared in the tomb. It was the light that had been resurrected from the darkness. It was a new light, and the dawning of a new day, whose direction now led to God.

Chapel of the Copts (22) Behind the tomb there is a small chapel belonging to the Coptic community. One legend from the sixth century relates that while Mary, the mother of Jesus, was traveling to Jerusalem she rested on a stone which she then blessed. The legend continues that the stone was later made into an altar destined for Constantinople. But the bulls drawing the cart carrying the altar-stone could not pass through the gates of Jerusalem. This was interpreted as divine intervention, and the stone was brought to the Holy Sepulchre and installed behind the edicule.

In the early sixteenth century, the altar was in the possession of the Franciscans. When they were imprisoned in 1537, the Turkish authorities gave possession of the altar to the Copts, who erected around it a small chapel. The monk on duty will gladly show you, beneath the altar, a piece of the original rock of the Holy Tomb.

The Syrian Orthodox Chapel (23) This chapel, which is used only on special occasions by the Syrian Orthodox community, is located in the western apse of the rotunda. Its appalling state is due to the restrictions imposed by the status quo which effectively prevent the Syrian Orthodox Church from carrying out repairs here. When the rotunda was constructed, the western apse cut across a rock tomb of the type known from the Second Temple period. Though part of the tomb was destroyed while the apse was being built, you can still see here a type of tomb that was in use in the time of Jesus. There is no evidence to support the very late tradition that this is the tomb of Joseph of Arimathea and Nicodemus.

Katholicon (24) The Katholicon is the best-preserved example of Crusader architecture in the Holy Sepulchre. Today it is difficult to visualize the degree of unity brought to the Church of the Holy Sepulchre by the Crusaders who built the choir in the Holy Garden and by means of a great arch joined it to the rotunda. Before the erection of the walls of the Katholicon in 1810, the tomb could be seen from all parts of the church, while in earlier periods the windows of the rotunda and the dome of the choir literally bathed the entire

Omphalos marking the center of man's salvation. From the Katholicon.

structure in light. The present walls also cut across the lines of the transept which runs north-south directly beneath the dome. The dome itself, 33 feet (10 meters) in diameter, is the largest built by the Crusaders in Jerusalem.

The altar lies in an apse which opens toward the west. Excavations carried out beneath this apse have revealed remains of the apse of the Constantine basilica. It lies directly below the present one but opens toward the east. The present altar is thus approximately in the same position as it was in Byzantine times and helps to verify where the Constantine basilica began.

As with the rotunda, we can only imagine the artwork that adorned the Crusader choir. The present floor is relatively new and in the style of Orthodox churches in Greece. The icons that covered the walls have been removed for repairs.

The Center of the World Near the entrance to the Katholicon is a vase containing a large ball with four intersecting lines. These lines represent the four cardinal directions, and the point at which they meet is called the Center of the World. In Crusader times this stood directly beneath the dome, but since then it has been moved westward to its present position.

There is a great deal of misunderstanding regarding this "center of the world." There are some that claim it is located in the wrong place, and to prove this they show that the early Church Fathers referred to Golgotha as the "center of the world." This is true insofar as the entire complex of Constantinian buildings was often referred to as Golgotha. Others claim that the idea originated in the words of Psalm 74:12, "For God is my King of old, working salvation in the midst of the earth." Cyril, the bishop of Jerusalem in the fourth century, often said in his sermons that "between Calvary and the tomb lies the center of our salvation." This "center of our salvation" was a spiritual center and not a physical one, though today it has come to mean the latter in popular understanding.

Having visited the tomb, you can now perhaps come a little closer to the true meaning of the term "center of the world." The monument which marks this center is called an *omphalos,* meaning "navel." In ancient Greece, for example, a rounded or curved stone called an *omphalos* stood in the Temple of Apollo at Delphi and reputedly marked the center of the world. The development of an embryo starts at the navel. When you visited the Temple Mount and looked at the traditions regarding the creation of the world, you saw that this creation was likened to the development of an organic body which develops outward from a central point. At the Church of the Holy Sepulchre this central point, symbolically marked by the *omphalos,* was the light of the new creation, which was to rise from the tomb and slowly spread its rays all over the world.

***The Latin Altar of St. Mary Magdalene* (25)** This altar commemorates events related in John 20:14–17. On the Sunday following the burial of Jesus, Mary Magdalene came to the tomb but found that the rock had been rolled away and the tomb was empty. Thinking someone had taken the body, she began to weep. Suddenly she "saw Jesus standing, and knew not that it was Jesus. Jesus saith unto her, Woman, why weepest thou? whom seekest thou? She, supposing him to be the gardener, saith unto him, Sir, if thou have borne him hence, tell me where thou hast laid him, and I will take him away. Jesus saith unto her, Mary. She turned herself, and saith unto him, Rabboni; which is to say, Master. Jesus saith unto her, Touch me not; for I am not yet ascended to my Father: but go to my brethren, and say unto them, I ascend unto my Father, and your Father; and to my God, and your God."

Tradition holds that this event took place within the confines of the Holy Garden, though the exact place was unknown. In the early eleventh century the spot was fixed at a point approximately below the present dome of the Katholicon. When the Crusaders built the choir, the commemoration of the event was moved to its present location, where a small oratory was built. Here a relic of the True Cross was kept. In the eighteenth century, the oratory was removed and in its place a new altar was built onto the ancient facade of the rotunda.

A portrayal of the gospel story hangs above the altar. The present floor is patterned after the eleventh-century floor that lies below it and which was revealed during excavations.

Franciscan Chapel of the Virgin Mary (*The Apparition of Jesus to His Mother*) **(26)** In 628 A.D., during repairs carried

Pillar of the scourging.
Chapel of the Virgin Mary,
Church of the Holy Sepulchre.

out by Modestus, a chapel to Mary was built to the north of the rotunda, very likely in the same area as the present chapel, which dates from the eleventh century. In the view of the Franciscans, although the event commemorated here is not related in the Gospels, the Church Fathers obviously felt that Mary would have been among the first to receive her son's consolation after his Resurrection.

To the right of the altar is a part of a pillar. It is said to come from Mt. Zion and to be part of the pillar to which Jesus was tied while being scourged. On the northern wall are a series of sculptures portraying the stages in the Passion of Jesus.

Franciscan Sacristy (27) On the wall to the left of the entrance is a glass-covered wooden case containing the spurs and sword of the Crusader knight Godfrey de Bouillon. Godfrey was overall commander of the forces that captured Jerusalem in 1099. He refused the title of king but was elected "Defender of the Holy Sepulchre." When Godfrey died in 1100, he was succeeded by his brother Baldwin, who was crowned first king of Jerusalem.

The Arches of the Virgin (28) This name derives from the proximity of these pillars and arches to the Franciscan chapel of the Virgin Mary. At first glance it is one of the most confusing areas in the Church of the Holy Sepulchre.

The Crusaders had two objectives in the Holy Sepulchre: to unify the existing structures under one roof, and, where possible, to preserve elements of the Byzantine church. The greater part of the Byzantine portico surrounding the Holy Garden could not be preserved; the construction of a new entrance, the southern arm of the transept, and the new

Arches of the Crusader transept built up against the arches of the Byzantine portico. A point of confusion in the Church of the Holy Sepulchre.

choir made this impossible. But in the north the portico could be preserved since the northern arm of the transept was designed to reach just short of it.

First, let us go to the northern side of the row of columns. This row, with the rounded arches and basket capitals, is what remains of the Byzantine portico built by Monomachus in the courtyard of the rotunda.

Now let us go to the southern side of the row of columns. Three columns and capitals of different design, supporting pointed arches, are built right up against the Byzantine portico. Their overall shape is the same as the entrance to the Holy Sepulchre and the southern transept. What we are seeing is the northern arm of the transept, which reached as far as the Byzantine portico and was built right against it.

***The Prison of Christ* (29)** The plan of the fourth-century church built by Constantine contains an anomaly. The northern portico of the Holy Garden (atrium) is slanted outward in order to include at its northeastern corner a small chapel. Here there was an altar commemorating the sacrifice of Isaac. Even before the fourth century, Abraham's sacrifice was seen as a symbolic forerunner of God's sacrifice of his own beloved Son. This is what is portrayed in the three mosaics in the Franciscan chapel on Calvary. In the central mosaic the witnesses to the sacrifice look on while to their right Jesus is nailed to the cross, and to their left Abraham raises the dagger to his son.

A chapel has existed in this area throughout all the reconstructions of the church. At some point its connection with the sacrifice of Isaac was forgotten and the name Prison of Christ appears, though it is not known when or why. The name was probably established in late Byzantine times, though it was first recorded in the early twelfth century. During the Crusader period, this chapel was one of the most popular places of pilgrimage.

Today it is still called the Prison of Christ by all except the Greek Orthodox, whose chapel it is. For them, it is the Chapel of the Women and commemorates (like the Armenian one to the south of the rotunda) the place where the women who followed Jesus stood and watched his execution.

As we leave this chapel, immediately to the left is a small altar and below it two holes in the floor. For the Greek Orthodox this commemorates the place where Jesus waited while preparations were being made for his execution. The holes were made to resemble those found in the Greek Orthodox Prison of Christ on the Via Dolorosa. The prisoner was made to sit on the floor, and his legs were placed in the holes and tied from below.

***Ambulatory* (30)** In the church of Monomachus there were three chapels to the east of the Holy Garden commemorating various events in the Passion of Jesus. These three, together with the Prison of Christ, formed a symbolic devotional route where prayers could be offered in relative safety in a hostile Muslim environment. The choir built by the Crusaders extended into the area occupied by these chapels. They were thus removed, and around the apse of the Crusader choir there was built a semicircular ambulatory containing three new chapels.

Greek Orthodox Chapel of St. Longinus (31) The Sabbath was approaching, and the families of the crucified asked Pilate to have the legs of the condemned broken (to hasten their death) and have their bodies taken down. The soldiers broke the legs of the two men crucified with Jesus. But when they came to Jesus they saw that he was already dead. Not believing he could have died so quickly, the Roman centurion Longinus drove his lance into the side of Jesus and at once there was a flow of blood and water (John 19).

Many legends arose concerning Longinus. One states that he suffered from a squint and when the blood of Jesus fell on his eyes he was cured. A second comes from Matthew 27, which relates that at the moment of Jesus's death there was a great earthquake and many strange events and miracles. When the centurion Longinus saw what was happening he was filled with awe and said, "Truly this was the Son of God." According to tradition, Longinus was converted, preached the Gospel, and later was made a saint.

Armenian Chapel of the Division of the Raiment (32) Here are commemorated events related in John 19:23–24: "Then the soldiers, when they had crucified Jesus, took his garments, and made four parts, to every soldier a part; and also his coat: now the coat was without seam, woven from the top throughout. They said therefore among themselves, Let us not rend it, but cast lots for it, whose it shall be: that the scripture might be fulfilled, which saith, They parted my raiment among them, and for my vesture they did cast lots."

Greek Orthodox Chapel of the Mocking (33) This chapel commemorates events in Matthew 27:27–31: "Then the soldiers of the governor took Jesus into the common hall, and gathered unto him the whole band of soldiers. And they stripped him, and put on him a scarlet robe. And when they had platted a crown of thorns, they put it upon his head, and a reed in his right hand: and they bowed the knee before him, and mocked him, saying, Hail, King of the Jews! And they spit upon him, and took the reed, and smote him on the head. And after they had mocked him, they took the robe off from him, and put his own raiment on him, and led him away to crucify him."

Below the altar is a fragment of a column upon which, it is said, Jesus sat while undergoing these trials.

Armenian Chapel of St. Helena (34) and Franciscan Chapel of the Finding of the Cross (35) Constantine's basilica began where you now see the apse of the Katholicon and extended eastward. Below the basilica there was a crypt and a cave.

Helena, the mother of the emperor Constantine, was converted to Christianity at the age of sixty-five, and visited the Holy Land at the time of Constantine's building projects. She came at the request of Bishop Macarius. Jerusalem was then still governed by non-Christians, and the Temple of Venus, beneath which was the tomb of Jesus, was still the most important pagan shrine in the city. Notwithstanding the emperor's order to destroy the temple, Macarius hoped to avoid unnecessary difficulties by lending to the project the prestige of a royal presence. By the end of the fourth century, pilgrim accounts attest to the popular belief that it was Helena herself who was responsible for the discovery of the Holy Sepulchre and the construction of the church. But there is little historical evidence to support this popular belief.

Crosses carved by Crusaders along the walls of the staircase leading down to the Chapel of St. Helena, Church of the Holy Sepulchre.

It is known that Helena dedicated the Church of the Nativity in Bethlehem and the Church of the Eleona on the Mount of Olives. But just how far her responsibilities went in regard to these two other basilicas built by Constantine is unknown. It is clear that the decision to build the Church of the Holy Sepulchre had already been taken by Constantine at the time of the Council of Nicea as a result of the irrefutable evidence brought by Bishop Macarius. Bear in mind that the evidence regarding the tomb of Jesus pertained equally to the mystic grottoes in Bethlehem and on the Mount of Olives.

Along the walls of the staircase leading down to the Chapel of St. Helena are crosses cut into the stone by the Crusaders.

The longitudinal axis of the chapel if extended westward coincides with the axis of the apse of the Constantinian church. Thus it would seem that the lateral walls of the present chapel are the remains of the foundations of the central nave of the fourth-century basilica. Archeological excavations have suggested that the northern wall may even date from the time of Hadrian (second century).

Whether there was a crypt here before the twelfth century or just an empty space containing foundations for the basilica, it was only in the Crusader period that the area received an independent function and dedication. The arches, vaults, apses, and dome are all the work of the Crusaders. Typical of their construction in the Holy Sepulchre is the use of materials from secondary sources. This is especially visible in the four columns supporting the dome. They are all different, with bases clearly too large for their use here. Some of the capitals are from the Umayyad period.

Today's chapel belongs to the Armenian community. The central altar is dedicated to St. Helena. To the left is an altar dedicated to the "good thief" crucified with Jesus. On the northern wall is a painting of Gregory, who brought the Christian religion to Armenia, here seen converting the Armenian nation. The mosaic on the floor before the altar depicts a number of famous Armenian cathedrals.

*Khatchkar (stone cross)
from the Armenian
Chapel of St. Helena,
Church of the Holy
Sepulchre. (See page 176.)*

To the right of the altar is a window which commemorates events connected with the "finding of the cross." According to legend, the cave below had been used for the dumping of refuse, and it was just there that Helena instructed the workers to dig for the True Cross. Because of the terrible smell the workers were reluctant to continue. So Helena sat here and threw gold coins down to them to keep them working.

A second staircase leads down to the former cave. Excavations indicate that this area was originally used as a quarry, which reached a depth of some 30 feet (nearly 10 meters). Later the walls of the quarry were plastered over and it was used as a well. The present dedication as the Chapel of the Finding of the Cross dates to the Crusader period. Above the altar is a bronze statue of Helena carrying the cross after its discovery. To the right of the altar a metal trellis indicates the exact spot of the discovery, which was commemorated by an altar in Crusader times. On the wall to the right are remains of paintings from the eleventh and twelfth centuries.

The earliest traditions do not link Helena to the finding of the True Cross. Eusebius in his *Life of Constantine* makes no mention of her in connection with such a momentous event. Even the pilgrim Egeria (who visited Jerusalem late in the fourth century), while recounting the popular legend that Helena was responsible for building the Church of the Holy Sepulchre, does not credit her with finding the cross. It is not until 395 A.D. that she is so credited, by St. Ambrose. He relates that Helena found three crosses (two others were crucified with Jesus), and that the cross of Jesus was identified by a plaque it bore containing the particulars of the condemned. In 401 a new version of the story maintained that the True Cross was distinguished from the others by its ability to cure a sick woman. Two years later it was claimed that rather than curing a sick woman, the cross had revived a corpse.

THE SIGN OF THE CROSS

The hill of Calvary is today completely enclosed by the monuments of the church. Only here and there is it possible to catch a glimpse of the rock itself. For the average visitor there is only the small rectangular opening at the top of the hill alongside the actual site of the Crucifixion, and the portion of rock visible in the Chapel of Adam. It also appears that at some time in its history the rock above ground level was cut down to a more or less rectangular or cubic shape so that it could be easily contained within the structure built to enclose it.

Excavations behind the Chapel of Adam have uncovered the rock to an impressive depth of some 30 feet (nearly 10 meters). There are some who claim that in its lower depths the rock of the hill extends eastward, and it is this rock that we see in the Chapel of the Finding of the Cross. Though it is difficult to either prove or disprove this claim, the chapel's symbolic meaning alone is enormous. Here was the place— the cave in the subterranean reaches of Calvary—chosen as the setting for the final part of Christ's drama.

While the historical circumstances regarding the finding of the cross are in doubt, it is clear that the real origins of these traditions and legends lie not in provable facts but in even earlier Christian mystic thought which sought to symbolically express Christ's role on earth. Adam had closed his heart to the light of God and had fallen into a world of darkness. He had condemned not only himself but all the generations of his children. And it was these, trapped in the world below, who cried out to God for deliverance.

For Jew and Christian alike, deliverance began with the exodus from Egypt. (Bear in mind that the Last Supper, Passion, Crucifixion, and Resurrection took place at the Jewish festival of the Passover, which commemorated this event.) In Exodus, God listens to the suffering of Adam's children. "And the Lord said, I have surely seen the affliction of my people . . . and have heard their cry . . . for I know their sorrows; and I am come down to deliver them. . . ." (Exodus 3). The act of deliverance begins with the marking or signing of those who are to be saved. The children of Israel are commanded by God to sprinkle the doors of their houses with the blood of a lamb: "For I will pass through the land of Egypt this night, and will smite all the firstborn in the land. . . . And the blood shall be to you for a token upon the house where ye are: and when I see the blood I will pass over you . . ." (Exodus 12). The sign of blood was to indicate to the Angel of Death those who belonged to God and to life.

By the time of the prophets the sign marking those destined for life was sealed on men's foreheads. In Ezekiel's vision of the destruction of Jerusalem he hears God say, "Go through the midst of the city, through the midst of Jerusalem, and set a mark upon the foreheads of the men that sigh and that cry out for all the abominations that be done in the midst thereof. And to the others . . . Go ye after him through the city, and smite: let not your eyes spare, neither have ye pity . . . but come not near any man upon whom is the mark" (Ezekiel 9). The Book of Revelation also speaks of the elect who have the seal of the living God as opposed to the seal of the beast (Revelation 7:2).

In an apocryphal writing, the *Descent of Christ to the Lower World* (sometimes included in the *Acts of Pilate*), the author describes how Christ, after being crucified, descended into hell and "raising his hand he made the sign of the cross over Adam and all the saints, and holding Adam with his right hand He ascended from hell and all the saints followed him."

The earliest Christians believed that Jesus had descended from heaven to save the world through the cross, which came to symbolize the power embodied in Christ. The Passion and Crucifixion symbolized the final merging of Jesus with his personified power. This merging signaled the appearance on earth of Christ, whose task was destined to take place in the chaos and darkness of the lower world. Like all cosmic heroes who descend the *axis mundi* to the land of death, he accomplishes his task by dividing the chaos and rendering it powerless. His weapon is the sign of the living cross, with which he seals the righteous and separates them

out from the world around them, thus initiating their ascent
to the world of light, and to God.

Thus we see that the legends of the finding of the cross—
its appearance in the depths of the sacred mountain, its
ability to cure the sick (in spirit), and to raise the dead to
life—are not facts from the profane history of mankind, but
a part of man's sacred history, and symbols of the great
cosmic events that took place here.

Ethiopian Chapel of the Four Beasts (*36*) Return to the
courtyard of the Holy Sepulchre and enter the Chapel of St.
Michael. A staircase to the left leads up to the Ethiopian
Chapel of the Four Beasts. On the wall of the chapel, to the
right, is a painting portraying the arrival of the queen of
Sheba at the court of Solomon. Ethiopians claim that Sheba

*The Holy Trinity surrounded by an eagle, ox, lion, and man.
From the Ethiopian Chapel of the Four Beasts, Church of the
Holy Sepulchre.*

was located in Ethiopia and that they are descendants of the
union of this queen with the Jewish king. At the left is a
painting depicting the Holy Trinity surrounded by twenty-
four elders. At the corners of the painting are the four beasts:
an eagle, an ox, a lion, and a man. This symbolism is met
with in both Jewish and Christian literature, and appears
frequently in Orthodox iconography. For Christians they
represent the four evangelists, Matthew, Mark, Luke, and
John, and symbolize the different character of each of the
four Gospels. Matthew is the man because he emphasizes
the human aspect of Christ's life; Mark is the lion, showing
Christ's power; Luke is the ox, representing Christ the priest
or mediator (the ox was used for sacrifices in the Temple);
John is the eagle (which soars above), emblem of Christ's
divinity.

Deir es-Sultan (37) Leaving the Ethiopian chapel, you come out onto the roof above the Chapel of St. Helena. This is the area where stood the basilica of Constantine. To the west is the outer wall of the ambulatory of the Holy Sepulchre, which approximately marks the spot where the basilica began. From that point the basilica itself extended eastward some 130 feet (40 meters).

In the latter half of the twelfth century, a cloister was built here for the Augustinian canons who served the Holy Sepulchre, in the abandoned space around the dome of the Chapel of St. Helena. Today the area serves as monastic quarters for Ethiopian monks. Minor remains of Crusader architecture (arches) can still be seen in the western (Crusader cloister) and southern (Crusader refectory) walls.

Leaving the Ethiopian monastery, walk eastward and you will soon arrive at the top of a staircase overlooking the Suq Khan es-Zeit. Constantine's basilica began at the ambulatory of the present church, which we can see in the distance to the west. It extended eastward some 130 feet (40 meters). Then there was a forecourt (atrium) and stairs which led down to the Cardo Maximus (today's Suq).

THE JEWISH TEMPLE AND THE CHURCH OF THE HOLY SEPULCHRE

For the early Christian Fathers the destruction of the Jewish Temple confirmed the prophecy that "not one stone shall be left upon another." Its continued ruin and desolation gave living proof of the failure and abandonment of the old covenant between God and Israel.

This view was largely born of the Hellenistic Christian milieu which saw in the death of Jesus the final fulfillment and rejection of the Jewish Law. The conquest by Christianity of the Greco-Roman world was aided in no small measure by the abandonment of the Jewish ritualistic system of precepts and prohibitions, which was completely foreign to pagan culture and civilization. But lost with this Law was an understanding of Jewish devotional obligations which in no way saw the destruction of the Temple as an ending.

Many Jews, both before and at the time of Jesus, saw the Temple as a "den of thieves" and predicted its destruction as a fitting punishment for sins. Their hopes became focused on a future incorruptible Temple which would be built by the hands of God and replace the one made by human hands.

Most extreme in their views at the time of Jesus was the Jewish sect of the Essenes, who rejected the Temple service of their day as defiled and corrupt. Setting themselves apart in a community which they considered a holy spiritual edifice, they professed the doctrine that prayer, strict observance of the Law, and rites of purity could serve as substitutes for the sacrificial service—though these substitutes were seen as only temporary expedients. In the Temple of the future, the Essenes believed, it would be they who would take over the service and offer the traditional sacrifices necessary for atonement.

Although the Essenes were extreme in their attitude toward the Temple, their belief in the efficacy of non-sacrificial devotion held outside the confines of the Temple was not unique. Throughout ancient Israel in the Second Temple period (and indeed, wherever Jewish communities existed), prayers were held in synagogues at times which corresponded with the times of the Temple service. These devotions symbolized the involvement of every Israelite in the worship being offered in Jerusalem. After the destruction of the Temple the synagogue itself became the main vehicle for Jewish worship, though prayers included the expectation that the Temple would be rebuilt by God and its service reestablished.

Christians, on the other hand, increasingly saw the restoration of the Temple as unnecessary. Sacrifice for the atonement of sin was no longer needed since Jesus, by his own sacrifice, had atoned for the sins of all mankind. The Church saw itself as a spiritual community united in the body of Christ. Just as the physical body of Jesus had been destroyed and a new spiritual body risen in glory, so the new spiritual Temple of the Christians was superior to the old material Temple of the Jews. Nor was Jerusalem itself spared, for Jesus had said, "Where two or three are gathered together in my name, there am I in the midst of them."

In the earliest Christian community of Jerusalem this sharp division was not so clear. The apostles had all been observant Jews who continued to fulfill their obligations to the Law even after the Crucifixion and Resurrection. James, the brother of Jesus and first bishop of Jerusalem, continued to pray at the Temple until his death. In the second century, mystic speculation born of the Judeo-Christian milieu of Jerusalem began to attribute to Calvary traditions associated with the sacrificial altar in the Jewish Temple. The place of Abraham's sacrifice of Isaac on Mt. Moriah became identified with the place where God had sacrificed His own beloved Son. The bones of Adam, buried beneath the altar of the Temple, were now said to be resting within the rock of Calvary to await his redemption by the blood of Christ.

In the early fourth century, the uncovering of the "mystic" grotto containing the tomb of Jesus, and the building of the Church of the Holy Sepulchre, unleashed a new wave of comparisons with the Jewish Temple. The cave was called the Holy of Holies, and the bishop its chief priest who, like the high priest of the Temple, entered its sacred confines while the congregation stood outside. The atrium between the cave and the basilica was the Temple court where Jesus found "them that sold and bought in the temple, and overthrew the tables of the moneychangers and the seats of them that sold doves" (Luke 11:15). The church itself, the new (spiritual) center of the world, was the New Jerusalem, "facing the one which was famous in former times." There were Temple parallels in the times and types of service. The dedication of the Church of the Holy Sepulchre and, later, the dedication of the finding of the cross were arranged to correspond to the date of Solomon's dedication of the Temple, which was on the Jewish festival of Tabernacles.

All these events—the creation of the world (center of the world), the fall of Adam, the sacrifice of Isaac, the dedication of the Temple—symbolize various points of beginning in the religion of the Jews. They are no less valid for Christians, who have never disclaimed their heritage. Whenever God enters the life of a people a new impulse is given to the world, a new beginning, a new center of creation. For the Jews, this center was the Temple Mount on Mt. Moriah, which gathered to itself and its history all the previous significant moments of divine intervention. For the Christians, it became the Church of the Holy Sepulchre at the moment of the triumph of Christ. And from here it spread to all the world.

The CHURCH OF THE HOLY SEPULCHRE is open daily, in summer 4:30 A.M.–8 P.M., and in winter 4:30 A.M.–7 P.M. Tel. 284213. (Here, and in all subsequent listings of visiting times, "summer" signifies April through September, and "winter" October through March.)

4

THE CHURCH OF ST. ANNE AND THE POOLS OF BETHESDA

The Church of St. Anne and the nearby Pools of Bethesda are not part of the present-day Way of the Cross, although they do have some minor connection with the route taken during the Crusader period. The best time to visit the two sites is just before proceeding along the Via Dolorosa. Any other arrangement would necessitate a special trip to this section of the city.

THE CHURCH OF ST. ANNE

Following the Crusader conquest of Jerusalem in 1099, a modest Benedictine convent was established just to the south of the present church on the spot now occupied by a small garden. Little is known about the origins of this convent except that its inhabitants were few in number and described as poor but pious nuns. In 1104 the convent's fortunes changed radically when its ranks were joined by two members of the royal family: Queen Arda, wife of Baldwin I, first Crusader king of Jerusalem, and Yvette, daughter of Baldwin II. In 1140 a church dedicated to St. Anne was built for the convent by a third member of the royal family—Queen Melisend, elder sister of Yvette and wife of Faulk of Anjou, third Crusader king of Jerusalem.

After the fall of the Latin Kingdom, Salah a-Din (Saladin) had the church converted into a Muslim theological seminary which was named Salahiya, after him. An inscription in Arabic commemorating the event still exists above the main door of the church. It is not clear how long the building was used as a school for Islamic law, though it is certain that it no longer functioned as one following the arrival of the Ottoman Turks in 1517. By the nineteenth century both the convent and the church had fallen into ruins and had been abandoned. In 1835 the convent was demolished and its stones used for building a Turkish military barracks on the site of the Antonia Fortress. At the close of the Crimean War in 1856, the site was given by the sultan of Turkey to Emperor Napoleon III in appreciation of France's role in the war. Restorations were undertaken by the French government in

1863 and completed in 1867. In 1878 the site was entrusted to the care of the White Fathers. (The White Fathers are officially called the Society of Missionaries in Africa. The society was founded in 1868 by Archbishop [later Cardinal] Lavigerie of Algiers. It is his bust that is in the garden on the site of the former convent.) The church was damaged during the Six Day War and repairs were carried out by the Israeli government. The opportunity was then taken to correct a number of mistakes made in the restorations of the previous century.

THE CHURCH

The church itself is one of those rare examples of religious architecture whose very structure directly imparts the lesson it has to teach—that of the Virgin Mary. It is often said that the Virgin, who appears in so many traditions, is the greatest mystery in the world. This is certainly so if we think in terms of our own lives, and what the Virgin means to us. We feel so far from God and our return to the source seems impossible. Yet within all of us there is something equivalent to the Virgin, which, despite all our acknowledged faults, remains pure, untainted, receptive, and destined to be filled by God's love. It is this deep and mysterious place, this Virgin within, which is capable of conceiving and giving birth to that which can save us and raise us from our fallen state.

The Virgin within is reflected by the interior of this Romanesque church which many have called the most characteristic example of Crusader architecture in Jerusalem. The only points of interest are the upper parts of the eastern pillars supporting the dome of the church. On the right-hand pillar are the remains of a man, and on the left an ox. Like those in the Chapel of the Four Beasts at the Church of the Holy Sepulchre, these represent the evangelists Matthew and Luke. Both figures were badly damaged during the long centuries of Muslim occupation. The two northern pillars once contained representations (now destroyed) of a lion (Luke) and an eagle (John). This is a relatively rare piece of symbolism. The dome of heaven, representing the heavenly or spiritual church, is being supported and joined to the earth by the four Gospels.

Architecturally the church resembles many others found in France from the same period, but its message is not a visual one. It is to be found rather in its extraordinary acoustical qualities. The first feature to strike the visitor to the church is its silence, which is heightened by the austere purity of its bare stone walls, the pale lighting, the virtual absence of religious art. If you sit here quietly for a while, you begin to realize that there is nothing to focus on and keep your attention within the church. The pure materiality of its form makes it feel limited and confining, and too small to enclose the spirit which seeks something larger.

The White Fathers disclaim any knowledge of a musical

tradition at St. Anne's, claiming that the echo in the church would prohibit it. But anyone who has sat and listened to the many pilgrims who come here especially to sing cannot help but be impressed by the very special acoustical qualities. Each new note is perfectly clear and not interrupted by the lingering vibrations of the previous ones which continue to fill the entire volume of the church. It is as if one were listening simultaneously to two separate and distinct sounds. When the music stops, one is struck by the sudden silence, which seems to be even greater than before. But now the church, which before seemed unable to contain the spirit, feels capable of absorbing all the vibrations in the world. It has become the pure, silent, infinitely receptive vessel which symbolizes the Virgin within.

The Crypt

The crypt, which is venerated as the birthplace of Mary, is reached by a staircase at the right of the church. The crypt was originally a grotto cut into the bare rock, which is still partly visible. Most of the present construction dates from the restorations of the last century. In the eastern part of the crypt there is an altar where daily morning mass is celebrated. In the western part there is a small shrine where an eternal light burns beneath an icon of Anne and Joachim and their newly born daughter, Mary.

Archeology has established that the crypt dates from the Roman period of Aelia Capitolina, and there is no evidence that the Roman structure replaced an earlier Christian sanctuary. Its relatively modern identification would seem to have been made on a very strong tradition identifying this general area with the birthplace of the Virgin. The tradition concerning Mary's birthplace is related to a former Byzantine basilica built over the Pools of Bethesda just to the north (which had not yet been discovered when the crypt's present identification was made), and the Crusaders themselves took no account of the little room beneath their church.

The tradition that Mary was born in a cave or grotto, however, is well founded and relates the story of the Virgin within to a theme we have already followed at the Church of the Holy Sepulchre—the descent of the cosmic or divine hero, his battle with the monster of the deep, his freeing of the divine light, and the resurrection of life. In the Middle Ages the adventures of the cosmic hero took the form of a virtuous knight who set off to a distant land to slay a wicked dragon. The dragon usually lived in a cave where he guarded a golden treasure he had stolen from a king, and where he kept a beautiful maiden in chains. The knight who slew the dragon reclaimed the treasure and set the maiden free. The knight is, of course, the cosmic hero. The dragon, which we also met at the Holy Sepulchre, is the monster of chaos, and his cave is the underworld. The golden treasure stolen from the king is the sun or divine light which has become trapped in the dragon's world of darkness and death. The knight kills the dragon, making possible the ascent and resurrection of the light, and the return of the treasure to its rightful owner (to God, the king, the source of life and light).

But the key to this ascent is the maiden for whose sake the knight sets out to slay the dragon in the first place. The maiden in distress arouses in the hero the image of ideal love which sends him on his way. She is the symbol of all that is receptive, fertile, and capable of bringing life into the world. Yet she is chained up and guarded by the dragon of darkness, and no man can reach her. Her condition symbolizes the real reason why life has come to an end in the underworld. She is the vessel through which the sun must pass on his journey. While she is held prisoner and unable to perform her part in the cycle of life, the sun cannot continue on his way. The monster of chaos and darkness uses her to attack the world of order and light. Only the cosmic hero can set her free. At the Holy Sepulchre we followed the journey of the divine hero through the three cosmic worlds of the universe to the underworld, and his slaying of the dragon of the deep. We also saw there that what is true in the macrocosm is equally true in the microcosm of man. Thus within the depths of human beings, as within the universe, lies the hidden cave where the Virgin who is infinitely receptive and infinitely fertile, and has been chained and hidden all our lives, awaits the coming of the divine hero, so that what is higher in us can be reborn.

The Name

Although the Crusader church was not built over any known previous Christian sanctuary, it seems that it was intended to commemorate the same event as the Byzantine structure slightly to the north, that is, the birth of the Virgin Mary. While the Byzantines called their church "Mary Where She Was Born," the Crusaders chose for theirs the name of St. Anne.

The source of the tradition locating the birthplace of Mary in Jerusalem lies in a Judeo-Christian text called the Apocryphal Gospel According to St. James. It is this Gospel which gives the names of Mary's parents, Joachim and Anne, which are unknown from other sources. The Gospel relates that Anne and Joachim were childless. While Joachim was in the desert and Anne in Jerusalem, it was divinely revealed to both of them that they would have a child, a special child, Mary. Joachim returned from the desert and Anne came out of their house to meet him. This meeting is a favorite subject of Christian religious art and is most often depicted as taking place in front of the Golden Gate, the eastern entrance to the Temple Mount, through which the Messiah will enter Jerusalem at the end of time. The Gospel continues with the birth of Mary, her childhood passed in the Temple, her betrothal to Joseph, the annunciation, and the birth of Jesus.

The story seems hard to reconcile with the accepted Gospel tradition that Mary was born in a village near Nazareth in the Lower Galilee. Why, then, does the apocryphal writing locate the early life of Mary in Jerusalem? Part of the answer may be that the author of this "Gospel" was aware of a number of very ancient traditions symbolically linking the life of Mary with the healing powers of the nearby waters of Bethesda.

The CHURCH OF ST. ANNE is open daily except Sunday, in summer 8:00 A.M.–12 noon, 2:30–6 P.M.; in winter, 2–5 P.M. Tel.: 283285.

THE POOLS OF BETHESDA

A few yards north of the Church of St. Anne lie the Pools of Bethesda. For Christians this is the place where Jesus cured the crippled man. "Now there is at Jerusalem by the sheep market a pool, which is called in the Hebrew tongue, Bethesda, having five porches. In these lay a great multitude of impotent folk, of blind, halt, withered, waiting for the moving of the water. For an angel went down at a certain season into the pool, and troubled the water: whosoever then first after the troubling of the water stepped in was made whole of whatsoever disease he had. And a certain man was there,

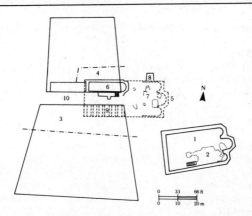

Fig. 20. The Pools of Bethesda and related churches.
1. *Crusader Church of St. Anne*
2. *Crypt of the Church*
3. *Excavated area of southern pool*
4. *Excavated area of northern pool*
5. *Byzantine church*
6. *Crusader chapel*
7. *Healing grottoes and pools*
8. *Mosaic from the Roman temple*
9. *Remains of 39-foot-high (12 meters) arched pillars supporting the floor of the Byzantine church*
10. *Dike between the two pools. Central part of Byzantine church was built on this dike.*

which had an infirmity thirty and eight years. When Jesus saw him lie, and knew that he had been now a long time in that case, he saith unto him, Wilt thou be made whole? The impotent man answered him, Sir, I have no man, when the water is troubled, to put me into the pool: but while I am coming, another steppeth down before me. Jesus saith unto him, Rise, take up thy bed, and walk. And immediately the man was made whole" (John 5:2–9).

The name Bethesda most likely derives from the Hebrew *Beit Hasda,* meaning "house of mercy," reflecting an ancient tradition connecting this place with the healing of the sick. Excavations carried out in this century have revealed that there existed here three independent sets of pools, all of which in time became associated with the tradition of healing. Although only a small area of the pools has been excavated, it has been enough to reconstruct a picture of their history. (The greater part of the pools lies beneath existing buildings, and it is unlikely that excavations will be extended in the foreseeable future.) The excavated area is, unfortunately, visually disappointing and confusing. What first strikes the eye is a vast disarray of pits of various sizes and depths, and assorted remains of ancient structures whose historical sequence is unclear. The White Fathers have attempted, by a small colored map in front of the excavations, to indicate the different periods and structures found at the site, but it is not so easy to follow without some clear picture of the events that took place here.

The Pools

In ancient times rainwater flowing down from the north cut a series of grottoes in the porous rock of Bethesda, which temporarily trapped the waters of the rainy season. These were apparently exploited by the kings of Judah, who built here a large reservoir that supplied water to the Temple Mount. This was the northernmost pool and today it is completely filled in. Only a very small corner of this pool lies within the excavated area. In the second century B.C. a second reservoir was built just to the south of the first, and separated from it by a broad dike. It is not yet clear for what purpose this pool was used or where its water led. (Facing the excavations, the large, very deep pit on the left is the northeast corner of this reservoir. The rest lies outside the area of excavations.)

During the reign of Herod the Great (37–4 B.C.) a completely new reservoir was constructed nearer to the Temple Mount, and these two great pools went out of use. Some traditions hold that while they were no longer needed to supply water to the Temple Mount, they may have continued in use for the washing of sacrificial sheep until the destruction of the Temple in 70 A.D. Hence the name Probatica, or "Sheep Pool." In times the pools of Bethesda became filled with silt, and their exact location was forgotten until rediscovered in 1957.

The Grottoes of Healing

Just to the east of the two great pools were a number of small natural grottoes long associated with the tradition of supernatural healing, and where it was believed that Jesus cured the crippled man. Some of these are still visible today, though access to them is difficult and there is not much to see.

Healing through water immediately recalls the act of baptism. In baptism the healing is spiritual in nature—the miraculous washing away of sin. But it must be recalled that for ancient man physical illness was widely believed to be God's punishment for evildoing. Thus Jesus says to the crippled man he has cured: "Behold, thou art made whole: sin no more, lest a worse thing come unto thee" (John 5:14). Just as the waters of baptism receive their curative powers through the spirit of Christ, so too the waters of Bethesda received theirs from the angel who came to bathe there and imbued them with his holiness.

The location of these curative waters in what was considered a sacred grotto tells us, however, an even more interesting story. These were quite literally perceived as the waters of chaos found in the underworld. The cycle of life that periodically passed through them did not simply come to an end. Death in these waters marked the physical annihilation of all that had become soiled and worn during the year. The life that was reborn here could begin freer and purer, washed clean of its burden of sin. For ancient man the new year was not simply a date in the calendar but represented the destruction and re-creation of the world in which each individual could also begin anew. The memory of this great event is still reflected in today's carnival, the new year's party. Once these were truly orgiastic feasts symbolizing the return to the primordial chaos that immediately preceded the creation of the world and of order.

The underworld and its waters were generally believed to be beyond the reach of man. Yet there were occasionally places on earth where worlds joined and the curative qualities of these waters became available to all. The sacred grottoes of Bethesda were such a place. This is reflected in the Gospel story which portrays an already ancient belief, and an even older tradition relating these pools to the place where Solomon tamed the devils of the underworld and forced them to work miraculous cures.

In early Christian times these waters and their ability to produce new and sinless birth became associated with the Virgin Mary, whose name was symbolically linked with the Latin word *mare*, meaning "sea," the pure undifferentiated matrix from which all life springs. Renewal through the Virgin was a special kind of birth, and it gave a new meaning to the waters of Bethesda.

The Birthplace of Mary

The bedrock experience of the Jewish people is the exodus from Egypt—the story of a God who intervenes in the life of a people to bring them out of slavery to freedom. This theme played a significant role in the life of the first Christian community of Jerusalem.

The story in the Gospel of St. John emphasizes the difference between the exodus of the Old Testament and the new exodus brought by Jesus. For St. John the Evangelist the exodus is symbolized by the angel who from time to time stirs up the waters of the Pools of Bethesda. Early Judeo-Christian thought associated this with the experience of the Children of Israel whose salvation from slavery in Egypt began with their miraculous crossing of the Red Sea. Led by Moses, they were the first to enter after the waters were stirred up and parted. They alone were saved while all others perished. The healing of the crippled man signaled the emergence of Jesus as the new Moses who would lead mankind to a new freedom. Salvation would no longer depend on the historical experience of Israel. All who were in bondage might escape to freedom through the curative waters embodied in Jesus himself.

The placing of the house of Anne and Joachim near the Pools of Bethesda was not fortuitous. The early Christians regarded the events of the Old Testament not just as historical facts but as symbolic predictions of what was to occur in the life of Christ. The Children of Israel were destined to build the Temple of God, but this could not happen while they were still slaves in Egypt. Only the exodus and the crossing of the Red Sea enabled them to begin to fulfill what had been predicted for them. Joachim and Anne were also destined to be the forebears of Christ—the new spiritual Temple—yet they were barren and without issue. Thus the miracle of their cure became associated by the Christians of Jerusalem with the Pools of Bethesda, where the exodus from Egypt and the mystery of the crossing of the Red Sea were believed to be symbolically reenacted.

The birth of Mary here also associated the pools with the legend of Miriam's well. According to this legend, a miraculous well appeared to the Children of Israel in the desert and accompanied them through their forty years of wandering. This miracle was wrought by God because of the merits of the prophetess Miriam, and hence its name. The name Mary is the western form of the Hebrew name Miriam, and the symbolic identification of Mary the mother of Jesus with Miriam the sister of Moses is found in the Qur'ān as well as in the beliefs of the early Christian community. Both women were instrumental in their people's exodus from slavery. According to tradition, while the old Miriam provided the life-giving waters needed to sustain the Children of Israel in their march to freedom, it was through the new Miriam that the living waters of Christ would bring salvation to all mankind. The two traditions met at the Pools of Bethesda, where the miraculous well of the old Miriam had come to rest to await the birth of the new Miriam, who would bring the world a different kind of healing waters. (While ancient esoteric thought associated this site with Miriam's well, later traditions claim that the well is at Nazareth.)

The Roman Temple

At the time of Aelia Capitolina, a Temple of Serapis (equated by the Romans with Aesculapius, the god of healing) was built north to south over the sacred grottoes, incorporating them into its structure. Part of a mosaic floor of this temple still remains. When the mosaic was discovered it was believed to be a part of a later Byzantine church because of the crosses in the design, but it is now known that these crosses have no religious significance. The temple extended southward, reaching the area now occupied by the Church of St. Anne. Thus, the remains of the pagan temple form the crypt of the church. Throughout the Roman period the memory of the sacred grottoes was kept alive by Judeo-Christians who continued to visit the site and worship there. The rites they carried out were constantly condemned by Hellenistic Christians, who themselves, in time, began to confuse the two large pools just to the west with the grottoes where the miracle of Jesus had taken place.

The Byzantine Basilica

By the fifth century the tradition of healing had been largely forgotten or suppressed, perhaps because the grottoes had become associated with a pagan shrine and Judeo-Christian worship. The Roman temple and much of the remains of the grottoes were destroyed when a Byzantine basilica was built here. The western part of the basilica rested on the dike between the northern and southern pools, while its eastern part was built over the remains of the Roman temple and grottoes. The dike was too narrow to support the entire width

Remains of 39-foot-high (12 meters) arched pillars that once supported the floor of the Byzantine church, Southern Pool, Bethesda.

of the church and the basilica's central and southern nave had to be supported on 39-foot-high (12 meters) arched pillars that reached down to the bottom of the southern pool. These are the pillars that are still visible today. The basilica was apparently built here because by now the two large pools had become definitely associated with the site of the Gospel story, and with the ancient Judeo-Christian tradition regarding the birthplace of Mary. The basilica, which escaped destruction during the Persian invasion in 614, was finally destroyed by the caliph Hakim in 1009.

The Crusader Churches

For some unknown reason the Crusaders separated the two memories brought together by the Byzantine church. In the midst of the ruins of the basilica they built a small chapel dedicated to the memory of Jesus's miracle, while just to the south of the ruins they built the Church of St. Anne commemorating the birthplace of Mary.

During this period there was an undercurrent of mystical speculation linking the healing powers of the waters of Bethesda (which for all intents and purposes had been thoroughly forgotten in the preceding centuries) with the history of salvation through Christ. It revolved around a legend which stated that King Solomon had been shown the wood on which the Christ would be crucified. The king had the wood submerged in the Pools of Bethesda, where it remained until the time of the Passion. It then floated to the surface and was taken to make the cross. It was believed that it was because of this wood, through which the world would be saved, that the angel came to bathe in the waters of the pool, giving it its curative powers. From this legend also grew the belief that the soldiers had brought Jesus here to take up the cross, and for a short while the event was commemorated on the road outside the Church of St. Anne.

5

THE VIA DOLOROSA

One of western Christianity's most important devotional routes is the Via Dolorosa, the Street of Sorrows, or the Sorrowful Way. It is also called the Via Crucis, the Way or Stations of the Cross. It commemorates the Passion of Jesus and the route taken by him from the place of his condemnation to the place of his execution and burial while bearing on his shoulders the cross on which he would be crucified.

Fourteen stations along the way mark specific events in the Passion. The first nine are located along the route itself, while five are found in the Church of the Holy Sepulchre. The events commemorated are: (1) Jesus is condemned to death. (2) Jesus receives the cross. (3) Jesus falls under the cross for the first time. (4) Jesus meets his mother. (5) Jesus is helped by Simon of Cyrene to carry the cross. (6) Veronica wipes the sweat from Jesus's face. (7) Jesus falls for the

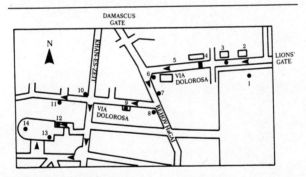

Fig. 21. The Via Dolorosa today.

1. First Station, the Antonia Fortress
2. Chapel of the Flagellation
3. Second Station, the Chapel of the Condemnation and the Taking Up of the Cross
4. Ecce Homo Arch and Ecce Homo Basilica
5. Greek Orthodox Praetorium
6. Third Station
7. Fourth Station
8. Fifth Station
9. Sixth Station
10. Seventh Station
11. Eighth Station
12. Ninth Station
13. Tenth–Thirteenth Stations, Calvary
14. Fourteenth Station, the Tomb of Jesus

second time. (8) Jesus talks to the daughters of Jerusalem. (9) Jesus falls for the third time. (10) Jesus is stripped of his raiment. (11) Jesus is nailed to the cross. (12) Jesus dies on the cross. (13) Jesus is taken down from the cross. (14) The body of Jesus is placed in the tomb.

Nine of the events are recorded in the Gospels, while five are the products of later traditions. The five events not mentioned in the Gospels are the three times Jesus fell and his meetings with his mother and with Veronica.

A SHORT HISTORY

It is not generally known that this devotional route is a relatively recent phenomenon whose origins lie in six-teenth-century Europe and whose stations were finalized only in the last century. Even less well known is the fact that this is a purely western rite, celebrated only by the Roman Catholic Church and its Protestant "offspring." There is no equivalent in Eastern Orthodox churches.

EARLY BYZANTINE TIMES

In the mid-fourth century, Cyril, the bishop of Jerusalem, instituted the innovative Easter practice of reading appropriate sections of the Gospels at a number of sites associated with the events leading up to the arrest of Jesus, his subsequent trial, and his Passion. Devotions began on the night before Good Friday at the Church of the Eleona on the Mount of Olives, where Jesus had taught the apostles. Just before dawn the worshippers went down to the site of the "agony" and to the place of the betrayal at Gethsemane, and from there straight to the Church of the Holy Sepulchre, where, before daybreak, they heard the account of the trial before Pilate. From the Holy Sepulchre they went to Mt. Zion to venerate the pillar of the scourging and then again to the Holy Sepulchre to pray at the site of the cross. At midday, while still at the Holy Sepulchre, they listened to the account of the Passion and then assembled before the tomb to commemorate the burial. Thus all the events commemorated along today's Via Dolorosa, from the trial to the burial, were celebrated in Cyril's time at the Church of the Holy Sepulchre.

For the next three hundred years, until the Arab conquest in 638, the principal points of the route remained essentially unchanged, though a number of sites were added to those established by Cyril. The procession still began on the evening preceding Good Friday on the Mount of Olives, then passed through Gethsemane. From there pilgrims proceeded to the Palace of Caiaphas the High Priest (today's St. Peter in Gallicantu), on the southern slopes of Mt. Zion, on to the Church of Pilate (St. Sophia), the site of the trial and condemnation of Jesus, and finally arrived at the Church of the Holy Sepulchre.

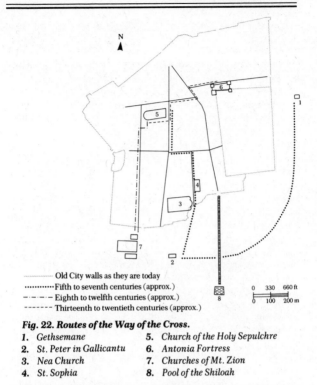

Fig. 22. Routes of the Way of the Cross.

Old City walls as they are today
·········· Fifth to seventh centuries (approx.)
– · – · – · Eighth to twelfth centuries (approx.)
- - - - - - Thirteenth to twentieth centuries (approx.)

0   330   660 ft
0   100   200 m

1. *Gethsemane*
2. *St. Peter in Gallicantu*
3. *Nea Church*
4. *St. Sophia*
5. *Church of the Holy Sepulchre*
6. *Antonia Fortress*
7. *Churches of Mt. Zion*
8. *Pool of the Shiloah*

THE PROBLEM OF THE PRAETORIUM

There are differences of opinion regarding the route actually taken by Jesus following his trial. This is the all-important route associated with the Way of the Cross. The key to this controversy lies at the site of Jesus's trial, traditionally called the Praetorium.

"Praetorium" was the Latin term for the residence used by a Roman procurator, or governor, when visiting a provincial town within his jurisdiction. After Herod's son Archelaus was deposed in 6 A.D., the judicial and military administration of the territories once under his control passed into the hands of a Roman procurator who had his capital at Caesarea. The procurator, however, often found his presence demanded in Jerusalem at the time of the Jewish festivals, when large numbers of pilgrims converged on the Temple Mount and the possibility of civil insurrection was at its highest. This danger was especially pronounced during the festival of Passover, with its emphasis on the theme of freedom. During these stays in the city the procurator used one of the palaces of Herod the Great as his praetorium. The question has always been, which palace? In the time of Jesus there were three palaces administered by the Roman governor in Jerusalem: the Antonia Fortress, at the northwest corner of the Temple Mount; Herod's new upper pal-

ace, at the Citadel near today's Jaffa Gate; and the old Hasmonean palace, in the area just opposite Robinson's Arch on
the Temple Mount.

For centuries the Antonia was widely believed to have been
the Praetorium. But archeological investigations carried out
over recent decades have shown conclusively that this identification is mistaken. Most investigators have therefore
turned to Herod's palace near the Jaffa Gate; but the problem
with this choice is that it holds no place in Christian tradition.
Excavations in the Jewish Quarter, however, have unearthed
evidence strongly favoring the third possibility: the old Hasmonean palace. The key piece of evidence lay in the discovery of the remains of the Nea Church. All ancient sources
confirm that the site of Jesus's trial (the Praetorium) was
commemorated in the early Byzantine period by a church
originally called the Church of Pilate. But there were apparently second thoughts about the appropriateness of naming
such a holy place after the very man who had condemned
Jesus, and the church was shortly afterward rededicated as St.
Sophia. The name was intended to indicate the place where
Divine Wisdom (Sophia)—Jesus—had been condemned by a
pagan judge. Father Bargil Pixner, a Benedictine monk and
archeologist from the Dormition Abbey, has convincingly
shown that all literary sources locate the Church of St. Sophia
near the Nea Church. Pilgrim accounts also mention the two
together. For example, the sixth-century Italian pilgrim from
Piacenza talks of "the basilica of St. Mary [St. Mary the New,
or "Nea"] at St. Sophia which was the Praetorium." It is these
two churches which, Father Pixner claims, are shown side by
side on the famous sixth-century Madaba Map. Thus the
route shown in Fig. 6 (see pp. 28–29) seems to have been the
one that the earliest Byzantine traditions held to be the actual
route taken by Jesus.

THE EARLY ARAB PERIOD

Both the Nea Church and the Church of St. Sophia were
destroyed in the Persian invasion of 614, which was closely
followed by the Arab conquest of Jerusalem in 638. The
Arabs began intensive building projects on the Temple
Mount (the Dome of the Rock and the al-Aqsa Mosque), and
occupied the area just to the west of al-Aqsa (today's Jewish
Quarter), including the sites of the two former churches.
The Nea Church was never rebuilt, but St. Sophia, which
was considered an important part of the Easter processional,
was eventually relocated on Mt. Zion. The Good Friday procession, then, began at Gethsemane (not further up the
Mount of Olives), and made its way to the House of Caiaphas, which by now was also relocated on Mt. Zion. After the
House of Caiaphas they visited the new St. Sophia, then
followed a road along the western wall of the city (today's
Armenian Quarter), and eventually arrived at the Church of
the Holy Sepulchre.

THE CRUSADER PERIOD

In 1172 a Crusader knight named Theodoric put forth the theory—which had no basis in any Christian tradition—that the actual site of the Praetorium had been the Antonia Fortress. The idea took hold, and a new route was established leading from the former fortress to the Church of the Holy Sepulchre. Because the twelfth-century Antonia was believed to be the remains of a once much larger structure, a number of sites connected with events that had taken place in different parts of the Antonia (the trial, scourging, crowning with thorns, condemnation, taking up of the cross) began to be "discovered" in the immediately surrounding area. It was these new sites that would eventually form the basis of today's Way of the Cross.

THE POST-CRUSADER PERIOD

After the fall of the Latin Kingdom the older Mt. Zion–Holy Sepulchre route was gradually abandoned. The new route became generally accepted and the occasional new "station" was added to those already "discovered" in the Crusader period. These additions no longer merely commemorated events that had taken place in the Praetorium, but were dedicated to episodes that had occurred along the road to Calvary.

A tremendous impetus was given to this trend by events that took place in fourteenth-century Europe. This was the time of the Hundred Years War. It was a terrible time, characterized by famine, plague, persecution, and intense human suffering. As conditions in Europe worsened, Christians began to meditate for the first time on the Passion and suffering of Christ as a way to understand and endure their own tragic fate. In the sixteenth century there swept through Western Europe a cult of the Passion whose devotees no longer saw Christ as the heavenly victor but rather, like themselves, as a very human sacrificial victim. It was an era oriented toward tragedy and pathos, glorifying the events of the Passion in literature, art, and mystery plays, and in routes of spiritual devotion in which the faithful followed Jesus on his journey from one station to the next. Historical or even biblical accuracy was no longer important. All that mattered was a growing revelation of the particulars of Christ's suffering.

In the seventeenth century one particular route, consisting of fourteen stations, was adopted by the Franciscans as a pious exercise and received official church backing in a series of papal briefs. By the eighteenth century a single Way of the Cross had been established in Europe, and its influence came to be felt in Jerusalem as well. Pilgrims to the Holy City wanted to see the stations they had become familiar with at home. In the nineteenth century, following the Crimean War, a period of liberalization under the Turks resulted in the intensive building of churches and chapels along the present Via Dolorosa, commemorating the fourteen stations of the cross popularized in Europe. As the stations became set, they were adopted by the Jerusalem Franciscans, and in 1880 they instituted a journey from the Antonia to Calvary as a route of spiritual devotion. This journey is still undertaken every Friday afternoon at three o'clock, starting within the Muslim El-Omariya School which now occupies the site of the Antonia.

THE CROSS AND THE TREE OF LIFE

In describing the Pools of Bethesda we mentioned a legend which existed in Crusader times concerning the finding there of the wood of the cross. This legend was actually one part of a popular medieval tale which associated the cross of Christ with the Tree of Life. According to this story, when Adam is nearly a thousand years old he sends his son Seth to the Garden of Eden to bring him the oil of mercy. Seth retraces Adam's footsteps, but when he arrives at the garden he finds its gates guarded by the flaming sword of the archangel Michael. Michael tells him that the time of Adam's pardon has not yet come, but that as token of this future pardon the wood on which mankind will be redeemed will grow from Adam's grave. Seth looks into the garden and at its center sees a great tree whose branches reach up into heaven. On the uppermost branch sits a child who, Michael tells him, is the second Adam, the one destined to redeem the sins of all mankind. The angel gives Seth seeds from the tree and tells him to place them on Adam's tongue when he dies. Seth does this and in time a magnificent tree grows from Adam's body.

The legend relates many episodes concerning this tree, which is eventually transplanted to Jerusalem by King David. His son, King Solomon, tries to use it as the main pillar of his palace but finds this impossible since the wood keeps changing its length. Finally Solomon buries it in a pit. Later he digs a pool on the spot, and the waters of the pool acquire healing powers. As the time of the Crucifixion approaches, the beam floats to the surface, where it is found by Roman soldiers who use it to make the cross on which Jesus is to be crucified. The cross is set up on Golgotha, at the center of the world, where Adam was created and died. The blood of the crucified Christ falls on the skull of Adam at the base of the cross, finally redeeming him, and through him all mankind.

The Tree of Life lay at the center of the Garden of Eden at the beginning of time, and will appear at the center of paradise at time's end ("And he shewed me a pure river of water of life, clear as crystal, proceeding out of the throne of God and of the Lamb. In the midst of the street of it, and on either side of the river, was there the tree of life."—Revelation 22:1–2). Adam's fall was a separation from this tree and from this center ("And the Lord God said, Behold, the man is become as one of us, to know good and evil: and now, lest he put forth his hand, and take also of the tree of life, and eat, and live for ever: Therefore the Lord God sent him forth from the garden of Eden."—Genesis 3:22–23).

Our legend tells of the establishment of the Tree of Life on earth, the lower world to which man has fallen. The earthly tree does not merely grow from the seeds of the heavenly tree, it is the same tree, for the seed is in the tree and the tree is in the seed. Its presence on earth as well as in heaven reveals it to be the cosmic tree. Like the cosmic mountain at the Church of the Holy Sepulchre, the cosmic tree, with its crown and branches reaching up to heaven and its roots descending to the abyss, symbolizes the cosmic axis which penetrates the three levels of creation (heaven, earth, and underworld), and makes communication between them possible. But the symbol of the tree is far more explicit than the mountain in describing the relation that exists between these levels. The leaves draw nourishment from the immaterial world of light above to the dark material world below, indicating the direction of the flow of consciousness and creation. The trunk is the medium for the transformation into sap of the life-giving liquids drawn up from the roots. In ancient times the rising of the sap in the sacred tree was equated with the production of the elixir of immortality, which was believed to flow up like a fountain of life to the fruit above.

The road that leads to salvation and redemption is the road that returns man to the Tree of Life at the center of the world. It is the road that leads to Eden, and paradise, and even to the heavenly Jerusalem. All earthly quests are attempts to find this hidden center where the *axis mundi* joins our own world. The earthly quest is a complicated and dangerous one. Labyrinths on certain church floors, and indeed in all places and times, symbolize the difficulty and complexity of this endeavor.

The Way of the Cross is such a quest. Although the cross is a very ancient symbol it was only in the fifth century that it was adopted to express the central meaning of Christianity—the sacrifice of Christ. Christ's instrument of sacrifice was probably at first represented by a simple pillar or stake (or even a tree) which symbolized the cosmic pillar (or tree) that stood at the center of the world. Later it was replaced by the cross, whose projected shadow on the ground indicated the place of sacrifice at the center of the four earthly directions, while the horizontal and vertical elements of the cross itself represented the union of opposites where all duality became reconciled (heaven and earth, time and eternity, etc.).

According to medieval legend, it was King Solomon who first recognized the significance of the cosmic tree. He changed it into a beam or pillar by stripping away its foliage. The foliage represents the world of change, which hides the unchanging vertical axis at its center—the immovable axis around which the visible world of change revolves. Solomon tried to establish this axis in his own house, to no avail. He cast it into a pit, where it remained until the coming of Christ, when the hidden center became visible to all men in the form of the wood of the cross, or the tree of sacrifice.

The revelation of the center is necessary so that men may be shown the way to it. The way is the Way of Jesus, symbolized by his journey along the Via Dolorosa, moving against the current of creation, and ordinary life, which leads from the fine to the coarse and always downward to death. To swim against the tide of nature must inevitably lead to a confrontation with all the passions and resistance that human and earthly life can offer. The way thus takes the outer form of terrible human suffering, as seen by those who look on from the periphery. Christ himself remains still and unmoving on the line leading to the center, where human passions and suffering come to an end. By doing so, he ascends the cosmic tree and transcends the level where these events take place. He becomes one with the axis of the universe, the tree of life, and is no longer limited by earthly existence.

This merging of Christ was described by one of the early bishops of Rome, Hippolytus: "This tree, wide as heaven itself, has grown up into heaven from the earth. It is an immortal growth and towers between heaven and earth. It is the fulcrum of all things and the place where they are all at rest. It is the foundation of the round world, the center of the cosmos. In it all the diversities in our human nature are formed into a unity. It is held together by the invisible nails of the spirit so that it may not break loose from the divine."

THE STATIONS OF THE CROSS

Aside from its role as a devotional route, today's Via Dolorosa is disappointing. Only a few of the stations are marked by churches or chapels which can be visited, and these are relatively modern. For the most part, the stations are token in nature and devotions are made at various points along the road itself leading to Calvary. Since its inception in the Middle Ages, the Way of the Cross has emphasized the external spectator's view of the Passion rather than Christ's inner experience of transformation, transcendence, and victory. Only certain Christian mystics have dwelt on this point. It is useful while following the Via Dolorosa to keep in mind the meaning that lies at the center and not just at the periphery, for celestial Jerusalem lies at this center and not in the stones and mortar we see at its outer edges.

THE FIRST STATION: *The Courtyard of the El-Omariya School (The Antonia Fortress)*

For the most part, the City of David was naturally defended by deep valleys bordering its perimeter. Only the northern part of the city opened onto a plateau and was vulnerable to attack. For this reason the kings of Judah built a fortress here called Hananel, which was sometimes known as Birah or, in Greek, Baris. When Herod came to the throne, the location of the old Baris interfered with his building projects on the Temple Mount and had to be removed. In its place, and just to the northwest of the newly extended Temple Mount, he built a new fortress which he named Antonia in honor of his friend Mark Antony.

Most reconstructions of the Antonia Fortress have been influenced by its erroneous identification (since the days of the Crusader knight Theodoric) with the Praetorium of Pilate. Its size, especially, has been greatly exaggerated. Thus the famous reconstruction by Père Vincent was made large enough to contain today's Chapel of the Flagellation, Chapel of the Taking Up of the Cross, the Lithostrotos at the Convent

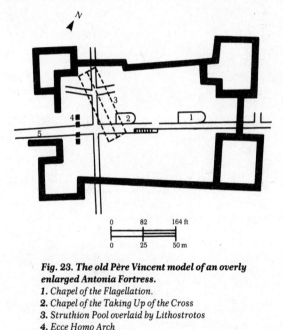

Fig. 23. The old Père Vincent model of an overly enlarged Antonia Fortress.
1. *Chapel of the Flagellation.*
2. *Chapel of the Taking Up of the Cross*
3. *Struthion Pool overlaid by Lithostrotos*
4. *Ecce Homo Arch*
5. *Via Dolorosa*

of the Sisters of Zion, and the Ecce Homo Arch—all events or architectural features associated in the Gospels with the Praetorium. It is now reasonably established that the Antonia was limited to the outcrop of rock to the northwest of the Temple Mount, where today's El-Omariya School is located.

The first station—where traditionally Jesus was condemned to death—is located in the courtyard of the school. Except for the weekly procession, which begins here every

Friday afternoon at three o'clock, there is nothing to mark it as a holy site. This is the only Station of the Cross that is not commemorated by a chapel of any sort. Earlier generations spoke of a Chapel of the Crowning with Thorns that once stood here, and eyewitnesses from different periods report seeing it used as a storeroom first for coal and later for fodder for horses, but it was apparently destroyed in an earthquake in 1927.

While it is clear that this was not the site of Pilate's palace, and that the Crusaders were in error on this point, their choice of route cannot simply be written off. The Latin Kingdom was a political and military entity, but there was also another, less well-known side to its nature that involved mystical speculations concerning the life of Christ and the very nature of Jerusalem itself. Thus, it cannot be overlooked that the route beginning here linked the three temples of Christian history: the old Temple of the Jews; the Temple of the body of Christ; and the Temple of the New Jerusalem, the Church of the Holy Sepulchre. While geographically the route is a horizontal one, spiritually it is vertical. Christ begins at the site of the old, the abandoned and dead (the old Temple). Through his Passion he climbs to the heights, achieving final victory at Calvary.

The Chapel of the Flagellation

The first church on this site was built by the Crusaders, who consecrated it to the memory of the events recorded in John 19:1–3. "Then Pilate therefore took Jesus, and scourged him. And the soldiers platted a crown of thorns, and put it on his head, and they put on him a purple robe, and said, Hail, King of the Jews! and they smote him with their hands."

Following the fall of the Latin Kingdom the church became successively a stable, a weaver's shop, and a refuse dump, and eventually lay in ruins. In 1838 the site was given to the Franciscans by Ibrahim Pasha of Egypt, and one year later it was reopened after restorations paid for by Duke Maximilian of Bavaria. In 1927–29 it was completely renovated in twelfth-century style. Remains of the Crusader church have been incorporated in the northern wall of the present chapel.

The decorations are relatively modern and have little relevance to the true meaning of the Passion. The only point of significance is the dome of the chapel, which contains a huge mosaic depicting the crown of thorns. Church domes always give a feeling of the ascent of the spirit, but here the ascent is met by the crown of thorns, which seems to descend from above to the material below. The impression is an unusual one for a Franciscan chapel, especially along the Via Dolorosa. This route, predominantly Franciscan in nature, is dominated by sixteenth-century European concepts of the Passion, that is, suffering as a result of human cruelty. Here, however, we get an inkling of a different meaning of the word "suffering." The crown of thorns that descends

The crown of thorns on the ceiling of the Chapel of the Flagellation.

from above is a spiritual one, that is, it comes from a higher, finer world than our own. What is this inner crown of thorns, consciously accepted by Jesus as a necessary part of his ascent to victory and freedom? Today's Via Dolorosa, which concentrates on the physical aspects and human agents of this drama, gives no answer.

The other decorations are of less interest. The three large stained-glass windows which close the arches of the vault of the dome represent, from left to right, Pilate washing his hands, the flagellation of Jesus, and the triumph of Barabbas. You might note the four paintings on the side walls of the chapel. These are St. Francis, the Virgin, St. John the Evangelist, and St. Paul. St. Paul is depicted here because he was held prisoner in the Antonia, which was once believed to have included this site. Take a look also at the iron door of the chapel, which contains twenty-two bronze panels depicting biblical symbols and quotations.

The CHAPEL OF THE FLAGELLATION is open daily, 8 A.M.–12 noon and 2–6 P.M. in summer; 1–5 P.M. in winter.

THE SECOND STATION: The Chapel of the Taking Up of the Cross

The station itself is located on the road outside the Franciscan compound opposite the chapel. The chapel is called by the Franciscans the Chapel of the Condemnation and the Imposition of the Cross, though the second station more properly commemorates only the latter. Although many writers claim that today's chapel was built on the ruins of an earlier Byzantine one, excavations carried out by the Franciscans have effectively disproved this hypothesis. The present chapel was built in 1903.

The windows of the dome show angels holding instruments of the Passion; while the two small side windows depict Pilate washing his hands, and the cross being taken up. In the apse there is a papier-mâché rendition of Jesus wearing the crown of thorns descending the steps of the Praetorium to take up his cross. To the right of the apse a second work in papier-mâché shows St. John trying to hide Jesus from his mother when they meet at the fourth station. These representations emphasize the cruel human aspect of the Passion. Compare this with the Church of St. Peter in Gallicantu, on Mt. Zion, where the emphasis is on the inner meaning of divine, compassionate sacrifice rather than on external human evil.

To the rear of the church are a number of large striated flagstones similar to the ones found in the Convent of the Sisters of Zion. These, and the bank outside the chapel, mark the beginning of the great pavement known as the Lithostrotos.

Before leaving the Franciscan compound, you should certainly pay a visit to the Museum of the Studium Biblicum Franciscanum, situated just to the left of the Chapel of the Flagellation. The Franciscans are responsible for some of the most interesting and important discoveries about the life of the early Judeo-Christians and the origins of the Church. These findings have been published by the Franciscan Printing Press, whose bookstore is located on St. Francis Street. The museum itself contains ten rooms of exhibits from early Christian sites in Israel.

The CHAPEL OF THE TAKING UP OF THE CROSS is open daily, 8 A.M.–12 noon and 2–6 P.M.

The Convent of the Sisters of Zion

The convent contains a number of remains once believed to be associated with the Praetorium of Pilate. Although the sisters now accept that the Antonia Fortress did not reach this far, the remains have historical and archeological value. Tours of the restored Struthion Pool and Lithostrotos are given without charge by the sisters, who provide a well-organized and detailed explanation before entry to the site. The site itself is well signposted, and diagrams along the way clearly explain what is being seen.

The Struthion Pool

A system of canals and reservoirs led water from various parts of the city to the Temple Mount. One such reservoir was an open double pool called the Struthion which collected water from the Tyropoeon Valley and the area to the north of the city. As a result of Herod's building projects on the Temple Mount, the Struthion was abandoned. When the area was developed a century and a half later by the Roman settlers of Aelia Capitolina, vaults were built over the pools to support the flooring of a new marketplace paved with large stones. This is the flooring known as the Lithostrotos. Both periods of construction are visible. The pool itself is cut into the natural bedrock while the overlying Roman vaults are built of stone blocks.

The Lithostrotos

The discovery of the Lithostrotos in the last century seemed at the time to prove that the Praetorium of Pilate was indeed the Antonia Fortress. According to the Gospel of John the Lithostrotos was the central courtyard of the Praetorium, where Pilate conducted the trial of Jesus. "When Pilate therefore heard that saying, he brought Jesus forth, and sat down in the judgment seat in a place that is called the Pavement, but in the Hebrew, Gabbatha" (John 19:13). Since then, however, similar pavements of large flagstones have been found at sites throughout Jerusalem, while this one has been shown to belong to the Roman marketplace built here some 150 years after Jesus's death.

The CONVENT OF THE SISTERS OF ZION is open daily except Sunday, 8:30 A.M.–12:30 P.M. and 2–5 P.M.

The Ecce Homo Arch

Leaving the convent, you are again on the road called the Via Dolorosa. Looking westward, you see an arch spanning the road outside the Ecce Homo Basilica. This is one of Jerusalem's most famous monuments associated with the Passion. In the thirteenth and fourteenth centuries it was linked with a rest taken by Jesus on the way to Calvary, and in the fifteenth century with the place of his interrogation. By the sixteenth century, pilgrims identified the arch with the entranceway to the Praetorium where Pilate presented Jesus to the people. "Then came Jesus forth, wearing the crown of

Part of a second century triumphal (triple) arch incorporated into the Ecce Homo Basilica. The higher, partial arch to the right continues on the street outside as the Ecce Homo Arch.

thorns, and the purple robe. And Pilate saith unto them, Behold the man!—Ecce Homo" (John 19:5).

In actuality, this was one of a number of "triumphal" gates or arches erected in Aelia Capitolina in the second century. It was originally part of a triple gate—consisting of a large central arch and two lower flanking ones—which stood at the western entrance of the Roman market, which was paved with the large stones known today as the Lithostrotos (see also Fig. 4, p. 26). Only the central part of this gateway spans the street. A small part of this central arch and the smaller adjacent northern one were integrated into the structure of the Ecce Homo Basilica. The southern arcade no longer exists.

The Ecce Homo Basilica

Take a quick look inside the basilica. It was built in 1868 in Roman-Byzantine style, and designed to incorporate in its structure a part of the Ecce Homo Arch. The northern arcade of the Ecce Homo stands behind the altar, and to the right of this is a part of the arch that spans the road outside. In the apse above the arch there is a golden mosaic with a Byzantine cross worth noting. At the corners of the cross are the four beasts associated in early iconography with the four evangelists. This is a really ancient symbolism whose source and exact meaning are unknown. It is also found in the prophet Ezekiel's vision of the four creatures who support the throne of God (Ezekiel 1:5–10) and in the Revelation of John (Revelation 4:6–8). The earliest known occurrence is in the Great Sphinx of Egypt, which has the body of a bull,

The cross of triumph from the Ecce Homo Basilica.

the legs of a lion, the wings of an eagle, and the head of a man. One of the most interesting interpretations of the four beasts was given by the Russian philosopher G. I. Gurdjieff, who claimed that the Great Sphinx symbolizes the four qualities necessary for man's inner development, with the four beasts representing the creatures in which these qualities were particularly manifest. Thus the bull represents the untiring energy necessary for such work. The lion embodies courage and faith in one's strength. The eagle indicates the requirement of continual meditation on higher questions, and not only on those related to everyday existence. The man expresses the need for the work to be performed with love and devotion. Note that there is no figure on the cross. This is because it is a cross of triumph and represents the victory of the Resurrection.

The ECCE HOMO BASILICA is open daily except Sunday, 8:30 A.M.–12:30 P.M. and 2–5 P.M.

The Prison of Christ

The structure known as the Greek Orthodox Praetorium or Prison of Christ seems to be based on a double misidentification. It is not the site of the Praetorium, and the imprisonment of Jesus is generally associated with St. Peter in Gallicantu on Mt. Zion. Although the Way of the Cross is not a part of the Greek Orthodox tradition, lately the Greeks have begun the practice of assembling here on Good Friday before going in procession to the Church of the Holy Sepulchre.

Opposite the entrance, and to the left, a narrow passage in the rock leads to a small room called the Prison of Christ containing a stone bench with two holes. It is claimed that the prisoner was made to sit on the bench, with his legs then being placed in the holes and tied from below. A staircase leads down from the entrance to two further levels of "cells." On the lowest level is one called the Prison of Barabbas. Despite the exotic interpretations given for the various chambers found here, their origins are rather prosaic. In the time of Aelia Capitolina, rooms and cells of various sizes and shapes were cut into the rock bordering the Roman market, and used as shops and storerooms.

THE PRISON OF CHRIST is open daily except Sunday. Regular hours in the morning, 9 A.M.–12 noon; in the afternoon, ring the bell.

THE THIRD STATION: Jesus Falls for the First Time

The third station is commemorated on the road outside a small chapel (usually closed) built on the site of a former Turkish bath. The tradition that Jesus—already exhausted from the agony in Gethsemane and the scourging in the

Praetorium—fell under the weight of the cross, does not appear in the Gospels. The site was bought by the Armenian Catholic Church in 1856, and the present chapel was built in 1947 with contributions made by Polish soldiers. For years the station was marked by two broken columns partially buried in the ground. Today these columns can be seen in the iron fence enclosing the entranceway.

THE FOURTH STATION: *Jesus Meets His Mother*

A few yards to the south is the entrance to the Armenian Catholic Patriarchate and the Church of Our Lady of the Spasm. The word "spasm" here refers to a state resulting from extreme sorrow or grief. The station itself is located a little further along the road, at the entranceway to a small oratory (almost always closed) which lies above the crypt of the church. This is the place where Mary met her son carrying the cross. The event is not mentioned in the Gospels, but does seem to have some basis in early Christian traditions and writings. In the Crusader period (twelfth century) it was commemorated at the site of St. Mary Major in the Muristan, near the Church of the Holy Sepulchre. In the thirteenth century it was moved to its present location. The crypt of today's church is located on an ancient street level and contains remains of this thirteenth-century chapel (which was then called Our Lady of the Fainting), and part of a mosaic showing two sandals pointing north. Some opinions hold that the thirteenth-century structure was built to incorporate the earlier mosaic, which seemed to symbolize the place where Mary stood.

THE FIFTH STATION: *Simon of Cyrene*

The fifth station commemorates events in Luke 23:26. "And as they led him away, they laid hold upon one Simon, a Cyrenian, coming out of the country, and on him they laid the cross, that he might bear it after Jesus." Simon's Jewish name probably indicates that he was a pilgrim from Cyrene (Libya) who had come to Jerusalem for the festival of the Passover, though nothing more is known of him. In the fifteenth and sixteenth centuries, this location was pointed out as the site of the house of Simon the Pharisee, where a sinful woman anointed the feet of Jesus. In 1850 it was chosen by the Franciscans to commemorate the story of Simon of Cyrene. The present chapel was built in 1895, before which the station was marked by the stone sealed in the wall at the right. The hollow in the stone was said to have been caused by a blow made by the cross of Jesus or the imprint left when Jesus put his hand on it while carrying the cross. Above the door is the symbol of the Franciscans: two crossed arms with signs of the wounds of Christ on their palms. The bare arm is Jesus, the clothed one St. Francis. This chapel, too, is almost always closed, and the event is remembered on the road outside.

THE SIXTH STATION: *Veronica*

The Via Dolorosa continues westward, rising from the fifth station to the Suq Khan es-Zeit above. Halfway along the lefthand side of the street, a pillar sunk into the wall marks the sixth Station of the Way of the Cross, commemorating Jesus's meeting with Veronica (not mentioned in the Gospels).

The legend of Veronica is both ancient and complicated. Its origins reach back to somewhere between the fourth and eighth centuries. It seems that eleventh-century Rome venerated a cloth bearing the image of Christ. One tradition claimed that it was used by Jesus to wipe his face at Gethsemane, while another related it to a story of a woman whom he miraculously cured. By the twelfth century the cloth came to be called Veronica, which probably derived from Vera Icone, or "true image" (of Christ).

Another version of the legend talks of a woman called Veronica or Bernice. This is the woman with the issue of blood cured by Jesus at Capernaum by the Sea of Galilee, who in gratitude followed him wherever he went. By the twelfth century Veronica's cure became associated with the area near the Pools of Bethesda.

At the end of the twelfth century the incident of Veronica somehow became linked with the story of the Passion, and by the fifteenth century it formed a part of what was then called the Sorrowful Way. The event was then localized outside of Veronica's house, which was believed to have been at the site of the present sixth station.

The legend of Veronica took its final form at that time. According to this version, a woman named Veronica wiped the sweat from the face of Jesus as he passed by her house on the way to Calvary. When she removed the cloth, the image of Jesus's face was impressed upon it. Later, when Veronica heard that the Emperor Tiberius was ill, she took the cloth to Rome and cured him by showing him the miraculous picture.

Today the House of Veronica belongs to a contemplative order of nuns called the Little Sisters of Jesus. The site was bought by the Greek Catholics in 1883, and a church was built in 1885. In 1953 it was rebuilt on two levels, the Church of Veronica above and a crypt and chapel below. The entrance to the crypt is through a little shop where the Little Sisters of Jesus make and sell icons. When the crypt was cleared, remains of a wall and arches of a building were found together with a Greek inscription mentioning the names of Cosmas and Damian. Although no excavations have taken place here, it is believed that these are the remains of the Monastery of SS. Cosmas and Damian, which was built in the sixth century as a hospice for nuns visiting Jerusalem.

THE SEVENTH STATION: *Jesus Falls for the Second Time*

The seventh Station of the Cross is commemorated outside a small chapel located at the intersection of the Via Dolorosa and the Suq Khan es-Zeit. The city street called Via Dolorosa comes to an end here, perhaps reflecting the fact that until the seventeenth century the Street of Sorrows, or the Sorrowful Way, itself ended at this point. The Suq runs along the route occupied by the Second Wall in the time of Jesus. During the Roman period of Aelia Capitolina this became the city's main street, the Cardo Maximus. From the thir teenth century onward, pilgrims began to point to this intersection as the site of the Gate of Judgment, where Jesus left the city on the way to Calvary. The name reflects the belief that sentences of death were read and posted here as the condemned passed through its gates. The importance of the site became established only after other sites along the Sorrowful Way were fixed in the sixteenth century. Here, it was believed, Jesus fell under the weight of the cross for the second time after his steep climb up the Via Dolorosa. In 1875 the site was bought by the Franciscans, who originally intended to build a school here. Instead they built the present chapel, which is used today by Coptic Catholics. The chapel, which is generally closed, contains a column still remaining from the Cardo Maximus.

THE EIGHTH STATION: *The Daughters of Jerusalem*

Cross over the Suq and up the steps to the street that continues westward. On the left is the German Lutheran Hospice of St. John and after that the Greek Orthodox Church of St. Charalambos. The station is marked by a stone set in the wall of the Greek church. The stone bears a cross with the letters $\frac{IC|XC}{NI|KA}$, meaning "Jesus Christ Conquers." The concept of a victorious Christ who will share his victory with those who follow him comes from John 16:33, where Jesus says: "In the world ye shall have tribulation: but be of good cheer; I have overcome the world." The Greek word for "conquer" was *nika,* which was sometimes abbreviated by Christians to the letter N. To show that the word *nika,* or N, referred to Christ, it was usually written in a sacred place or accompanied by other signs that had some relation to him. Here it is accompanied by a cross and two groups of letters, IC and XC. These latter are formed from the first and last letters of the two Greek words IHCOYC XPICTOC, Jesus Christ. Thus, "Jesus Christ Conquers."

In the time of Jesus this was the site of an open field just

The eighth Station of the Cross, "Jesus Christ Conquers."

outside the city wall. Today Christians commemorate here Jesus's warning to the daughters of Jerusalem. "And there followed him a great company of people, and of women, which also bewailed and lamented him. But Jesus turning unto them said, Daughters of Jerusalem, weep not for me, but weep for yourselves, and for your children. For, behold, the days are coming, in the which they shall say, Blessed are the barren, and the wombs that never bare, and the paps which never gave suck" (Luke 23:27–29).

This event has been located at various places during the centuries. It was only in the nineteenth century that the Franciscans moved it to its present location. Although we are now very close to Calvary, we can no longer follow a direct route and have to return once again to the Suq.

THE NINTH STATION: *Jesus Falls for the Third Time*

Return to the site of the seventh station and turn south. A short walk along the Suq will bring you to the stairs leading up to the Coptic Patriarchate. This is where Constantine's Church of the Holy Sepulchre led down into the Cardo Maximus. A column to the left of the entranceway of the Patriarchate marks the ninth station, where Jesus is said to have fallen for the third time. The event was originally commemorated in the courtyard of the Church of the Holy Sepulchre and was moved here sometime between the fourteenth and sixteenth centuries.

From here we can see the Church of the Holy Sepulchre. A doorway to the left of the pillar opens onto Deir es-Sultan, the Ethiopian monastery on the roof of the Holy Sepulchre's Chapel of St. Helen. It is possible to reach the courtyard of the Church of the Holy Sepulchre by cutting across Deir es-Sultan and descending through the Ethiopian Chapel of the Four Beasts. But the way is not always open, and it is usual for pilgrims who wish to follow the Way of the Cross to return yet again to the Suq. The double change in direction caused by the eighth and ninth stations is an inconvenience. It has thus been suggested that the eighth station be moved to the Suq somewhere south of station seven, and the ninth station relocated to its original site in the courtyard of the Church of the Holy Sepulchre.

THE LAST FIVE STATIONS OF THE CROSS: The Church of the Holy Sepulchre

The last five Stations of the Cross are located in the Church of the Holy Sepulchre. (*See* p. 100 et seq.) Stations ten through thirteen commemorate events of the Crucifixion and are located on Calvary (Jesus is stripped of his garments, Jesus is nailed to the cross, Jesus dies on the cross, Jesus is taken down from the cross). Station fourteen commemorates the burial of Jesus and is located at the tomb (*see* p. 106).

These last five stations are of the greatest symbolic significance. The stripping of the garments (station ten) is reminiscent of the first stage of baptism. From the earliest days of Christianity, baptism was looked upon as analogous to the Passion of Christ. In baptism the candidate began by removing, in imitation of Christ, the old earthly garment of sin and corruption with which he had been clothed by God after the fall. This outer garment represented the changeable physical body and its passions, the prison which kept man tied to the lower world, but which could be abandoned when he achieved the primitive innocence of the center. The nailing to the cross (station eleven) represents the irrevocable joining to this center, which Hippolytus described as being accomplished with "the invisible nails of the spirit so that it may not break loose from the divine." The twelfth station represents not only the death of Jesus on the cross but the raising of the wood of the cosmic cross, or the establishment of the vertical axis at the center of the world. Only when the axis is raised and established is the link between heaven and earth fully forged and one can die to the earthly by rising above it.

Stations thirteen and fourteen (the taking down from the cross, and the placing of the body in the tomb) form part of an incomplete story. Once the *axis mundi* is erected, a divine link is forged between heaven, earth, and the underworld. These two stations represent Christ's journey downward to the lower regions, where he establishes the axis in the world of darkness. Here the axis takes the form of a cosmic ladder for those whom Christ has marked with the sign of the cross (his personified power). Thus Adam and the saints are set free.

The ascent of Jesus, Adam, and the saints along this center is missing in today's Way of the Cross, with its emphasis on tragedy and pathos. Today there is a growing feeling that this emphasis has cut us off from the true meaning of the events that took place here two thousand years ago. It has been proposed that this could be expressed by adding a fifteenth station commemorating the triumph of the Resurrection.

6

MOUNT ZION

THE CHURCH OF ST. PETER IN GALLICANTU

The Church of St. Peter in Gallicantu ("at the cock's crow")
is situated on the eastern slope of Mt. Zion. Its location fits
the description by the anonymous fourth-century Pilgrim of
Bordeaux whose accounts have proven accurate time and
again. He writes that leaving the Pool of Shiloah at the
southern end of the City of David, he climbed to Mt. Zion,
and before entering Zion's wall arrived at the site of the
palace of the high priest Caiaphas. This is the place where
according to the Gospels Jesus was imprisoned and interrogated by the high priest before being handed over to the
Roman governor, Pontius Pilate; and where Peter denied his
master three times before the crowing of the cock. To the left
of the church there can still be seen the remains of a set of
ancient steps leading up to Mt. Zion from an area just to the
north of the Pool of Shiloah. Traditions locating the palace of
Caiaphas further up the hill—on the site of today's Armenian
cemetery—belong to a later period.

The church, which was consecrated in 1931, belongs to
the Assumptionist Fathers (the Augustinian Fathers of the
Assumption). The atmosphere here is unique. There is a
lightness that contrasts sharply with the heavy feeling of
tragedy found along the Via Dolorosa. Here too, the theme is
the Passion and suffering of Christ, but the many mosaics
which fill the walls of the church attempt to portray the
inner meaning of this suffering rather than concentrating on
its cruel physical aspects. What is apparent here is divine
compassionate sacrifice, repentance, and forgiveness.

The theme of divine sacrifice begins with the Creation,
when "the Lord God formed man of the dust of the ground,
and breathed into his nostrils the breath of life" (Genesis
2:7). The gift of life meant that God had to sacrifice a part of
his own living breath and spirit. What would become of this
seed planted by God? Would it be used to transform the gross
matter into which it had been placed? Or would it be swallowed up in this matter, fall away from its source, and be lost
forever? Part of the answer is given at St. Peter in Gallicantu,
where the theme of sacrifice is intimately related to an-

other—that of forgiveness. Man is not abandoned in his
inevitable fall, nor does divine sacrifice end with the Creation. The fall of Adam is followed by the sacrifice of Jesus,
who descends the cosmic axis to the earthly world in order to
awaken the conscience of man to his state and open his
heart to forgiveness. Forgiveness is the return to innocence
and the way back to the source.

The story of St. Peter exemplifies this theme. Peter is
destined to lead the Church after the death of Jesus, but
first Peter himself must be awakened, seek forgiveness, be
transformed and brought back to the source. Peter's trial
begins at the Last Supper. Jesus, who knows what is about
to take place, says to the apostles: "Little children, yet a
little while I am with you. . . . Whither I go, ye cannot
come" (John 13:33). "Simon Peter said unto him, Lord,
whither goest thou? Jesus answered him, Whither I go,
thou canst not follow me now; but thou shalt follow me
afterwards. Peter said unto him, Lord, why cannot I follow
thee now? I will lay down my life for thy sake. Jesus answered him, Wilt thou lay down thy life for my sake? Verily, verily, I say unto thee, The cock shall not crow, till
thou hast denied me thrice" (John 13:36–38).

Following the Last Supper, Jesus and his disciples departed for Gethsemane, where, unknown to his disciples,
Jesus awaited his arrest and the beginning of his Passion.
The Gospel of St. Mark tells us that when Jesus was arrested
his disciples fled in fear, though Peter followed his master
from afar. Since it was too late an hour for him to be taken
before the Roman governor, Jesus was led to the palace of
the high priest Caiaphas, where he was interrogated and
imprisoned overnight. While Jesus was being questioned,
"Peter sat without in the palace: and a damsel came unto
him saying, Thou also wast with Jesus of Galilee. But he
denied before them all, saying, I know not what thou sayest.
And when he was gone out into the porch, another maid saw
him, and said unto them that were there, This fellow was
also with Jesus of Nazareth. And again he denied them with
an oath, I do not know the man. And after a while came unto
him they that stood by, and said to Peter, Surely thou also art
one of them; for thy speech bewrayeth thee. Then began he
to curse and to swear, saying, I know not the man. And
immediately the cock crew. And Peter remembered the word
of Jesus, which said unto him, Before the cock crow, thou
shalt deny me thrice. And he went out, and wept bitterly"
(Matthew 26:69–75).

A mosaic on the lefthand wall of the church depicts Jesus,
with hands tied, confronting Peter at cockcrow. This meeting exemplifies the meaning of sacrifice that is portrayed
throughout the church. Jesus suffers in the palace of the
high priest. It is the beginning of his Passion. The tied hands
at last reveal what he really is—the divine breath and spirit
held prisoner in the fallen world of man. But Peter too suffers. At the crowing of the cock he suddenly awakens to the

full implications of his denial, and understands that the divine prisoner whom he has denied is not only the one who stands before him but also the one who stands within. What others are doing to Jesus he too has done to the divine seed and master within himself. In this moment of recognition Peter is at last capable of accepting God's compassionate gift and sacrifice and weeps bitter tears of repentance. They are tears which lead to release, forgiveness, and reorientation— and Peter is transformed.

The Assumptionist Fathers draw special attention to the fact that sacrifice, as represented here, is not one-sided. Both Christ and Peter are wounded in the exchange that permits each to accomplish what is destined for him. Only by both suffering, both sacrificing, can God and man come closer and begin to work together. They point out that this is the theme in the story of Jacob's struggle with the angel. Jacob defeats the angel, but the angel wounds Jacob. Only then does he become Israel, and the father of the nation that will work together with God to transform the face of the world.

Other mosaics in the church also portray this theme. The mosaic behind the altar shows Christ, the divine prisoner, at the trial before Caiaphas, while flanking this scene are panels depicting sinners who have repented and been forgiven. To the left is St. Dismas, the good thief, who received Christ's forgiveness on the cross, and the inhabitants of the Holy Land who did penance for their sins. To the right are women who were sinners, repented, received forgiveness, and were transformed. These include Mary Magdalene and Mary of Egypt. On the righthand wall there is a mosaic depicting the Last Supper. Note that there are only eleven

Repentance and forgiveness, the theme at St. Peter in Gallicantu. This is a mosaic of Mary Magdalene and Mary of Egypt, representing female sinners who have repented and received God's forgiveness.

apostles shown here. Judas Iscariot, who represents the earthly forces which close the heart to divine love and forgiveness, is not represented.

The Palace of Caiaphas (Hebrew: Armon Caiaphas)

While perhaps it cannot be proved that this was the actual site of the palace of the high priest Caiaphas, the archeological remains found here are certainly intriguing and bear consideration. These can be seen from a balcony that surrounds the outside wall of the apse of the church. The ruins we are looking at served as the foundations for a Byzantine church that existed here in the late fourth or early fifth century. It is claimed that these are not merely foundations but the remains of an even earlier structure upon which the Byzantine church was built, possibly even the palace of Caiaphas itself.

Forecourt of the Palace

Descending to the level below the present neo-Byzantine church, you come to a floor with two chapels built over what are believed to be the dungeons below the forecourt of the palace of the high priest. In the construction of this floor much of the natural rock was retained and incorporated into the structure. This level belonged to the forecourt of the palace of Caiaphas, where Peter met Jesus and wept. When the Byzantines built their church, this level was kept as a crypt where Peter's repentance was remembered.

The center of this floor is built over the place where Jesus is believed to have been imprisoned. The hole in the floor is where the prisoner was lowered down. The mosaic on the northern exterior of the church shows the bound Jesus with ropes under his arms being lowered down into this pit. Note the crosses on the walls of the opening of the pit. Crosses are also found along the walls of the pit itself. It is believed that these crosses were made by early Christians who here venerated the place where Jesus was imprisoned. Today a staircase leads down to the room itself.

The Place of the Scourging

To the side of this "prison" (and reached by a separate staircase) is an area called the guardroom and common prison. It is said that between the first and second pillar there was once another pillar. This was reputedly the pillar to which Jesus was tied and scourged, and which was later removed to the Church of the Pillar on Mt. Zion.

The early Byzantine church was destroyed in the Persian invasion of 614. Another church was built in its place but was also destroyed, this time by the caliph Hakim in 1009. In the Crusader period a church was built which was given the name Sanctus Petrus-in-Gallicantu (St. Peter's at Cockcrow), signifying that by that time only St. Peter's repentance was commemorated here. By then the older tradition of Jesus's trial before Caiaphas had been transferred to a small chapel not far from the house of the Last Supper on Mt. Zion, on the site of the present Armenian cemetery.

The CHURCH OF ST. PETER IN GALLICANTU is open daily except Sunday, in summer 8:30–11:45 A.M. and 2–5:30 P.M.; in winter, 2–5 P.M. Tel.: 283332.

THE BASILICA OF THE DORMITION ABBEY

Following the Crucifixion, Mary the mother of Jesus resided with the apostles and other members of the earliest Christian community in the place called the Upper Room, where Jesus and the twelve apostles had celebrated the Last Supper. This fact, briefly mentioned in the Acts of the Apostles (Acts 1:12–14) does not convey the true significance of Mary's presence in the heart of this first community. Today it is known that the family of Jesus played a much more significant role in the leadership of this early group than is presented in the New Testament. Jesus was not simply regarded as the Messiah, but the Messiah from the promised line of David. It was this Davidic line, and thus the family, that was all-important, and which constituted the true heart of this early community. For this reason it was not an apostle but James, called the brother of Jesus, who was chosen, mainly by the family, to be the first bishop of Jerusalem. After James, Simon was chosen—the son of Mary, wife of Cleophas, a woman described as the sister of Jesus's mother. The popular picture of these early days is one of Mary living with the apostles and being cared for by them. In actuality it was the opposite. The apostles and early community clustered around Mary and the family of Jesus.

The importance of Mary, however, went beyond the family. The cult of the Virgin, which was later to erupt with such force, already had its origins in the earliest community. But even at that early period the cult of the Virgin was not new. It had already existed for millennia in the religions of the ancient world, most notably in Egypt in the cult of Isis.

The Virgin is regarded by many as the greatest mystery of the world. She is at once always fertile and always a virgin. She is the beloved of God, the one pure element worthy of being the vessel through which the Most High can enter and renew the world. Within ourselves she represents the secret hidden place which can nurture and give birth to the higher man. In churches she is often identified with the portal or door through which God descends out into the world, and through which man can enter into a different and higher realm. Mary's special role is described in such early Judeo-Christian apocryphal writings as The Book of James, The History of Joseph the Carpenter, and The Assumption of the

Virgin. In the last-named, especially, Mary is presented as the one who guides the twelve apostles and the early church. In this role she is described as the fertile vine and mother of the twelve branches. She is the mother of all who are saved, and God blesses the church planted by her hands.

Mary's death, which is commemorated here, is not a simple matter, but hides a mystery related to her role in the salvation of man. One ancient tradition relates that Mary asked her son why she had to die. In answer Jesus took her to the underworld and showed her all the lost souls. When she saw them she was filled with pity and asked what had to be done to save them. Jesus told her that to save them she had to die for them. Mary then said that to save these souls she would be willing to die many times. Here began the intercession of Mary and the cult that surrounded her. She was no longer merely the door through which Jesus had entered the world, but the very gates of mercy through which the sinner and damned could achieve salvation.

The dormition of Mary symbolizes this mystery. Mary dies. But Mary cannot die, or rather she must die over and over again for the salvation of many. Thus the word "dormition," which comes from the word to sleep. Mary falls into an eternal sleep, the state between life and death. It is between these two states that she has placed herself to help the fallen.

The Church of the Dormition

The building where Mary lived with the apostles was called the Church of the Apostles or the Mother of Churches. In the earliest apocryphal writings Mary too is alluded to as the mother of churches. In the late fourth century, Hellenistic Christians built their own church just to the north of the older one. It was called the Church of the Pillar (or Church of the Column of the Flagellation) because it contained the pillar from St. Peter in Gallicantu on which Jesus had been scourged. In the early fifth century the Byzantines enlarged this church, renaming it Hagia Sion (Holy Zion), and dedicated the northwest corner to the place where Mary lived and where she died. Here began the tradition of the dormition, or falling asleep, of Mary. In 1009 Hagia Sion was destroyed by the caliph Hakim. A century later the Crusaders rebuilt the church, joining Hagia Sion with the older Church of the Apostles, and named it St. Mary on Mt. Zion. In 1219, shortly after the fall of the Latin Kingdom, this church too was destroyed. From that time until the present century, no church was dedicated to the dormition of Mary. In 1898 German Catholics acquired the present site of the Dormition Abbey. The site lay just to the northwest of the Crusader church, and within the northwest corner of the area occupied by the Byzantine church, Hagia Sion. The construction of the Church of the Dormition was entrusted to the Benedictines, and the church was consecrated in 1910.

The Mosaic Floor: The Circle and Star as Symbols in Christian Representational Art

The church is especially rich in religious representational art. The Dormition Abbey has produced a superb booklet with color photographs minutely describing all that is seen. It is highly recommended that visitors to the church purchase this inexpensive booklet at the abbey's new bookshop.

A few words, however, need to be added about the mosaic floor, which portrays, in concentric circles, the spreading of the word of God in space and time. The mosaic contains two symbols used by Christians since the earliest days of the original Judeo-Christian Church: concentric circles and the star. Early Christians, like many people before them, saw the circle as a symbol for God and the completeness of life because it had no beginning and no end. Most often Christians drew three concentric circles to indicate the Holy Trinity. The Constantinian Chi-Rho monogram, which consisted of the first two letters of the Greek word for Christ

Mosaic floor portraying the spread of the word of God in space and time, Dormition Abbey.

(XPICTOC), was sometimes engraved on these circles. Here the circles represented the three heavens or levels of the universe which were united in the being of Christ. In time these concentric circles became the moving heavens that turned about the fixed point of the universe—the source of all creation. In Europe this came to be expressed in the wheel-shaped stained-glass windows of Romanesque churches, and later in the more developed windows of Gothic cathedrals where God himself was the one unmoving point at the center of a vast elaborate universe of life and light which turned around him. The further from the center, the greater the movement and thus the greater the instability. Churches with windows of this sort often had floors with labyrinths, which represented the way from the unstable

The Chi-Rho monogram. Mosaic floor, Dormition Abbey.

periphery to the unmoving center. These were symbolic maps of man's inner struggle and search to find the center and stability of his own being. To achieve this center was to achieve one's balance where all human motion stopped. This was also the point of the *axis mundi* around which all the levels of creation turned.

Motion, however, was indicated not only by space but by time. Thus zodiacs, as we also see here, represent the movement of finite time around the fixed point of the eternal. The fixed point was often seen as a star. For many traditions this was the polestar, which appears as the fixed point in the heavens around which our own world turns. This imagery is found in the Coptic apocryphal Gospel, where it is written that "this star was not a star like others, but a big star in the form of a wheel."

For the early Christians the star was the symbol of Christ. They found this symbolism in the prophecy of Balaam (Numbers 24:17) which foretold that "there shall come a star out of Jacob." As the symbol of the star developed, it became a star with rays. These were usually twelve in number, representing the apostles. To make the association even clearer, Jesus was often called "day" and the apostles "hours"; or Jesus was called "year" and the apostles "months." Whatever the name, it was clear that the light of the world, the celestial light of the eternal, was diffused into the finite world by the twelve apostles who revolved about the master, as the year or zodiac revolved about the sun. While the mosaic of the Church of the Dormition is clearly modern, all the elements of early Christian symbolism are here.

Body to the Earth, Spirit to the Sky

The Basilica of the Dormition Abbey is one of those architectural rarities that transmits its teaching directly to the senses of the observer. It is said that masters of ancient sacred architecture knew certain laws that are unknown to us today. Travelers have often written about this experience. But to find it in a structure as modern as the present Church of the Dormition is surprising.

When you have finished your visit to the main floor of the church and seen all its interesting points, take a few minutes to sit or stand quietly. Try not to concentrate on any particular feature, but let your eyes wander at random and feel the volume of the space enclosed by the walls and dome. When you are ready, descend the stairs to the crypt. As you reach the bottom of the stairway you may begin to notice a physical feeling of heaviness in the stomach, legs, and lower part of the body. It is as if there is a force pulling you down to the floor of the crypt. Do not force it. If it is there it is clear. It requires only a certain inner silence and attentiveness to the body. Use the abbey's booklet as you look around the crypt. When you are ready, return again to the church above. As you reenter the church and take in the dome and the volume, you may have a sudden feeling of expansion in the chest and upper part of the body. Something light and silent seems to want to flow up and beyond the physical limits of the body and fill the space enclosed by these walls and dome.

Many ancient traditions have different ways of expressing this experience and the great truth being taught here. Ancient Egypt called it "Body to the earth, spirit to the sky." In Christianity it can be found in Jesus's exhortation to render unto Caesar that which is Caesar's, and unto God that which is God's. But, more important, it represents the two currents of life that exist in all human beings. It is these two currents which mingle and form the basis of all inner conflict and struggle and which can be reconciled only at the still point at the center whose silence is capable of englobing all life.

The BASILICA OF THE DORMITION ABBEY is open daily, 8 A.M.–12 noon and 2–6 P.M.

THE CENACLE (*Coenaculum; the Upper Room*)

The Last Supper and the Symbol of Bread and Wine
This bare medieval room has, since Crusader times, been associated with the events surrounding the birth of the Christian Church. Even before these events, the Upper Room had been the scene of the Last Supper, where Jesus set in motion the events of his Passion. The sacrifice of flesh and blood that Jesus was about to make is still symbolically remembered here in the carving of a Crusader capital above the stairway leading down to the lower floor. Here we see a pelican whose young are eating its living flesh and drinking

its blood. The image of the pelican, which is known to give its living body to its starving young, seemed to the Crusaders a perfect representation of Jesus's own words and actions at the Last Supper: "And as they did eat, Jesus took bread, and blessed, and brake it, and gave to them, and said, Take, eat: this is my body. And he took the cup, and when he had given thanks, he gave it to them: and they all drank of it. And he said unto them, This is my blood of the new testament, which is shed for many" (Mark 14:22–24).

A pelican offering its starving young its own flesh and blood, symbolic of Christ's own sacrifice. The Room of the Last Supper.

Jesus and the apostles were celebrating the Jewish feast of Passover, which commemorates the exodus from Egypt. This movement from slavery to freedom can be seen on many levels, that is, both as a unique historical experience and as an ever-recurring inner, spiritual one. A central feature of this festival is the sacrifice of the Passover, or Paschal, lamb: "And the Lord spoke unto Moses and Aaron in the land of Egypt, saying . . . Speak ye unto all the congregation of Israel, saying, In the tenth day of this month they shall take to them every man a lamb . . . and the whole assembly of Israel shall kill it in the evening. And they shall take of the blood, and strike it on the two side posts and on the upper door post of the house wherein they shall eat it. And they shall eat the flesh in that night. . . . For I will pass through the land of Egypt this night, and will smite all the firstborn . . . and when I see the blood, I will pass over you" (Exodus 12).

The symbol of Jesus as the lamb sacrificed for man's spiritual freedom is well known. But there is something else that was also seen as being significant by early Christians. This was the symbol of Jesus as the door. In the Gospel of St. John, Jesus says, "I am the door: by me if any man enter in, he shall be saved, and shall go in and out, and find pasture" (John 10:9). This "door" was seen to correspond with the Old Testament account of the doorposts marked with the blood of the lamb which saved the Children of Israel. St. Justin wrote that, "As the blood of the Pasch freed those who were in Egypt so the blood of Christ freed from death the believers." For Christians the blood on the doorposts prefigured the salvation of man which was to be brought by the blood of Christ.

Despite all that has been written about the Last Supper, the sacrifice of blood and wine remains a mystery in the true sense, and the Crusaders called this room the Room of the Mysteries. Today the event is repeated in the sacrament of the Eucharist, where the worshipper continues to partake of the living flesh and blood of Christ. Many interpretations have been given for this symbolism, but the solution seems to lie in a deep and hidden past. The real meaning of sacrifice itself is unknown. At the Church of St. Peter in Gallicantu we saw that the creation of man depended upon God sacrificing a part of His own breath and spirit. Thus at the beginning of time, God is not just king but high priest who offers sacrifice so that man may be born and live. This heavenly role is mirrored in the earthly world by the legendary king Melchizedek. It is important to recall here a few of the things said about Melchizedek in Chapter 1. The name is composed of two Hebrew words, *melech* ("king"), and *zedek* ("righteousness"). The first implies his role as king and the latter as priest. This Melchizedek is described by St. Paul in the Epistle to the Hebrews as "first being by interpretation King of righteousness, and after that also King of Salem, which is, King of peace. Without father, without mother, without descent, having neither beginning of days, nor end of life; but made like unto the Son of God; abideth a priest continually" (Hebrews 7:2–3). It is this Melchizedek who comes out to meet Abraham after the latter's defeat of the four kings: "And Melchizedek king of Salem brought forth bread and wine: and he was the priest of the most high God. And he blessed him, and said, Blessed be Abram of the most high God, possessor of heaven and earth: and blessed be the most high God, which hath delivered thine enemies into thy hand. And he gave him tithes of all" (Genesis 14:18–20). The symbolic offering, or sacrifice, of bread and wine made by Melchizedek to Abraham is seen by many as a passing on of the earthly obligation given to Melchizedek by God: "The Lord hath sworn, and will not repent, Thou art a priest for ever after the order of Melchizedek" (Psalms 110:4). The obligation given to Abraham and his children is to maintain the continuous sacrifice that God began at the beginning of time so that men may find life. (In the apocryphal Testament of Levi, which describes the enthroning of the high priest,

one of the presentations made to him is of bread and wine.)
For St. Paul (Epistle to the Hebrews) Jesus was the last true
inheritor in the line of Melchizedek, for he was not only high
priest in the line of Aaron, but king in the line of David. For
Paul, Jesus's very real sacrifice of flesh and blood represented the end of sacrifice and the beginning of man's salvation. But the mystery of sacrifice does not end here. At the
Last Supper, Jesus himself passes on the offering of bread
and wine to the apostles, who in turn take on the role of
priests, and pass it on, through the sacrament of the Eucharist, to all the world. In this sacrament not only does the
bread and wine blessed and offered (sacrificed) by the priest
mystically turn to flesh and blood, but it requires each re-
cipient to discover within himself the obligation demanded
by this gift. It is interesting to note that Melchizedek was
king of Salem, which is equated with Jerusalem. Thus, the
spread of Melchizedek's kingdom through the succession of
priests over the whole of the world became in reality the
extending on earth of God's holy city, Jerusalem, fulfilling
God's promise that Israel was to become a nation of priests.

The Descent of the Holy Ghost: *The Symbol of the Cross at the Center of the World*

Following the death of Jesus, the Upper Room became the
center of the new community. The apostles lived here with
Mary and the family of Jesus. Here Jesus appeared again to
his disciples, and Matthias was chosen to replace Judas Iscariot. But most important, for the establishment of Christianity as a church and its subsequent spread, was the descent
of the Holy Spirit on the apostles on the day of Pentecost. To
understand the significance of this event, and the relationship between Christ and the Church, we must yet again turn
to the symbol of the cross.

The meaning of this symbol is to be found in the inner
teachings of certain ancient traditions where it is seen as a
cross of three dimensions inscribed within a sphere. The
cross itself consists of three axes. Taking as example our
own planet, the principal axis is the vertical one. This is the
fixed line (the polar axis) around which the world rotates.
Two additional axes, perpendicular to the vertical one, are
found at the plane of the equator. One is called the
north-south axis and is formed by the two points which join
the solstice, while the other is the east-west axis which joins
the equinox. The resultant figure is a cross of three dimensions oriented to the six directions of space: zenith, nadir,
north, south, east, and west. A seventh part completes the
cross. This is the center, which integrates the six directions
and is in direct contact with them all. This central point,
which itself has no dimensions, is seen as the hidden source
of life, which in many traditions corresponds to the mysterious creative Word.

This form symbolically describes the three levels of the universe. The upper part of the vertical axis corresponds to the upper world with all its ascending states of being and consciousness. The lower part corresponds to the lower world with all its states of darkness, obscurity, and ignorance. Between these lies an intermediary world (seen here as a circular plane determined by the four horizontal directions), whose tendency is neither ascending nor descending, and where a particular point in the vertical line of being is reflected in all its possible manifestations and aspects. Our world is such an intermediary level, at the center of which is the point that represents the fixed vertical axis. This point is the meeting place between two kinds of events: the vertical immobile activity of heaven, and the cyclic vicissitudes of the phenomenal world which endlessly revolves around it. To reach this center has been the goal of all great teachings, and our model shows the type of activity necessary to achieve this aim. The way to the center, the way of the master, is the way of inner immobility and silence. This silence is more than a passive detachment from all that is transitory. Rather it is an inner movement by which the master reassembles all his powers around the vertical axis of his own being, which alone can actively hold them in perfect balance and repose. Whether for man the microcosm or the greater macrocosmic world, the point at the center of the cross is the site of Jerusalem, in its meaning of the City of Peace. (The Hebrew letters *sh, 1,* and *m,* which make up the name Shalem—Salem—the city of Melchizedek, and which form the latter half of Yerushalem—Jerusalem—means "wholeness" or "peace"). The view offered along today's Via Dolorosa of external suffering and cruelty can at best be a subjective vision glimpsed at the periphery of the events. Hostility and other manifestations of external opposition cannot exist for the being who has achieved the harmony of the center and is beyond all opposition.

The arrival of the master at the center is a turning point in the life of mankind. The Passion of Jesus, for example, the way to the center, is one story. But then the story becomes a very different one. The central point of the cross unites the peace of the vertical, the heavenly city of peace, Jerusalem, with the peace of Christ. As long as the center of Christ's being is actively maintained at the center of the cross, his influence spreads through the horizontal earthly world reflecting the world above. This influence is no longer dependent upon the physical presence or action of the Christ who partook in the changing events and history of the world. The influence of the Christ at the center (or any true master for that matter) is a permanent one whose power lies beyond the ability of the earthly world to affect or touch it. This new Christ (the Christ at the center) is the Christ of the Holy Ghost. It was this Spirit that appeared to the apostles in the Upper Room on the day of Pentecost, and which changed them and sent them out to establish the Church that would reflect throughout the world the image of the·heavenly Jerusalem.

The CENACLE is open daily, 8:30 A.M. to sundown, except for Friday afternoons, when it is closed.

DAVID'S TOMB (*Hebrew: Kever David*)

The Church of the Apostles and the New Zion
It is not always clear to the visitor that both the room containing David's Tomb and the room of the Last Supper (the Cenacle or Upper Room) are situated in the same building. This is because they are located on different floors with separate entrances, on opposite sides of the building. Even after Pentecost, the Upper Room continued to be used by the members of this new community to celebrate rites proper to them alone. The best known of these rites was the Eucharistic banquet. There was, however, another side to this first Christian community. These were Jews, who adhered to Mosaic law and continued to follow Jewish traditions regarding ritual prayer. From early Christian writings it would seem that prayers were usually recited at the Temple. After the destruction of the Temple in 70 A.D. this was no longer possible, and in 75 A.D. Simon bar Cleophas, a cousin of Jesus, and the second bishop of Jerusalem, built on this site a Judeo-Christian synagogue. It has become known to us through history as the Church of the Apostles and consisted of an upper room for the celebration of the Eucharist, and a lower room which served as a synagogue for ritual prayer.

The role of the present room as an ancient synagogue has been noted by almost all observers. On the northern wall, behind the monument called the Tomb of David, there is a large semicircular niche, which all writers have claimed points northward to the Temple Mount. Here, it is said, the liturgical books and the holy scrolls were kept. The niche and holy ark (in which the scrolls of the Law, or Torah, are kept), like the *mihrab* in mosques, determines the direction of prayer. The question of orientation is important. It is always toward a center where the heavenly world joins our own. The orientation of the worshipper toward this center is not only an external physical act but an internal one which directs his very essence to turn to that which is higher. For Jews all over the world this orientation is always toward Jerusalem and the Temple Mount. The present room, however, presents a problem. While it indeed points northward, its orientation is not in the direction of the Temple Mount but instead toward Calvary and the Tomb of Jesus.

This deviation from accepted Jewish custom is important for understanding the significance of Mt. Zion for early

Christians. The present Mt. Zion is not the Mt. Zion of the Old Testament. That Zion referred to an area to the south of today's Temple Mount and was the site of the Jebusite fortress ("the stronghold of Zion") captured by the Israelite king and subsequently called the City of David. As the city extended northward (to include Mt. Moriah, the site of Solomon's Temple) so did the name Zion, which was sometimes used by the prophets to refer to all of Jerusalem and sometimes just to the Temple Mount. It was this latter usage which became predominant by Maccabean times, when the Temple Mount was called the "mountain of Zion." By the time of Josephus (a witness of the Jewish War of 66–70 A.D.) the "stronghold of Zion" was also identified with the new area that had grown up to the west of the City of David and which included the hill that is today's Mt. Zion. For early Christians this new identification, coupled with the destruction of the old Zion in 70 A.D., was of immense significance.

Investigations of the foundations of the northern, eastern, and southern walls of David's Tomb show that they are made of large blocks which may well be Herodian in origin. Some have voiced the opinion that they may be not only Herodian, but blocks rescued from the destroyed Jewish Temple itself. This would support the belief held by this early community regarding the Church of the Apostles, which though not necessarily seen as a successor to the Temple was certainly seen as the site of the new Zion. This belief found its greatest support in the descent of the Holy Ghost at Pentecost. This event marked the real beginning of Christianity as a church and a new order in the world. The word "order" should be taken quite literally, for the Christ at the center represented a new world of heavenly laws and order as opposed to earthly chaos. This new world, activated in men by the Holy Ghost (or spirit of Christ at the center), began its work here by descending on the apostles at Pentecost. This event seemed to thus confirm the words of Isaiah, "For out of Zion shall go forth the law, and the word of the Lord from Jerusalem" (Isaiah 2:3). That this was indeed the new Zion seemed to be further confirmed during the reign of Hadrian (135 A.D.) when the synagogues of Jerusalem were destroyed and only those of the Judeo-Christians on the new Mt. Zion (strictly speaking, outside Hadrian's new city of Aelia Capitolina) were left standing.

The Tomb of David

Growing animosity between Judeo-Christians and Hellenistic Christians resulted in the latter's abandoning the Church of the Apostles, or Mother of Churches, which they increasingly saw as a synagogue of Jews. In 383 the Byzantines built their own church on Mt. Zion next to the ancient synagogue. It was called the Church of the Column of the Flagellation because the portico contained a column, brought from St. Peter in Gallicantu, to which it was believed Jesus had been bound and scourged. In 415 the church was enlarged. This was the famous Hagia Sion (Holy Zion) Basilica. It was badly damaged during the Persian invasion of 614 but was rebuilt. It was finally destroyed, as were so many other monuments in the city, in 1009 by the caliph Hakim.

In 1105 the Crusaders built a new church on Mt. Zion, called St. Mary on Mount Zion. It was much smaller than Hagia Sion but included a number of interesting features. First of all, it contained the Upper Room today known as the Cenacle and then called the Chamber of Mysteries. A second feature was the ancient synagogue which was now included within the church and was dedicated as a cenotaph to King David.

David, of course, is not buried here. His burial place was somewhere in the City of David, the Zion of the Old Testament. There is no difference of opinion among scholars— religious or secular—on this matter. Traditions linking him to this site derive from the early Christians, who saw his presence here in terms of his seed or Davidic line, who were the real living remains of the Israelite king. It is this that St. Peter spoke of in Acts 2:29–32: "Men and brethren, let me freely speak unto you of the patriarch David, that he is both dead and buried, and his sepulchre is with us unto this day. Therefore being a prophet, and knowing that God had sworn with an oath to him, that of the fruit of his loins, according to the flesh, he would raise up Christ to sit on his throne; He seeing this before spake of the resurrection of Christ, that his soul was not left in hell, neither his flesh did see corruption. This Jesus hath God raised up, whereof we are witnesses." We have already mentioned on a number of occasions the importance of this Davidic line to the Judeo-Christians. In Byzantine times the living presence of this line was perpetuated by celebrating here the feast of David on the same day as the feast of St. James, the brother of Jesus and his heir as first bishop of Jerusalem, whose seat was later transmitted to Simon, also of the Davidic line.

By Crusader times the old and new Zion had become thoroughly confused in the minds of both Christians and Jews. The Crusaders built the present cenotaph to commemorate the tradition of their link with the Jewish king (a cenotaph is a sepulchral monument to someone whose body is elsewhere). But within a very short time the symbolic meaning of the monument was forgotten and its presence led even Jews to believe that this was Mt. Zion where David was buried, and David's actual tomb. This fervent belief by both Christians and Jews eventually led to the appropriation of the site by the Muslim rulers of Jerusalem, who built here a mosque in honor of the prophet David. The remains of this mosque are still visible in the *mihrab* in the southern wall which points to Mecca. The site, which was alternately in the hands of Muslims and Christians at various periods, came under Israeli control after the War of Independence in 1948. During the period of 1948 to 1967, it became one of the most sacred Jewish holy sites, largely because it was the closest point to the Old City and Temple Mount then under Israeli control. Pilgrimages were made here on all three Jewish festivals, but especially on the festival of Shavuot, the traditional date of David's death.

THE ARMENIAN MONASTERY OF ST. SAVIOUR
(*House of Caiaphas; Armenian Cemetery*)

Take a brief look around this enclosure, which contains the "House of Caiaphas" and the Armenian cemetery. The Persian invasion of 614 resulted in the destruction of a number of Jerusalem's churches, including two which lay along the early Byzantine Good Friday route commemorating the events of the Passion, and were eventually relocated to Mt. Zion. These were the Church of St. Sophia, which commemorated Jesus's trial before Pontius Pilate, and the House of Caiaphas, which commemorated his imprisonment and trial before the high priest. It was this relocation which resulted in the establishment of the Easter Mt. Zion–Holy Sepulchre route, which lasted well into Crusader times. An interesting discovery can still be seen in the center of the Armenian cemetery: flagstones which formed a part of the actual road that led from Mt. Zion along the western wall of the city and then to Calvary.

Although this is called a monastery, there is no one now living here. The name St. Saviour was given because of the suffering that Jesus was believed to have undergone here for the redemption of the world. The site is in a state of transition. A new church is in the process of being built, while the small twelfth-century Crusader church (House of Caiaphas) is undergoing repairs and is closed to the public. The structure surrounding the church is from the seventeenth century, while in front of the church are the burial places of the Armenian patriarchs.

THE ARMENIAN CATHEDRAL OF ST. JAMES

This is certainly one of the most impressive places to visit in Jerusalem, though unfortunately it adds very little to the knowledge of the inner meaning of the city or the many great events that have taken place here. The cathedral is generally open to the public only during the brief daily afternoon service, but this is an opportunity to approach the question of what is meant by a sacred place from another point of view.

Ancient man saw the sacred as the penetration of our earthly world by the divine, which occurred at a particular place. This line of communication is almost always described as some sort of vertical axis which connected—in the spiritual rather than geographical sense—our own earthly world

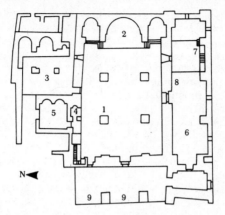

Fig. 24. The Armenian Cathedral of St. James.

1. *Throne of St. James the Less*
2. *Altar of St. James the Less*
3. *Chapel of St. Stephen*
4. *St. James the Great*
5. *St. Menes*
6. *St. Etchmiasin Chapel*
7. *Altar of the Three Stones*
8. *Pictorial tiles*
9. *Khatchkars*

---

to upper or higher worlds. Descriptions of the earth's polar axis and its relation to the axis of the polestar were simply physical analogies of a much more real and essential connection that linked the world of man to finer worlds above and beyond his sight. The point of earthly contact represented the miracle of the appearance in our world of the laws belonging to a higher world. Many ancient temples are described as being in the image of heaven. This did not mean that the temple was the exact physical counterpart of heaven, but rather that it reflected the same laws of cosmic order as its heavenly source. The temple marking a sacred place was seen as a kind of bridgehead of divine order in the earthly world of chaos. Its walls clearly marked the dividing line between the two. Only the temple door opened onto both worlds, permitting the divine spirit to descend further into the world, and the pilgrim to ascend out of spiritual darkness.

In the Cathedral of St. James it is possible to get a sense of this otherworldliness, and a feeling of abrupt transition from the profane to the sacred. Pushing aside the heavy leather curtain covering the doorway of the cathedral, you are suddenly plunged into an entirely different world. What is true of St. James's is equally true of many churches of the eastern rite throughout the world, but in Jerusalem it is unique. The visitor is completely cut off from the outside world. The only lighting comes from candles or the high dome. The ears take in the sound of singing, the nose inhales the smell of incense; the eyes see the icons, the decorations, the paintings, the architecture, the vestments of the priests. There is touching of the cross, taste in holy communion, and prostration of the body in prayer. Standing on one's feet (there are no chairs) makes it more difficult to sleep or daydream. One is always at the very center of what is going on. Even an observer who does not really know what is meant by prayer and whose intellect tells him that these are but the external trappings of faith cannot help but feel that there is something true here, that prayer is not just a recitation of words but an immersion in a completely different reality.

The cathedral was built by the Armenians during the Crusader period. Parts of it are more ancient, though many of the interior decorations date from the early eighteenth century. It is a treasure trove of Armenian art which can be studied in detail in a beautiful book published in Israel, titled *Armenian Art Treasures in Jerusalem* (edited by Bezalel Narkiss). The history of the cathedral and of the Armenians in Jerusalem is also a fascinating subject. Both have been dealt with in a small book written by Mr. Kevork Hintlian, secretary to the Armenian Patriarch. This book, *History of the Armenians in the Holy Land*, is published by the St. James Press (the printing press of the Armenian Patriarchate). Unfortunately it is not always in print, though it may be possible for serious students to obtain photocopies.

The cathedral is not really related to the symbolic history of the early Christian Church. The name St. James is in honor of the apostle James (St. James the Major), who was beheaded by Herod Agrippa in 44 A.D. It is not known when the site became identified with the place of his burial, though by Crusader times it was definitely considered to be the burial place of his head. (From the ninth century, his body was believed to have been miraculously transferred to Compostela in northwest Spain, which subsequently became the center of a number of very important pilgrimage routes.) The church also claims the remains of St. James, the brother of Jesus and first bishop of Jerusalem (St. James the Less, who was martyred in 60 A.D.), whose throne is opposite the altar. Other saints and martyrs honored here can be identified by the names of their chapels.

One point of interest is the khatchkars (stone crosses) inserted in the walls of the courtyard of the church. These are decorative stone engravings of crosses set up for various purposes, such as marking the completion of a church, to commemorate important historical events, or as votive offerings. There are literally thousands of these throughout the world and no two are alike. A close look at some of these, especially those in the Church of the Archangel (the Armenian parish church located within the Armenian compound), reveals leaves growing from the ends of the cross. These represent a relatively rare symbolic identification of the cross with the Tree of Life. (See p. 142 for more on the cross and the Tree of Life, and also photo on p. 120.)

It is worth a trip to the Armenian museum, which is open

*Khatchkars in the Church
of the Archangel.*

all day. It is located in the former theological seminary and
covers two floors of exhibits. The lower floor contains litho-
graphs and pictures depicting the fascinating history of the
Armenian people. The upper floor contains a large represen-
tative sample of art and religious treasures as well as other
objects belonging to the church. Special note should be
made of a tapestry in room 28—an altar frontal depicting an
angel bringing a head to the Virgin Mary. This is not the
head of St. John the Baptist, but of the apostle St. James the
Major.

The ARMENIAN CATHEDRAL OF ST. JAMES is open to the public only during
the daily afternoon service, 3–3:30 P.M. Monday to Friday, and 2:30–3:15
P.M. Saturday and Sunday. The ARMENIAN MUSEUM is open daily except
Sunday, 10 A.M.–4:30 P.M.

THE SYRIAN ORTHODOX CONVENT
(St. Mark's House; The Upper Room)

St. Mark's Church, or, as it is more popularly called, St.
Mark's House, is located on the northern slope of Mt. Zion,
on the borders of the Jewish and Armenian quarters. It
presents an interesting puzzle that has never been taken
seriously. The Syrian Orthodox Church is one of the oldest

in the Christian world. Its origins lie in Antioch, where the Gospel was preached soon after the events of the Pentecost. It was there that the followers of Jesus first received the name Christians. At the Council of Nicea in 325 A.D. (the First Ecumenical Council of the Church), Antioch became one of the great sees, or patriarchates, of the Church. Its traditions are thus ancient, as is its presence in Jerusalem. For the Syrian Orthodox, St. Mark's House is the site of the Last Supper (the Upper Room). Today it is almost universally acknowledged that the Upper Room was on the site of the building now containing the Tomb of David and the Cenacle, and the Syrian Orthodox claim is rejected out of hand. This rejection in itself is unusual. It is common in Jerusalem to find churches of different traditions celebrating single events at different places. (Note, for example, the number of churches that commemorate the events which took place at Gethsemane.) While there is often a "friendly" rivalry between these churches, it is uncommon to find such a universal rejection of any one claim, particularly when it belongs to a tradition as ancient as that of the Syrian Orthodox. But if this is not the Upper Room, then what is it? And what lies behind the tradition found here?

Part of the answer may lie in certain events commemorated here which are not remembered elsewhere in Jerusalem. These are depicted in the paintings over the entranceway to the church. To the left an angel frees an imprisoned Peter, while at the right Peter is portrayed at the door to this house. The picture in the middle shows Mary with the apostles in the Upper Room. The story of Peter's imprisonment and miraculous release, and subsequent appearance at the house of Mark, plays a central role in the tradition of this church. The events are related in Acts 12:1–17: "Now about that time Herod the king stretched forth his hands to vex certain of the church. And he killed James the brother of John with the sword. And . . . he proceeded further to take Peter also. . . . And when he had apprehended him, he put him in prison. . . . Peter was sleeping between two soldiers, bound with two chains. . . . And, behold, the angel of the Lord came upon him . . . and raised him up. . . . And his chains fell off from his hands. And the angel said unto him . . . Cast thy garment about thee, and follow me. And he went out, and followed him; and wist not that it was true which was done by the angel; but thought he saw a vision. . . . They came unto the iron gate that leadeth unto the city; which opened to them of his own accord: and they went out, and passed on through one street; and forthwith the angel departed from him. And when Peter was come to himself, he said, Now I know of a surety, that the Lord hath sent his angel. . . . And when he had considered the thing, he came to the house of Mary the mother of John, whose surname was Mark; where many were gathered together praying. And as Peter knocked at the door of the gate, a damsel came out to hearken, named Rhoda. And when she knew Peter's voice, she opened not the gate for gladness, but ran in, and told how Peter stood before the gate. . . . But Peter continued knocking: and when they had opened the door, and saw him, they were astonished. But he, beckoning unto them with the hand to hold their peace, declared unto them how the Lord had brought him out of the prison. And he said, Go shew these things unto James, and to the brethren. And he departed, and went into another place."

The tradition that this is indeed the site of the house of Mark is a fairly strong one. As you enter the church, on the wall immediately to the right there is a plaque discovered in 1940 during restorations and written in ancient Syrian script. In translation it reads: "This is the house of Mary, mother of John called Mark. Proclaimed a church by the holy apostles under the name of Virgin Mary, mother of God, after the ascension of our Lord Jesus Christ into heaven. Renewed after the destruction of Jerusalem by Titus in the year 73 A.D." The present structure is basically of twelfth-century Crusader origin. Prior to the Crusader period this was the site of a mosque which was built on the ruins of a seventh-century Byzantine church called St. Peter in Chains. The inscription itself is generally considered to be of sixth-century Byzantine origin, and may well refer to an even earlier tradition reaching back as far as the days of the apostles.

There thus seems to be strong evidence relating this site to the story of the imprisonment of Peter and the house of Mark which, it would appear, were the events originally commemorated here. But does this necessarily imply that this was the Upper Room? Christian tradition holds that the apostles and the family of Jesus were living in the Upper Room following his Crucifixion and Ascension, but the account in Acts 12 seems to indicate that not all the members of the community were. When those present at Mark's house opened the door, Peter told them to repeat the events to James and the brethren (the apostles), indicating that they lived elsewhere. This elsewhere was most certainly the Upper Room at the site of today's Cenacle. When did the confusion and association of the house of Mark with the Upper Room begin? It is hard to say, though it must have been after the early Byzantine period since no mention is made of it in the sixth-century plaque.

The Church Interior

The interior of this restored Crusader church reflects this mistaken change in emphasis, and largely remembers events associated with the Upper Room. The paintings along the walls are only some 100 to 150 years old, while the facade of the altar is not much older. Among the treasures of the church are a baptismal font (against the wall opposite the entranceway) which is claimed to have been used to baptize Mary, the mother of Jesus; and above this, a miraculous painting of the Virgin which Syrian tradition claims was painted by St. Luke himself.

To the left of the altar is a small room used today as a vestry. According to Syrian tradition, this was the room of Mary. There is a small well here from which she reputedly drank, and in former times water was taken from here for blessing and healing. The chair to the left of the altar represents the throne of St. James, the first bishop of Jerusalem. To the right of the altar, behind the grillwork, are the relics of saints and martyrs from Turkey, brought here as a blessing. Beneath the floor here is the burial place of the archbishops of the church.

Note the Gospels written by hand in a dialect of Aramaic, the lingua franca of the Middle East in the time of Jesus, and a language still used by the Syrian Orthodox Church. The book used for the liturgy was written by hand with a bamboo quill by the present archbishop for his consecration service here—an ancient tradition which still survives.

ST. MARK'S CHURCH is open to the public daily. Regular hours in the morning, 9 A.M.–12 noon; in the afternoon, 3:30–6 P.M., one may ring and ask for the key.

7

GETHSEMANE

Almost all guidebooks to Jerusalem include the sacred places of Gethsemane (Hebrew: Gat Shemanim—"the Oil Press") in a section dealing with the Mount of Olives. Gethsemane, however, which appears to lie at the base of the Mount of Olives, is in fact located in the valley which separates the Mount of Olives from Mt. Moriah (on which is located the Temple Mount). This valley is called the Valley of Jehoshaphat. The name is composed of two Hebrew words, *Jeho* ("God") and *shaphat* ("judged"). According to the prophet Joel (and in Jewish, Christian, and Muslim traditions), it is here that God will judge the nations at the end of time. This idea of a final judgment is intimately related to the story of the sites of Gethsemane, and it is not by chance that they are located here.

THE CHURCH OF THE AGONY
(*THE CHURCH OF ALL NATIONS*) (*Hebrew: Kneisiat Gat Shemanim; Kneisiat Kol HeAmim*)

THE GARDEN OF OLIVES

In order to reach the entrance to the church, you must walk around a small olive grove. This is called the Garden of Olives. There are pilgrims who still believe that these are the same olive trees which witnessed the agony of Jesus, or, at the very least, offshoots from those trees. This belief, which was once more widely accepted, was fostered by the often repeated statement by Pliny that the olive tree does not die but takes on new life from its stump. However, there is no historical reference to olive trees before the fifteenth century; and by the seventeenth century they are described by pilgrims as burned, cut down, or dead of old age. Even the Franciscans, whose property this is, readily admit that there is no evidence that the present trees are in any way related to more ancient ones. The grove, however, does serve to remind us how the area must have looked in Gospel times. The name Gat Shemanim is an ancient one, and in the time of Jesus this was most likely part of an agricultural property which contained olive trees and an oil press.

THE CHURCH

The church is built on the site of a Byzantine basilica erected in the late fourth century, and probably destroyed by fire during the Persian invasion of Jerusalem in 614. It also partly overlies the remains of a medieval church built by the Crusaders. All three churches were built to commemorate the agony of Jesus and the place where he prayed before his Passion.

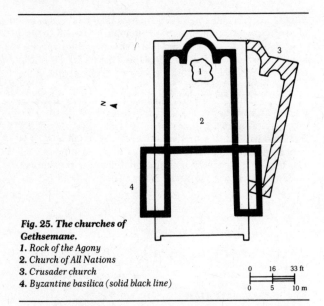

Fig. 25. The churches of Gethsemane.
1. *Rock of the Agony*
2. *Church of All Nations*
3. *Crusader church*
4. *Byzantine basilica (solid black line)*

The present building was constructed in 1924. The architect's stated intention was to create an atmosphere that would recall the scene of the agony, and he succeeded brilliantly. He sought to evoke the sense of depression he imagined Jesus must have felt by means of relatively low walls and a ceiling of twelve low, blue, star-studded domes (with olive trees reaching up from their corners). While it cannot be said that the visitor experiences any depression, the domes, combined with the semidarkness of the church, convey the feeling of the closeness of a clear night sky. Each dome contains a shield with the name of a country that helped pay for the building, and it is for this reason that it is also known as the Church of All Nations. The coarsely hatched windows interspersed with violet-colored glass and alabaster (forming a cross) give the effect of being in a wood at night where the dim light is seen through the branches of trees.

The church follows the general plan of the earlier Byzantine basilica though on a larger scale. The location of the walls and columns of the Byzantine church are marked on the present floor by flagstones of gray marble. The two zigzag lines to the north and south of these "walls" symbolize water and cover cisterns and water channels belonging to the ancient building. The mosaics on the floor, too, follow the original Byzantine designs, patches of which can still be seen here and there preserved under glass.

The Mosaic of the Central Apse

The mosaic behind the main altar of the church depicts the agony of Jesus and commemorates events related in Luke 22:39–46. After the Last Supper, Jesus "came out, and went, as he was wont, to the mount of Olives; and his disciples also followed him. And when he was at the place, he said unto them, Pray that ye enter not into temptation. And he was withdrawn from them about a stone's cast, and kneeled down, and prayed, Saying, Father, if thou be willing, remove

The agony of Jesus. Mosaic, Church of All Nations.

this cup from me: nevertheless not my will, but thine, be done. And there appeared an angel unto him from heaven, strengthening him. And being in an agony he prayed more earnestly: and his sweat was as it were great drops of blood falling down to the ground. And when he rose up from prayer, and was come to his disciples, he found them sleeping for sorrow, And said unto them, Why sleep ye? rise and pray, lest ye enter into temptation."

In his book *The New Man*, Maurice Nicoll points out that we cannot understand the Gospels if we do not appreciate that they constantly speak about an inner evolution called "rebirth." The model for this inner development is found in the life of Jesus. That Jesus too had to undergo inner growth becomes clear when we see how at the agony (as elsewhere) he suffered temptation and experienced despair. Had he been born perfect he would not have experienced these emotions, nor would he have been able to carry out the task that had been ordained for him—to show men the way to reestablish the link between the two levels called heaven and earth that had been severed at the time of Adam's fall. Jesus constantly refers to the fact that he has received the knowledge and understanding of what he must do from above. He has no doubts as to its source. But the doing must be done by him alone, and it is not always as the human within him would wish or choose. By his faithfulness to his task and his example, Jesus became, for those in our world who could understand, what the word from above had been for him. Thus he says of himself, "I am the way."

A number of important points in this inner teaching called "The Way" are represented in the story of the agony. The first of these are those of temptation and prayer. The events of his Passion were irrevocably set in motion by Jesus at the Last Supper, and it was here at the base of the Mount of Olives, in the Valley of Jehoshaphat (the Valley of God's Judgment), that he chose to await the final stage of his evolution called his glorification (after Jesus sends Judas Iscariot out from the Last Supper to complete the betrayal he says, "Now is the Son of man glorified"). Until this moment Jesus had nothing to fear, for the time of his final trial had not yet come, but now the moment was all too real. Throughout the Gospels Jesus is in constant contact with the forces of a higher level that have sent him. Yet when his very life is at stake, his earthly senses threaten to overpower this contact. That Jesus is indeed tempted by the lower level is shown in his words, "Father, if thou be willing, remove this cup from me."

Jesus's response in the face of temptation is prayer. Prayer is the directing of consciousness to what is above. Jesus has led his disciples to a grotto at Gethsemane and left them there admonishing them to pray so as not to fall into temptation. The disciples do not yet know what is to come and the only way to prepare them for the event is to ask them to find some inner purpose that they must serve. He then leaves them and comes to this place ("about a stone's cast") and prays himself.

The scene in the mosaic before us depicts the true nature of the moment, the starting point of the Passion that is to follow. It is night, symbolically the lowest point of the human condition, when we are afraid and alone and only glimmers of light reach us from above. Our human senses are now at their strongest, binding us to the earth. It is here that most is demanded of us. In terrible prayer (his sweat fell to the ground like thick drops of blood) Jesus turns his consciousness inward to what is highest in himself, in order to strengthen the vision of what is being offered to him (in the mosaic)—the hand of God from above offering the crown of ultimate victory. Only this vision permits him to conclude his prayer, "not my will, but thine, be done."

The Rock of the Agony

The bare rock raised above the floor before the altar is the one featured in the center mosaic with Jesus seated upon it. This rock existed in the Byzantine church and is today called the Rock of the Agony. It is surrounded by an iron wreath in the form of a crown of thorns. Birds in front of a chalice represent souls who wish to share the cup of Christ's Passion. But more important are the two silver doves caught in the thorns. As with Christ, the pain and temptation of the senses have momentarily ensnared them, but finally they extend their necks to the higher will that has determined their fate.

The Sacrificial Altar and the Sacred Mountain

In the mosaic, Christ is seen seated on the Rock of the Agony, which resembles a sacrificial altar. In ancient times, altars were of stone and were places of sacrifice. We tend to forget that even today's church altar is the place where Christ's sacrifice is reenacted in the mass.

The Gospels remind us time and again that God and man are not on the same level, and that regardless of what the faithful of various religions may say, contact between these levels is not simple. A wave of religious emotion may momentarily bridge the gap between levels, but to bridge the gap permanently a man must make a complete change within himself. As Jesus taught, the higher level, called in the Gospels the Kingdom of Heaven, is within us.

What is the starting point for such an inner evolution? The New Testament indicates that it begins on a much higher level than is generally imagined. Using the terminology of the Gospels, Maurice Nicoll calls this the level of "stone," representing esoteric truth, or truth of a higher order in its most external and literal sense. This form is necessary for making these truths available to even those who are not capable of seeing in them any deeper meaning, and it provides the firm foundation for a deeper understanding. Thus the Ten Commandments were written on stone. In the story of the Tower of Babel, men wished to build a tower that would reach to heaven. In other words, they wanted to make a bridge between heaven and earth. But, we are told, they "had brick for stone," and their efforts came to nothing. Without the firm foundation of "stone," that is, without a true esoteric teaching, there can be no solid basis on which to build a higher understanding of inner evolution. When you visited St. Peter in Gallicantu we discussed the repentance and conversion of Peter. It was Jesus who renamed Simon as Peter, which in Greek (*petros*) means "stone." In Matthew 16:18 he says, "Thou art Peter, and upon this rock [or stone] I will build my church." Yet stone is not sufficiently flexible to lead to inner evolution. The basic teaching must be understood, not just followed blindly or literally. As long as Simon Peter remains a stone or rock he is incapable of really understanding the master or his aims. As the "stone" he can see only the visible, earthly part of the teaching represented by the actual presence of the master. Thus when Jesus tells his disciples that he must die, "Peter took him, and began to rebuke him, saying, Be it far from thee, Lord: this shall not be unto thee. But he turned and said unto Peter, Get thee behind me, Satan: thou art an offence unto me: for thou savourest not the things that be of God, but those that be of men" (Matthew 16:22–23). Only when Peter realizes that the understanding of the teaching lies within does he reorient himself to the things of God.

The sacrificial altar of stone as seen in the mosaic forms the base of the cosmic mountain. Without this base the mountain (which bridges heaven and earth) cannot be formed; and yet, as it is, it can serve only as the base. The rest of the mountain must be formed of the material of inner understanding, which is invisible to the senses. To do this, to go beyond the external and literal, one must, like Peter, sacrifice what orients us to the world below and reorient ourselves to the world above.

The Dome Above the Rock of the Agony
This dome is different from all others in the church. It represents the summit of the cosmic mountain whose base is the Rock of the Agony, and whose body of inner understanding remains invisible to our eyes. This summit is supported by four angels holding the tabernacle of the temple of the heavenly Jerusalem.

The Mosaics of the Side Apses
These two panels depict the betrayal and arrest of Jesus following the agony. On the left is the kiss of Judas, while on the right Jesus affirms to those who come to arrest him that he is Jesus of Nazareth. Since the story of the betrayal is associated with the Grotto of Gethsemane, we will wait until then to comment upon it. Thus, it is well to keep these pictures in mind until you get there.

The Valley of Jehoshaphat (Hebrew: Emek Yehoshaphat)
As the name of the valley indicates, the final judgment is God's and not man's. The events at Gethsemane show that this judgment is irrevocable and cannot be thwarted by human effort. With the words "not my will, but thine, be done" Jesus surrenders to God. This is symbolized by his passing through the valley and back to Jerusalem with his captors. He is tried, humiliated, and executed by men whose judgment seems to be done, but in reality the journey across the valley leads to his Passion, and ascent up the cosmic mountain to celestial Jerusalem. The final victory is Jesus's, for judgment here belongs to God.

The Porch

As you leave the church take a look at the outside of the door with its bronze paneling, which contains a number of motifs you have seen before. Note the cross in the form of the tree of life. Four branches issue from the tree, forming volutes which encase the symbols of the four evangelists. Below these volutes are panels containing the respective Gospel texts concerning the agony.

The Facade

The facade is very impressive, mainly because of the very lovely mosaic of the tympanum (the triangular area over the portal). Flanking the great archways are four pillars bearing statues of the four evangelists. Above the tympanum two stags stand on either side of a cross. These latter refer to a line in Psalms, "As the hart panteth after the water brooks, so panteth my soul after thee, O God" (Psalms 42:1). In the language of the New Testament "water" denotes a special kind of understanding called living truth: "Whosoever drinketh of this water shall thirst again: But whosoever

The tympanum of the Church of All Nations.

drinketh of the water that I shall give him shall never thirst; but the water that I shall give him shall be in him a well of water springing up into everlasting life" (John 4:13–14). Water is fluid and flexible, and represents a truth or teaching of a higher inner level than that of "stone."

The mosaic is interesting and can be seen on two levels. On the ordinary level, it represents Christ as mediator between God and man, for whom he offers his heart (seen here being received into the hands of the angel). On Christ's left are simple people who look to him with hope while on his right the powerful and learned admit the uselessness of all their might and learning. Jesus makes the prayers of all these his own, as is represented in the words below the mosaic, Jesus "offered up prayers and supplications with strong crying and tears unto him that was able to save him from death, and was heard in that he feared" (Epistle to the Hebrews 5:7).

On another level, the mosaic is far more interesting in that it summarizes the mission of Jesus. Above Jesus, God sits on His throne. He holds in His lap a plaque with the first and last letters of the Greek alphabet, denoting that He is the alpha and omega, the first and the last, and the original heavenly unity of all things. Below God is the world of men cut off from the heavenly world. It is a world of duality where conflict, opposition, and division prevail. The bridge between these two worlds is the Christ. Here we see Christ portrayed with his head in the realm of heaven, and with his two arms extended outward encompassing the duality of the human world. Christ here also englobes both worlds in his being. Thus, in him, all is reconciled. This reconciliation of all things is symbolized by the triangle behind God's head. This is the Trinity, the three in one, where all is completed.

THE GROTTO OF GETHSEMANE
(Hebrew: Ma'arat HaYisurim)

Over the centuries there has been much confusion over the two sites, the Grotto of Gethsemane and the Place of the Agony. Today it is fairly well established that after the Last Supper, Jesus led the apostles to this grotto, where he left them, while he himself went a little way off to the Place of the Agony. After praying, Jesus returned to the grotto, where he found the apostles sleeping, and where he was subsequently betrayed by Judas Iscariot and arrested.

According to Christian tradition, the grotto had been used by Jesus and the apostles on a number of occasions. Its primary use was probably agricultural, during the olive harvest, and at other seasons.

In the fourth century, the grotto was adapted to serve as a chapel. An ambulatory was formed around it, remains of which can still be seen along the south and west walls. Four pillars supported the roof, which had an opening. Below the opening, a cistern collected rainwater. The floor of the grotto was originally paved with white mosaic tiles, which were damaged during the fifth to eighth centuries, when the grotto was used as a burial place. It still functioned as a burial site in Crusader times. The cistern in the northwest corner still retains part of an inscription, "*ke anapaus . . .*" ("Lord, grant rest . . ."").

During the Crusader period the chapel was repaired and redecorated. The floor was paved with flagstones and mosaics, while the ceiling was painted with stars. Some of these stars can still be seen. They are eight-pointed stars, which in very early Christian times symbolized angels. Thus it is hard to know if, like at the Church of the Agony, they were meant

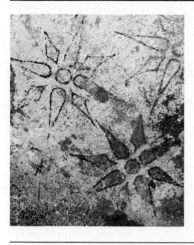

Eight-pointed stars on the ceiling of the Grotto of Gethsemane.

to portray a starry night, or the presence of heavenly forces at this very important moment in the life of Jesus. Most of the decoration, however, was reserved for the area of the altar. Traces of this can still be seen (two haloes, clothing, and an angel's wing). On the basis of these remains it has been suggested that there were three representations here: the prayer of Jesus in the garden, Jesus with the apostles, and the angel comforting Jesus. Three lines of inscription are also visible: "Here the king sweated blood," "Christ the saviour frequented . . . ," and "Father if it is your wish let this chalice pass from me." The present entrance was opened in the seventeenth century, when flooding forced the Franciscans to block up the one from the Byzantine period.

In modern times a new floor was laid and three new altars were erected. The scene behind the central altar shows Jesus praying in the olive press with eleven apostles. Behind the altar to the left is the assumption of Mary, while behind the altar at the right is the betrayal by Judas Iscariot.

Sleep in Gethsemane

Following his baptism, Jesus went into the wilderness to be tempted by the devil. Here he was offered what are essentially external power and authority, which he rejected with the words, "it is written, Thou shalt worship the Lord thy God, and him only shalt thou serve." This was the first indication that Jesus's mission was not of this world. He was not to be an earthly king who would help those who believed in him by bringing them earthly rewards. Instead, he turned his vision to helping men reach a higher level within themselves.

Throughout the Gospels Jesus indicates that he is not free, but under the will of a higher force, which he calls his Father in Heaven, even when it means that to accomplish the aim set for him he must give up his own life. Part of

Jesus's agony arose from the realization that his disciples did not really understand the purpose of his mission. Thus when he tells them that he must suffer and die and is rebuked by Peter, he calls the apostle Satan because he prefers the things of man to the things of God. This association of the devil with the love and temptations of this world is important for understanding the events that took place here. Gethsemane lies in the Valley of the Lord's Judgment, where a man's fate is ultimately decided by his own inclinations and desires. The way to the higher, inner world, called in the Gospels the Kingdom of Heaven, cannot be reached by serving the will of the lower world.

Jesus teaches that men choose the material world by default as a result of the state known as sleep. References to this are constantly being made throughout the New Testament in words such as "watch," "awake," "sleep not." In the parable of the sower, Jesus tells us that the "kingdom of heaven is likened unto a man which sowed good seed in his field: But while men slept, his enemy came and sowed tares among the wheat" (Matthew 13:24–25). The field is humanity on earth. The good seed is the divine word concerning the kingdom of heaven sown by higher forces. The tares are the work of the devil (the enemy) who overpowers men through the world of the senses so that teachings concerning inner evolution appear remote and unreal. The work of the devil can be done only while men sleep. This is not physical sleep, but the very real and deep identification men experience in their waking lives. In physical sleep a man is passive and subject to dreams and thoughts which are beyond his control yet seem utterly real. But in his waking state his condition is not much different. A man appears to be master of his actions, but in reality he cannot control the constant flow of thoughts, imagination, and emotions that take place within him, and which color his world and prevent him from seeing things as they really are. It is into this state of waking sleep that the devil enters and sows the seeds of earthly temptation that drown out and weaken the call of a true teaching and the way to it.

The Gospels tell us that the apostles slept in Gethsemane. "And when he rose up from prayer, and was come to his disciples, he found them sleeping for sorrow, And said unto them, Why sleep ye? rise and pray, lest ye enter into temptation" (Luke 22:45–46). In Matthew (26:36–46), the account is even more telling. In this version Jesus leaves eight of the apostles in the grotto and takes with him Peter and the two sons of Zebedee, James and John, to the Place of the Agony. These three had been present at his transfiguration on Mt. Tabor and had thus witnessed his true nature. Yet they, too, sleep. That the disciples "sleep from sorrow" again does not mean a physical sleep. Rather, as yet unable to comprehend the master's true mission, they are asleep to the source of this mission and see all that is happening through the dreamy eyes of earthly senses which lead them to the temptation of sorrow.

This moment in Gethsemane is an important one in the teaching of Christ. It is not only nighttime in the physical sense, but the nighttime of the soul, when Christ must show by example the way for men to cross over to the heavenly Jerusalem. The apostles are there to witness the event and the teaching. But their presence in this cave and their description as being asleep show that they are swallowed up by the things of this earth. Yet even here they are not alone and the word from above reaches them through Jesus, who tells them what they must do, both for their own souls in their own final judgment and in order to understand what is about to take place. They must leave this cave and go out into the night to meet the events that are ordained from above. To do this they must wake up and stop confusing the things of God with the things of men. And to keep awake they must pray, that is, turn their attention to higher causes, so as not to be tempted by the lower world.

The Grotto of the Betrayal

This cave is also known as the Grotto of the Betrayal because it is from here that Jesus went out to meet Judas Iscariot. The story of Judas Iscariot and the betrayal and arrest of Jesus is certainly one of the most curious episodes recorded in the New Testament. If you recall now the mosaic in the Church of the Agony, of Judas betraying Jesus with a kiss, and remember all that has been said about Gethsemane, you will realize that Judas Iscariot acted in such a way as to lead to the fulfillment of Jesus's role. The other apostles were no help to Jesus at this most difficult time: their very actions ran counter to divine will. When the soldiers were about to arrest Jesus, Peter tried to defend him by force, for which he was rebuked by the master with the words, "Put up thy sword into the sheath: the cup which my Father hath given me, shall I not drink it?" (John 18:11). It is clear from the Gospel account that Jesus could easily have overcome the earthly forces sent against him if he had so wished. Continuing to rebuke Peter he says, "Thinkest thou that I cannot now pray to my Father, and he shall presently give me more than twelve legions of angels?" (Matthew 26:53). That these are not empty words is shown by Jesus's continued ability to work miracles: "Then Simon Peter, having a sword drew it, and smote the high priest's servant and cut off his right ear" (John 18:10). "And Jesus answered and said, Suffer ye thus far. And he touched his ear and healed him" (Luke 22:51). The Gospels tell us that when the soldiers took Jesus, the apostles forsook him and fled.

In the New Testament's long list of characters only three are recorded as fulfilling, or playing, a role which is known to them beforehand. The first is, of course, Jesus himself, who constantly refers to the fact that he is accomplishing the will of his Father. Even the darkest moments of his sojourn on earth seem to have been known to him, for he says of them, "for this cause came I unto this hour."

The second is John the Baptist, who heralded the coming of the Christ, who said, "He that sent me to baptize with water, the same said unto me, Upon whom thou shalt see the Spirit descending, and remaining on him, the same is he which baptizeth with the Holy Ghost. And I saw, and bare record that this is the Son of God" (John 1:33–34).

The third person, strangely enough, is Judas Iscariot, the betrayer of Christ. It is clear that Judas was chosen for this role by Jesus himself. At the very beginning of his ministry, while still by the Sea of Galilee, Jesus says, "Have not I chosen you twelve, and one of you is a devil. He spake of Judas Iscariot, the son of Simon: for he it was that should betray him, being one of the twelve" (John 6:70–71). Yet there is nothing in the Gospels to suggest awareness on Judas's part of having been selected for such a role, at any time during the three years he accompanied the master (that is, during the full period of Jesus's ministry). Nor is there the slightest indication that the other apostles—with whom he was in daily intimate contact—in any way suspected him of being other than a worthy disciple. Even at the Last Supper, when Jesus told the apostles that one of them would betray him, "the disciples looked one on another, doubting of whom he spake" (John 13:22).

Nonetheless, that Judas did indeed have some knowledge of the part he had to play is indicated by the understanding that existed between him and Jesus concerning the betrayal. At the appropriate moment in the Last Supper, Jesus merely says to him, "That thou doest, do quickly" (John 13:27), and Judas gets up and leaves. Not even the other apostles understood this exchange, thinking that Judas, who "had the bag" (that is, was the treasurer), had gone out "to buy those things that we have need of against the feast; or, that he should give something to the poor" (John 13:29).

The true motivation behind Judas's act may never be known. There are those who contend, or hint, that he acted consciously; that he was the only apostle who truly understood the master's mission and had the faith to carry out the terrible deed that would set in motion the events of the Passion and Resurrection. Others, however, follow more closely the Gospel account which relates that when the disciples asked Jesus which one of them would betray him, he answered, "He it is, to whom I shall give a sop, when I have dipped it. And when he had dipped the sop, he gave it to Judas Iscariot, the son of Simon. And after the sop Satan entered into him" (John 13:26–27). The passage leaves one uneasy, however, for it indicates that Judas, who until then had been a simple and loyal apostle, after receiving the sop was suddenly possessed of the power to do evil. While we have no basis for determining which of the two positions is correct, it would be well to keep in mind the definition given by many esoteric teachings concerning the difference between white and black magic. White magic is usually defined as being done with the consent and understanding of the subject, while black magic—even if performed for the best of reasons—is done without the subject's knowledge or consent.

But why does the Gospel trouble itself with such an elaborate and complicated story such as that of Judas Iscariot and the betrayal in Gethsemane? Jesus could have arranged to have been arrested at any time and begun his Passion in any number of ways. Why is the story included, and what does Judas Iscariot really represent? In many places in the Gospels the apostles—especially Peter—are shown as denying Jesus. This is always because they are not yet fully developed, and thus do not fully understand the master's purpose and ways. Judas represents, however, not denial but rejection, which is something completely different. Moreover, it is rejection by one who is supposedly close to the teaching.

In Luke 18:8, Jesus asks a question about the future of the inner meaning of the teaching that he brings: "When the Son of man cometh, shall he find faith on the earth?" Here Jesus voices one of the most fundamental laws of our world. Around the still center everything is in motion, and either develops and evolves in its pilgrimage to the center, or falls and disintegrates and is lost forever. The teaching enters this world of motion like seeds falling on the earth. Here and there they find fertile ground and are nurtured as the bearer brings them ever closer to the light and living waters of the center. Most, however, are lost as they descend in external rituals and endless intellectual arguments about words. The prophet Zechariah talks of this failure of God's teaching by saying that it was valued by the people at thirty pieces of silver (in other words, a lowly sum). This is also the sum received by Judas for betraying his master. Judas thus represents what Jesus knows in the future must eventually come to pass for the greater part of mankind—the failure of the teaching and its inner meaning. The spirit of the teaching will be rejected (valued little), and Christ, who is this spirit, betrayed. That the betrayal takes place in Gethsemane is significant, for here will take place God's final judgment, based not on externals but on what is still alive in a man's heart.

The GROTTO OF GETHSEMANE is open daily—in summer, 8:30–11:45 A.M. and 2:30–5 P.M., except that closing time on Sunday and Thursday is 3:30 P.M.; in winter, 2:30–4:30 P.M.

THE TOMB OF MARY (*Hebrew: Kneisiat Kever Miryam*)

As you stand at the head of the broad Crusader stairway and look down into the underground church that contains the

Tomb of Mary, you cannot help but feel a sense of the mysterious. At the foot of the staircase, looking toward the entrance, the feeling is increased. Except for periods when prayers are in progress, most of the church is kept in darkness. Ask the monk there to turn the lights on so you can have a good look around (the Greek Orthodox and Armenians are in charge on alternate days). Look at the ceiling and walls, and experience the volume of the structure, especially in relation to the tomb; then look back up the stairs to the entranceway, where the light flows down to the darkness below. Despite the many changes that have taken place over the centuries and the gradual darkening of the church, it is still possible to recapture some of the original atmosphere of the place.

The Tomb of Mary.

The Ephesus Tradition
Today it is often claimed that the Tomb of Mary is located not here but at Ephesus. This is largely the result of the visions of a German mystic, one Catherine Emmerich, who located Mary's dwelling place where she died on the site of the discovered remains of a Byzantine chapel near Ephesus. Those who believe that Mary accompanied the apostle John to Ephesus support their belief with the statement made by Jesus on the cross: "When Jesus therefore saw his mother, and the disciple standing by, whom he loved, he saith unto his mother, Woman, behold thy son! Then saith he to the disciple, Behold thy mother!" (John 19:26–27).

Both the Eastern and Western Churches (both of which venerate the Tomb of Mary here in the Valley of Jehoshaphat) approach the claim made for Ephesus with a great deal of caution. The visionary aspect of the claim is easily countered by similar visions concerning the Jerusalem site (such as that of St. Bridget of Sweden). Also it has always been the opinion of the Church Fathers that St. John settled in

Ephesus at a relatively advanced age; certainly not before 56
A.D., and perhaps even after the Jewish War of 70 A.D. Even
if Mary was only about fifteen years of age at the birth of
Jesus, this would place her somewhere between seventy and
eighty-eight years of age when called upon to accompany
John—an almost unimaginable age at which to make such a
journey. More telling (and suspicious), however, is that the
vision of Catherine Emmerich, at least in its published form,
contains almost all the elements present in early Christian
apocrypha which clearly situate Mary's death in Jerusalem.

The Jerusalem Tradition

The presence of a shrine in the Valley of Jehoshaphat containing the Tomb of Mary is first mentioned in texts dating
from the fifth century. As early as the second or third century, however, Judeo-Christian apocryphal texts such as the
Transitus Mariae (The Passing of Mary) already place her
tomb in this area, and no doubt reflect traditions reaching
back to the time of the event itself. The marked absence of
any historical reference to the tomb before the fifth century
by the Fathers of the Hellenistic Church should come as no
surprise. There is a similar silence regarding the Church of
the Annunciation in Nazareth, and almost as complete a
silence regarding the Room of the Last Supper on Mt. Zion.
This silence originally made it difficult for scholars to admit
the presence here of a tomb before the fourth or fifth century. Today, thanks to archeological excavations (largely carried out by the Franciscans), a great deal is known about the
Judeo-Christians and the first three centuries of Christianity
in Israel, and there can be little doubt that a tomb did exist
here from the earliest years. The silence, here as elsewhere,
arose from the fact that the tomb was in the hands of the
Judeo-Christians, and was avoided by the Gentile Church,
which considered the former schismatics or heretics. Thus it
is only around the fourth or fifth century, when the tomb fell
into Gentile hands, that official mention is made of it. It is
further known that Judeo-Christians did not believe in erecting shrines around their holy places, and that the first shrine
built here dates from the Byzantine period, when the Hellenistic Church first took control of the site.

The Tradition Behind the Jerusalem Tradition

There are a number of extant versions of the Judeo-Christian
apocrypha dealing with the falling asleep, or dormition, of
Mary, her burial, and her bodily assumption into heaven. All
contain certain elements in common. According to these
texts, as Mary is about to die, the apostles are all miraculously transported to Jerusalem (including St. John, who was
in Ephesus). She dies on Mt. Zion and her soul is taken up
into heaven by Jesus and the archangel Michael. The apostles are then commanded by Jesus to take the body of Mary
("which at one time was my abode") and to bury it in a new
tomb that they will find in the "flowery garden of Jehosha-

phat" (that is, Gethsemane), and to wait there until he speaks to them again. After 206 days (seven months) Jesus appears in a heavenly chariot accompanied by the soul of the Virgin. He calls out over the tomb, and Mary's body ascends to embrace its own soul. Some of the text also contains references to Mary's intervention in the saving of the damned. (*See* p. 163.) Here Jesus promises her that wherever there is a memorial in her name, all that call on her will be heard.

The Zoroastrians believed that the body would meet its soul on a bridge over which the dead would have to pass. For the good man the bridge was wide and spacious, and on it he would encounter his own soul coming to meet him. For the evil man it became razor-thin, causing him to plunge into the abyss. Essentially the same belief existed in Islam, except that instead of a bridge, a string as black as night, as thin as a hair, and as sharp as a sword would be strung from the Mount of Olives across the Valley of Jehoshaphat to the Temple Mount, over which the just would pass safely, but from which the evil would fall to eternal doom.

It is not generally known that many of the ideas concerning the "final days" found in early Christian, as well as Jewish and Muslim thought, are actually Zoroastrian in origin (the battle between good and evil, the prince of light and the prince of darkness, the last judgment, heaven and hell). While these ideas no doubt found their way into Judaism during the period of the Babylonian captivity, they seem to have entered Judeo-Christian thought through the Essenes, whose basic beliefs were similar to those of the Zoroastrians, and who are known to have been instrumental in the founding of certain of the early Judeo-Christian sects. The Tomb of Mary was revered by the Judeo-Christians as a place of the mysteries. It was for this reason that they were severely condemned by the Hellenistic Church. Exactly what these mysteries comprised we cannot tell, though a clue to their content may come from traditions related to Mary's power of intervention. Mary's bodily assumption into heaven and her meeting with her own soul were possible because she was pure and had not known corruption during her earthly life. According to Zoroastrian belief, all souls originally come from the kingdom of light. They enter the world of their own free will to help the prince of light in his battle against the prince of darkness. In this battle many of these souls are corrupted and must suffer the agonies of hell until all is purified following the final battle at the end of time. But, as was explained in the description of the Church of St. Anne, Mary was not just thought of as the mother of Jesus, but represented the hidden part of each man's soul that remains forever uncorrupted and pure and beloved by God. Thus the mysteries practiced here must have taught the way for a man to reach this hidden place, and to contact the one element within himself that might intervene with higher forces and permit his safe passage to the heavenly Jerusalem.

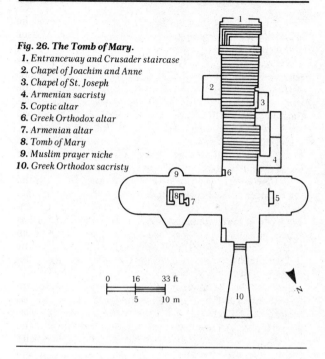

Fig. 26. The Tomb of Mary.
1. *Entranceway and Crusader staircase*
2. *Chapel of Joachim and Anne*
3. *Chapel of St. Joseph*
4. *Armenian sacristy*
5. *Coptic altar*
6. *Greek Orthodox altar*
7. *Armenian altar*
8. *Tomb of Mary*
9. *Muslim prayer niche*
10. *Greek Orthodox sacristy*

0   16   33 ft

5   10 m

N

The Church

When the Hellenistic Christians decided to build their first church here in the fourth or fifth century, they faced many of the same problems encountered at the Tomb of Jesus, though on a much smaller scale. The tomb itself was cut into rock and surrounded by other burial chambers. In order to isolate the burial place of Mary, a number of these surrounding tombs were simply cut away, being of no cultic interest. Around it was then built a cruciform structure similar in plan to the one today. This constituted the lower church or crypt, while above it the Byzantines built an octagonal upper church, which was destroyed by the Persians in 614. Note the similarity of its overall form to the Church of the Holy Sepulchre, with its commemorative tomb surrounded by apses. In the Church of the Holy Sepulchre the tomb is located on the main floor of the church—Christ had first to descend to the lower world before ascending again. The tomb of the Virgin, however, was located on the lower level of the Byzantine church, which represented the lower world in which she had remained pure and from which she was assumed directly up into heaven.

It is unclear whether the upper church was rebuilt immediately following the Persian invasion, and if so whether it was again destroyed in 1009 during the reign of the caliph Hakim. What is clear is that the Tomb of Mary and the lower church were saved from destruction during the early Arab period by the fact that the Muslims themselves venerated Mary as the mother of the prophet Jesus.

An upper church was rebuilt by the Crusaders following their conquest of Jerusalem in 1099, while the lower one was enlarged and redecorated. The present staircase with its adjacent shrines was added to the original structure, the ceilings and walls were covered in frescoes (as in Byzantine times), while the tomb was covered with marble and mosaic and crowned with a canopy of marble and gold.

After the fall of the Latin Kingdom in Jerusalem, the upper church was destroyed. The lower church again survived because of its veneration by Muslims. With time the ground level rose, covering the windows of the lower church, and the structure was plunged into the darkness we still find it in today.

The present church must certainly be a far cry from what it once was. The disappearance of the upper church, especially, makes it impossible to reconstruct it in full.

The remains of the facade are Crusader, in typical Romanesque style. The low triangle on the summit, however, dates from the last century; and a low set of ascending steps has been placed before the entranceway to protect the church from flooding.

The broad Crusader staircase constitutes the southern arm of the church, and is today reminiscent of a darkened entrance to an underground cave. The staircase is divided into three sections. The first part has a ceiling of sharply descending ridges. To the right can be seen the outline of a doorway that once led to the Grotto of Gethsemane or to the upper church. To the left is one of the windows that once lit up the church. The second section has a ceiling with rounded vaults and contains two side chapels. To the right is a chapel dedicated to Joachim and Anne, the parents of Mary. This dedication began only in the sixteenth century. The chapel itself was originally built to contain the remains of Queen Melisend, the wife of Faulk of Anjou, third Crusader king of Jerusalem. If you have a flashlight, you can shine it up and see the dome that was built above the chapel (it too contains windows to let in light). To the left of the stairway is a chapel dedicated to St. Joseph, but which in reality contains the remains of Crusader princesses. With the third section of the southern arm we enter the cruciform church built by the Byzantines, which is certainly one of the oldest existing churches in Jerusalem.

The tomb itself lies in the eastern arm of the cross. Its exterior is largely reconstruction, though parts of the original rock can still be seen behind the sections of glass that cover it. There are today two entrances to the tomb (to the north and to the west), though one of these must have been a later addition in order to facilitate the movement of worshippers and pilgrims. On the northern exterior you can still see the bases of the pillars that surrounded the tomb in Crusader times.

The interior is a rectangular rock-cut room. To the east are the remains of the stone bench on which the body of Mary was laid. Marble slabs cover the bench, the upper one being used as an altar. The holes in the bench are the work of pilgrims who took pieces of the holy tomb for souvenirs. The damage must have been done at an early period, since by Crusader times the bench was covered in marble. On the southern wall you can see a niche. This is most likely a prayer niche (*mihrab*) used by Muslims. Another, larger prayer niche is formed by the recess on the southern wall of the eastern arm. A similar recess (this time not a *mihrab*) exists on the northern wall, and these two recesses constitute the northern and southern apses of the church. On the upper part of the northern recess there is a metal grate behind which were discovered other burial chambers that existed in the cemetery where Mary was placed.

Before leaving, stand toward the rear of the eastern arm, and ignoring the modern paintings and decorations, once more take in the tomb and the general volume of the church in which it lies. The presence of this small structure in this darkened underground chamber leaves you with a sense of something silent and pure and, as we said at the beginning, a certain feeling of the mysterious.

The TOMB OF MARY is open daily, 6:30 A.M.–12 noon and 2–5 P.M.

THE CHURCH OF ST. MARY MAGDALENE

The church, strictly speaking, has nothing to do with Gethsemane, though this association is made by the Russian Orthodox. It was built by Tsar Alexander III, in imitation of the Muscovite style of the sixteenth and seventeenth centuries. The church is open only on Tuesdays and Thursdays, but in any case should really be visited in the afternoon at about four-thirty, when the nuns sing the Office. Their singing is quite extraordinary, and it is well worth the effort to hear them—but you will have to check beforehand to make sure of being admitted.

The CHURCH OF ST. MARY MAGDALENE is open only on Tuesday and Thursday, 9 A.M.–12 noon and 2–4 P.M. Tel.: 282897.

8

THE MOUNT OF OLIVES

DOMINUS FLEVIT

The present church was built in 1955 on the site of a seventh-century monastery. The dome of the church is in the shape of a teardrop to remind us of the tears that Jesus wept over Jerusalem while prophesying the destruction of the city and its sanctuary (*Dominus flevit*, "The Lord wept"). "And when he was come near, he beheld the city, and wept over it, saying, ... For the days shall come upon thee, that thine enemies shall cast a trench about thee, and compass thee round, and keep thee in on every side, and shall lay thee even with the ground, and thy children within thee; and they shall not leave in thee one stone upon another" (Luke 19:41, 43–44).

According to the Gospels, this event took place during Jesus's triumphal entry into Jerusalem. There is no way of knowing if the site of Dominus Flevit lay on the actual route taken by Jesus, though it is fairly certain that in Byzantine times the Palm Sunday procession, celebrating the event, did pass here. There is nothing to indicate that the Byzantine monastery was in any way connected with this procession. In medieval times pilgrims began to point to a particular rock as the actual place where Jesus wept, though no church or monument commemorating the event was ever built here by the Crusaders themselves.

The Entry into Jerusalem

The triumphal entry into Jerusalem is recorded in the Gospel of Matthew. In this account, Jesus sends two of his disciples to the village of Bethphage (Hebrew: Beit Pagi, or "House of Pagi"), to bring him an ass upon which no man had previously ridden. This, we are told, was in order to fulfill the prophecy, "Tell ye the daughter of Sion, Behold, thy King cometh unto thee, meek, and sitting upon an ass" (Matthew 21:5). What follows became the basis of the Palm Sunday procession. Jesus, seated on the ass, proceeds toward Jerusalem and the eastern gate of the Temple Mount through which the Messiah will pass at the end of time. "And a very great multitude spread their garments in the way; others cut down branches from the trees, and strawed them in the way. And the multitudes that went before, and that followed, cried, saying, Hosanna to the son of David: Blessed is he that cometh in the name of the Lord; Hosanna in the highest" (Matthew 21:8–9).

The key to the symbolism of this event is to be found in the mythology of ancient Egypt. Here the sun represents the source of life and movement. But the sun is variously portrayed, in one case with the ears of an ass (or alternately a seated sun god with the head of an ass). This represents the negative aspect of the sun, that is, obstinacy, opposition to movement, and rebellion. This dual nature of the sun symbolizes the inner conflict that exists everywhere in the universe. On the larger, macrocosmic scale it is the conflict that exists between good and evil, light and darkness. In man, the microcosm, it is the conflict between his spirit which wishes to return to its heavenly source, and the lower elements which tie him to the earth.

The soul instinctively knows its home, but must languish in the world until it understands and can accomplish its mission—to expand the rule of light over the rule of darkness. The morsel of darkness which is the responsibility of each individual soul is the body in which it is born. The body is the ass. It is what is lowest in man, and its movements are chaotic and without order. The body, left to itself, will carry the soul ever deeper into darkness. To reach the light the soul must learn to tame the ass by getting to know it, speaking a language it can understand, and finding a way to convince it to carry the soul toward the light.

The successful accomplishment of this task leads to the expansion of the light by the spiritualization of matter (the ass). But it also leads to the further development of the soul, made possible by its constant struggle to acquire the understanding necessary to convince the ass of the unity of purpose which alone can lead to mutual salvation. This process begins with the introduction of a third force capable of englobing the opposing tendencies of body and soul. This was the teaching concerning inner evolution brought by Jesus, and called by him "The Way."

The triumphal entry of Jesus into Jerusalem riding on an ass represents the act of salvation that can result from the inner growth of man. It represents a new unity which was not possible before. Jesus represents the soul which, possessed of new knowledge, is capable of overcoming the natural resistance of the ass and guiding it. The ass itself is described in the Gospels as never having been ridden by man, that is, until the coming of Jesus and the teaching brought by him such a working relation between body and soul was impossible. The man who creates such a unity within himself is the Messiah. The word "messiah" comes from the Hebrew *mashiach*, "the anointed one." We are used to hearing this word in connection with the anointing of kings and high priests. But in the time of Jesus it was given another meaning by the disciples, who "cast out many devils and anointed with oil many that were sick and healed them" (Mark 6:13). The true king and anointed one is the one who is made well, that is to say, made whole again. It is the one who reconciles within himself the battle of opposing forces which enfeebles him, and brings them peace. This new unity is the Christ, whose kingdom is symbolized by Jerusalem.

DOMINUS FLEVIT is open daily, 8–11:30 A.M. and 3–5 P.M.

THE JUDEO-CHRISTIAN CEMETERY AT DOMINUS FLEVIT

This first- to fourth-century necropolis is one of the most important archeological discoveries ever made in Israel. Until the middle of the present century, it was generally believed that Christian communities did not exist in Jerusalem prior to the period of Constantine. Excavations carried out here in 1953 completely changed this picture, and formed the basis of much that is now known concerning the Judeo-Christians. Two periods are represented here. The most significant is the one stretching from the first century A.D. to the end of the Second Jewish War in 135.

The excavators (the Franciscans) clearly recognized that this was a Jewish cemetery. Yet it contained a number of important elements which distinguished it from other Jewish burial grounds. First of all, there was the widespread presence of ossuaries, or receptacles for the bones of the dead—like the ones you see here. These presuppose exhumation. While this is sometimes permitted under Jewish law (such as for reburial with one's family), it is generally shunned by Jews, who consider the touching of human bones, or any contact with the dead, as resulting in ritual or legal impurity. Christians, on the other hand, consider human bones to be sacred, a belief connected to the doctrine of the mystical body, and which resulted in the veneration of relics.

Most important, however, not only for identifying these as Judeo-Christian burials, but for understanding so many of the ideas of this early group, are the symbols engraved on these ossuaries. A list of these symbols with their interpretations and origins would be much too long and complicated to attempt here. Anyone wishing to pursue this fascinating subject in English is referred to a publication of the Studium Biblicum Franciscanum in Jerusalem by Father Bellarimo Bagatti, entitled *The Church from the Circumcision*. It can be purchased at the bookshop of the Franciscan Printing Press on St. Francis Street in the Old City.

Most of the more interesting ossuaries are located at the Flagellation Museum on the Via Dolorosa. On the ossuaries here we see only one of the many symbols used by the Judeo-Christians, the six-pointed star. This belongs to a very large group of symbols, beliefs, and doctrines concerning Christ in relation to the angels. Sometimes he is merely associated with them, though at their head and with power over them, while in other instances he himself takes on the guise of an angel. In one apocryphal version of the Immaculate Conception, for example, Christ states that it was he himself who descended upon Mary. To do this he had to pass through the various levels of heaven ruled by the angels. Wishing to carry out this mystery in secret, he says, "I passed in front of the archangels and angels in their likeness, as if I were one of them."

The six-pointed stars we see here place Jesus in relation to the six angels of creation (one for each day), each of which was believed to have presided over one of the things created. These six angels, however, are only external manifestations of what was already at the beginning before the creation, that is, Jesus as the Word ("In the beginning was the Word"—John 1:1). The Word is the point at the center of the star. It is the hidden source of all that becomes manifest. Judeo-Christians saw the world in terms of the history of the salvation of man by Jesus Christ, and many of the events in the Old Testament were believed to contain prophecies concerning the future role of Jesus in this history. Thus in Exodus 23:20, God says, "Behold, I send an Angel before thee, to keep thee in the way, and to bring thee into the place which I have prepared." For Christians this referred not only to an earthly place but to the route taken by the soul from its earthly abode to its heavenly one. The one who guides man's soul on its way is Jesus, seen here in his manifestation as the six angels of creation.

It is worth mentioning that Judeo-Christian symbolism was apparently well known to the Hellenistic Church Fathers. From the fourth century onward, as the power of the Hellenistic Church spread, Church councils became increasingly opposed to the use of this symbolism, which, they claimed, easily degenerated into superstition, and fostered beliefs and practices contrary to accepted Church dogma. We now know that the Judeo-Christians did not completely disappear until the sixth century, while their symbols increasingly became the possession of mystics.

THE TOMBS OF THE PROPHETS
(Hebrew: Kivrei HaNevi'im)

It is quite a strenuous climb to the top of the Mount of Olives. In the hot summer months a visit to this cool underground chamber will provide a very welcome break. There is little of real interest to see here. If you plan to look around, be sure to take a flashlight with you, or ask the guardian to show you around with a lantern. Only the central chamber receives light from the hole in the roof. The corridors, containing the niches that once were tombs, are in total darkness.

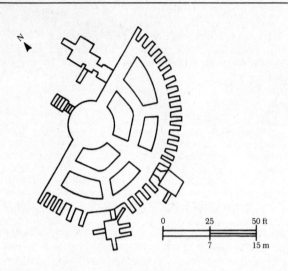

Fig. 27. The Tombs of the Prophets.

The association of these tombs with the prophets Haggai, Zechariah, and Malachi came rather late, certainly not before the fourteenth or fifteenth century. The association is clearly a false one. These prophets lived in the fifth and sixth centuries B.C., while the graves here are from a period some thousand years later. The large central chamber with an opening in the ceiling has caused some to speculate that this might have been in origin a cistern or well. Today it is generally believed that the graves date from the fourth or fifth century A.D., and belong to pilgrims who died while on pilgrimage.

THE JEWISH CEMETERY
(*Hebrew: Beit Kevarot HaYehudi*)

Make your way to the observation point just below the Intercontinental Hotel. This provides a magnificent view of the city and many of its important sites and features. Directly in front of you, and continuing down to the valley below, is the Jewish cemetery. This is the largest Jewish cemetery in Israel, and for Jews certainly the holiest one in the world. Today there is little reminder of the extensive damage caused by the Jordanian army in the period prior to the Six Day War, when countless gravestones were taken from here for paving roads. The cemetery dates from the fifteenth century. Before that time Jews buried their dead on the slope of Mt. Moriah, just outside the eastern wall of the Temple Mount. This practice was brought to an end by the ruling Mamelukes, who established in its place the Muslim cemetery we still see today, forcing the Jews to retreat to the nearby Mount of Olives.

The name "Mount of Olives" no doubt derives from the groves of olive trees that once grew on its slope. The only reminder we have of these today are the few, relatively modern trees in the garden alongside the Church of the Agony, and in the ancient name of Gethsemane, or in Hebrew, Gat Shemanim ("the Oil Press").

Even before the fifteenth century the Mount of Olives played an important role in Jewish life and thought. According to legend, at the time of the great flood, it was from the Mount of Olives that the dove brought back the olive leaf to Noah in the ark. When asked why it chose an olive leaf, whose taste is very bitter, the dove replied, "May my food be bitter as the olive but given by the hands of God, rather than sweet as honey, but given by man." In biblical times the southern part of the mountain was known as the Mount of Anointing, in Hebrew Har HaMishchah, for here were prepared the fine olive oils needed for anointing the kings and high priests of Israel. After King Solomon settled a number of his foreign wives here and established for them places of idol worship, the name was changed to Har HaMashchit, "Mount of Corruption." Today this is usually translated as "Mount of Scandal."

After the destruction of Solomon's Temple the Divine Presence first wandered over the Temple courtyard, then made its way to the wall of the city, and from there to the Mount of Olives ("And the glory of the Lord went up from the midst of the city, and stood upon the mountain which is on the east side of the city"—Ezekiel 11:23). Here it dwelt for three and a half years waiting for the Children of Israel to repent. Each day it called out, "Seek ye the Lord while he may be found, call ye upon him while he is near" (Isaiah 55:6). But Israel did not repent and the voice was finally heard to say, "I will go and return to my place, till they acknowledge their offence, and seek my face" (Hosea 5:15). Then the Presence ascended to heaven. The place from which the ascent took place was called, in popular belief, the footstool of God. (Its exact location is unknown today.)

The Mount of Olives played an especially important role in Jewish life and thought during the Second Temple period, when practices carried out here were linked to the activities of the Temple itself. Most important was the burning of the red heifer at a point directly opposite the opening of the sanctuary. The law regarding this sacrifice as a purification for sin is found in Numbers 19, and includes the injunction that "the priest shall take of her blood with his finger, and sprinkle of her blood directly before the tabernacle of the congregation seven times" (Numbers 19:4). Also important was the lighting of beacons on the Mount of Olives to announce the starts of months, years, festivals, and holy days. These signals were passed on rapidly through a network of high places to Jewish communities throughout Israel, and even to the large Jewish community in Babylon, thus linking all Jews to the times of the Temple service in Jerusalem.

From the ninth century onward, Jews were forbidden entry to the Temple Mount by the Muslim rulers of the city, and so the Mount of Olives—because of all the religious associations mentioned above, its closeness to the city, and the fact that it directly overlooked the Temple Mount—became an alternate center for religious gatherings and pilgrimage, as well as a place where Jews came to pray and rend their clothing as a sign of mourning for the Temple. When, in the fifteenth century, further restrictions forced the Jews to abandon their traditional burial place on Mt. Moriah, it was quite natural for them to establish their new cemetery on this nearby uninhabited slope.

Other factors, too, played a role in making this decision. God had abandoned the world from the Mount of Olives, and one day he would reappear there in the form of the Messiah. The sound of the shofar (the ram's horn) would signal the resurrection of the dead and the ingathering of the exiles for the final judgment. Both Jews and Muslims believe that those buried here, close to the wall of the Temple Mount, will be the first to be resurrected and enter the new Jerusalem to achieve salvation and eternal life.

The Mount of Olives forms a divide between the desert to the east, and civilization, represented by Jerusalem, to the west. Before the city spread eastward this division was far clearer, and the summit of the hill represented the separation between the land of the living and the land without life. From where you are standing you can see that the eastern wall of the Temple Mount was built especially low, so that the Temple, which faced eastward, and whose doors opened onto the Mount of Olives, was visible from here. Looking at the Dome of the Rock today it is clear that the Temple dominated the field of vision of anyone arriving at the summit of the Mount of Olives from the desert to the east. Thus the division here between desert and civilization was not just horizontal and geographical, but also vertical and spiritual: a separation between the desert and barrenness of the ordinary human level and the higher level of God's city and tabernacle on earth.

This division, however, is not absolute, or rather will become so only at the end of time. As long as the present world exists, it remains as a point of passage, joining the two worlds and showing that man's inner evolution to a higher level of existence remains a possibility. But this possibility will come to an end with the last judgment at the end of time when, according to the prophet Zechariah, God shall stand "upon the mount of Olives, which is before Jerusalem on the east, and the mount of Olives shall cleave in the midst thereof toward the east and toward the west" (Zechariah 14:4).

The cleaving of the Mount of Olives also symbolizes God's judgment of all nations. The day when Israel repented and was again worthy of God's stewardship would be a terrible one for those who had been God's instrument in chastising his chosen people. God would judge these nations, rise against them, and cut them off forever from his kingdom. God's justice here toward those who have served his purpose is difficult to comprehend. It is the same justice found in the story of Judas Iscariot. At Gethsemane we saw how Judas was chosen by Jesus to set in motion the events of the Passion and Resurrection. Yet Jesus says, "The Son of man goeth as it is written of him: but woe unto that man by whom the Son of man is betrayed! it had been good for that man if he had not been born" (Matthew 26:24). Part of the answer to the mystery of this justice lies in Zoroastrian thought, which left its mark on both Judaism and Christianity. Here, in the struggle between good and evil, the good is essentially defenseless against the onslaught of evil, whose methods it cannot employ. This is its danger. Its weapon against evil lies not in force but in its divine knowledge of its own possible evolution. Only by evolving can it raise itself to a level that evil cannot reach, thus condemning evil to vent its destructive energies upon itself until it is devoured. The instrument of this evolution is the man in whom the struggle between good and evil is locked. Here evil is given the opportunity of attacking the good, which can passively succumb or awaken to its state and actively seek within itself the hidden source of divine understanding which alone can guide it to the safety of a higher level. This active search, in the face of evil, is epitomized in the symbolism of the Passion and Resurrection of Jesus, which, taken to its end, results in the birth of a glorified body on a new level of life. As with Judas Iscariot, only evil can set this process in motion and keep it going. But once the new level of being is reached, evil is overcome and condemned to darkness, forever separate from the light.

THE CHURCH OF THE PATER NOSTER

The present building lies above the remains of the Eleona basilica built by the emperor Constantine in the early fourth century. The name apparently derives from the Greek *elaion*, meaning "of olives." The fourth-century pilgrim Egeria called it "on Eleona," which today is understood as meaning the church on the Mount of Olives. This was one of the three basilicas built by the emperor on the site of a mystic grotto believed to have been illuminated by the Divine Presence. In Byzantine times the grotto was incorporated as a crypt beneath the choir of the church, while now it is found in the courtyard of the cloister of the Carmelite convent. (The cloister is the only part of the church and convent open to the public.)

Here again is the conflict that existed between the understanding and practices of Jewish and Hellenistic Christians in the early centuries of Christianity. Judeo-Christians' beliefs concerning the sacred grotto were of a more mystical nature than those of their Hellenistic counterparts, and their practices here had less to do with matters of faith than with the inculcation of the inner meaning of various aspects of the life of Christ. These practices were severely condemned by the Hellenistic Church, which, in uncompromising terms, warned its pilgrims to beware of the "sect of the impious" who call their caves the Lord's house. With the growth of Byzantine political support of the Hellenistic Church in Jerusalem, the nature of these grottoes began to change. Eventually they all fell into the hands of Hellenistic Christians, who, contrary to Judeo-Christian practice, built churches or shrines around them. While these structures succeeded in drawing the interest of pilgrims, and keeping alive the memory of the events that had taken place there, religious practices were reduced to the form of faith and devotion, and the inner meanings of the teachings were eventually suppressed or forgotten.

The three mystic grottoes—at Bethlehem, the Holy Sepulchre, and the Eleona—were bound up with the solely Judeo-Christian doctrine of the descent and ascent of divine light into the world. We have already discussed the Holy Sepulchre at length. At Bethlehem, the Grotto of the Nativity was the place where the light first descended into the world. The cave was likened to the world of men which until then had been in darkness and separated from the world of light above. This descent reestablished the link between heaven and earth broken at the time of Adam's fall. Of the three sacred caves, least is known concerning the Eleona. It is often proposed that Bethlehem, the Mount of Olives, and the Holy Sepulchre correspond to the three great events of Jesus's career: his birth, teaching, and Resurrection. Thus the Eleona would be the site of the divine light of knowledge. Most scholars contend that this was the knowledge, conveyed by Jesus to the disciples, concerning the final battle between good and evil at the end of the world (Matthew 24). The site, situated near the summit of the hill that was destined to play such an important role in those final days, would certainly have been an appropriate place for such a teaching.

The Grotto

Today's grotto can give only the most general impression of how it once was. In addition to the vast changes time has wrought, it was badly damaged during the First World War, when German and Turkish troops used it as a field kitchen. Its present form is the result of an overall reconstruction undertaken in 1927. Over the two entranceways are quotations taken from the diary of Egeria (the fourth-century

Spanish nun who visited Jerusalem). The southern lintel refers to the cave where Jesus used to teach his disciples, while the northern one refers to the cave where he taught the apostles.

The Burial Cave

During the reconstruction an additional opening was made in the grotto joining it to the adjacent burial chambers to the west. The exact relation of the grotto to these chambers is unknown (they originally had their own entranceway to the south). The cave appears to have been constructed in the second or third century, that is, before the building of the Eleona, and to have been reused at a later date for burying a number of the bishops of Jerusalem. Burial chambers and graves are found almost everywhere on the Mount of Olives, including here, and beneath the Pater Noster church.

The Pater Noster

The Eleona was destroyed during the Persian invasion of Jerusalem in 614. By the Crusader period the identification of the site as the place where Jesus had taught the disciples was virtually forgotten, and the small chapel built here was dedicated, rather, to the prayer known as the Pater Noster ("Our Father"). Some of the Gospels associate this prayer with Jesus's ministry in Galilee, immediately following the Sermon on the Mount. The Gospel of Luke, however, clearly places it on the Mount of Olives. This tradition has been continued in the decoration of the present cloister, where the

The Pater Noster,
Pater Noster Church.

Pater Noster, or Lord's Prayer, appears on tiled panels in some fifty languages. (The number constantly changes as panels are removed for repairs or other reasons.)

The prayer itself was given by Jesus in response to a request made by one of the disciples. "And it came to pass, that, as he was praying in a certain place, when he ceased, one of his disciples said to him, Lord, teach us to pray" (Luke 11:1). To this request Jesus replied, "When ye pray, say, Our Father which art in heaven, Hallowed be thy name. Thy kingdom come. Thy will be done, as in heaven, so in earth. Give us day by day our daily bread. And forgive us our sins; for we also forgive every one that is indebted to us. And lead us not into temptation; but deliver us from evil" (Luke 11:2–4).

It is clear that the disciples were not asking Jesus to teach them to pray in the ordinary sense. For them, as observant Jews, prayer was a daily part of life. At Gethsemane we discussed at length the nature of prayer in the Gospels, and saw that it referred to the reorientation and turning of a man to that which is higher. In making this request the disciples were asking Jesus how to turn to the hidden source and find the knowledge and understanding to illuminate their own path. Jesus replied by instructing them in the Lord's Prayer, which must thus be seen as the essence of his teaching.

The CHURCH OF THE PATER NOSTER is open daily except Sunday, 9–11:45 A.M. and 3–4:30 P.M.

The Tomb of Princess de la Tour d'Auvergne
Following the fall of the Latin Kingdom the Crusader church was destroyed by Salah a-Din. In 1866 the property was bought by the princess de la Tour d'Auvergne, who financed the building of the present church (1874), which was entrusted to the Carmelite sisters. According to her request her remains were brought here after her death and placed in the sarcophagus at the entrance to the church. The church itself is generally closed to the public.

The Basilica of the Sacred Heart
Above the sacred grotto are the remains of an uncompleted church called the Sacred Heart (of Jesus). The idea was conceived in France during the First World War and was intended to be a symbol of world peace. The cornerstone was laid in 1920. Work stopped for lack of funds and was never continued. The reconstructed grotto was meant to be the crypt of this new building.

A slightly different version of the story can be read on a note of explanation on the wall of the cloister. According to this, in 1915, a "bogus visionary" claimed that a Sacred Heart basilica had to be built here so that France could win the war and peace be brought to all men. Work begun destroyed part of the cloister and transformed the chapel of the crypt. The plaque goes on to claim that the church will never be built because it cannot serve the purpose of one segment of mankind but belongs to all.

THE CHURCH OF THE ASCENSION
(*Hebrew: Kneisiat HeAliyah*)

This site was given by Salah a-Din, as a religious trust, to two of his followers, and has been a Muslim possession ever since. It is thus not open to the public on the same regular basis as are the churches of the city. If it is closed when you get there, ask the guardian to open it for you. If he is not there, almost anyone in the vicinity can find him within a few minutes.

The ascension of Jesus to heaven stands at the center of Christian traditions, and almost all the churches at, or near, the summit of the Mount of Olives are somehow related to this event. The Russian Orthodox assign it to the area of the tower of the nearby Russian monastery. The site of Viri Galilaei ("Ye men of Galilee"), where the angel addressed the disciples, and today the seat of the Greek Orthodox patriarch, commemorates the events immediately following the

The Church of the Ascension.

ascension. Even the Eleona was often associated with this event. Eusebius, the bishop of Caesarea who witnessed the construction of the Eleona, described it as the place where Jesus revealed the mysteries of the end of the world to his disciples and then ascended into heaven.

The first real historical evidence concerning the present site of the ascension comes from the diary of Egeria. According to her, the event was commemorated at a place not far from the Eleona called the Imbomon. This name is believed to derive from the Greek meaning "a high place," or "on the hillock." Strangely enough, she records that Ascension Day itself was not celebrated at the Imbomon (which she describes as "the place from which the Lord ascended into heaven"), but at Bethlehem. If you recall all that has been said about the *axis mundi*, you will see that there is a certain logic in this. Christ had descended into the world at Bethlehem, and there is no reason why he would have ascended from it at any other place. Egeria's description of the place as the Imbomon, that is, a high place or hillock, confirms that in her day there was as yet no church there. A church was, however, built on this site very soon after Egeria's visit. This was the Church of the Holy Ascension, built by Poemenia, a member of the royal family. It was apparently a round structure whose center, which marked the spot of the ascension, was open to the sky. Legends about the building of the church say that its dome kept collapsing and the flooring flew from its place, until the builders realized that ground touched by Jesus and his path to heaven were not to be covered.

In the twelfth century the Crusaders built a new church, whose plan has been largely reconstructed from discovered remains. It was no longer a single building as in Byzantine times, but octagonal in shape, and essentially a central shrine or edicule (the structure we see today), surrounded by a fortified monastery. The shrine contained the rock from which Jesus reputedly ascended to heaven and which contained his footprints (in Byzantine times these footprints were shown in the dirt of the floor), and had an open dome which indicated the path of his ascension. Open domes exist or have existed on a number of Jerusalem's monuments. The rotunda of the Holy Sepulchre until relatively recently had such a dome, and one can still be seen above the edicule in the Tomb of Mary. These symbolize the soul's ability to pass freely beyond the earthly confines of this world.

When the site was taken over by the Muslims in the time of Salah a-Din a number of changes were made: The open dome was replaced by a closed one, and the spaces between the arches of the edicule were filled in. A *mihrab* (a prayer niche facing in the direction of Mecca) was built in the south wall, and the stone of the ascension was moved closer to the niche. The shrine has survived because of its sacredness to Islam, while the rest of the Crusader church has slowly disappeared. A number of Christian communities are permitted access to the compound to celebrate the event of the ascension. Bases of columns that lie against the ancient outer wall of the site, and which once carried the arches of the Crusader church, serve as altars for these different groups. The Franciscans alone are permitted to pray in the edicule itself.

Origins of the Tradition

The most important factor in both Jewish and Christian traditions concerning the ascent of the divine from the Mount of Olives is that in neither case is the ascent a permanent one. At the end of time both the Divine Presence of the Jews and the glorified Christ of the Christians will reappear on the mountain to resurrect the dead, judge the nations, and lead the saved into the new Jerusalem. For Muslims it is the prophet Muhammad who will appear on the Mount of Olives, but this is clearly a later version of the same tradition, which, by the Muslim period, had lost all connection with the essential element of the ascent of the divine from the summit of the hill.

The source of this tradition lies in a particular Jewish belief concerning God's relationship with Israel and the city of Jerusalem which arose following the destruction of Solomon's Temple—the belief that Jerusalem is not one city but two. This is reflected in its Hebrew name, Yerushalayim, whose plural form denotes the two Jerusalems—the heavenly and the earthly one, described in Psalms (122:3) as a city that is joined together, that is to say, the Jerusalem on high is directed to face the Jerusalem below. Most significant, however, is the order of their creation. Rabbinic commentaries state quite clearly that God created the heavenly Jerusalem out of his great love for the one below, and built it as a city in the heavens that would be joined with the one on earth. However, God swore that his Divine Presence would not enter the heavenly city until the earthly city had been rebuilt. One rabbinic commentary has God saying, "From the day that the wicked Nebuchadnezzar came up and destroyed my home, and burned my court, and exiled my children among the nations of the world, I have not entered into my throne." And again, "Said the Holy One, Blessed be He, to Israel: My children, from the day I destroyed my house below, I have not gone up to dwell in my house on high, but have dwelt in the open, in the dew and the rain."

The early Jewish tradition concerning God's ascent from the Mount of Olives thus represented not an abandonment by God of His people, but the withdrawal of the Divine Presence to a place of exile, which corresponded to Israel's own exile on earth. The point of contact with this hidden place of divine exile is at the summit of the Mount of Olives. We have already seen the significance of this location, which symbolically divides the land of the living in the west, represented by Jerusalem, from the land without life to the east, whose desert and barrenness represented the exile of ordinary human existence from its living source. God's contact with this earthly point acts as the bridge which joins these two worlds and makes passage between them possible. It is the bridge that is kept open for a repentant Israel which will one day reorient itself and return to its source. When Israel reenters the earthly Jerusalem, God will enter the heavenly one, and the bridge between worlds will cease to exist. It will be the final judgment.

There can be little doubt regarding the origin of the tradition of Jesus's own ascension from the Mount of Olives. As with the Divine Presence, Jesus as the Way was the bridge over which men could travel from their fallen state to a promised higher level. The older Jewish tradition passed easily and naturally into the hands of the early Judeo-Christians who understood its significance, and for whom terms such as Mount of Olives, Jerusalem, the lands of the living and the dead, symbolized inner truths rather than mere geographical places. It was by understanding these truths, and recognizing them within themselves, that men could shed light on their own inner chaos and exile and by doing so bring to it the divine order that was their birthright. The rejection of these earliest followers of Jesus by their Jewish brethren on the one hand, and their Hellenistic counterparts on the other, led to their disappearance. The Hellenistic Church, which grew up divorced from Jewish tradition and rejecting Mosaic law, inherited a teaching whose symbols largely derived from a culture they did not understand, and whose inner meanings were thus lost.

SOME USEFUL DATES

4th mill. B.C.   First permanent settlement of Jerusalem, adjacent to the Gihon Spring.

19th cent. B.C.   Name Ushalmes (Ushames) appears in Egyptian texts.

18th cent. B.C.   Abraham meets Melchizedek, king of Salem (Jerusalem) and priest of the Most High God.

13th cent. B.C.   Exodus from Egypt.

12th–11th cent. B.C.   Jerusalem a Jebusite city.

1000 B.C.   David captures Jerusalem and establishes it as the political and religious center of the state.

960–928 B.C.   Reign of Solomon and the building of the Temple.

928 B.C.   Death of Solomon and dissolution of the state into a northern kingdom (Israel) and a southern kingdom (Judah) with its capital at Jerusalem.

928–586 B.C.   Jerusalem the capital of the kings of Judah.

725–697 B.C.   Reign of King Hezekiah of Judah. Construction of Hezekiah's Tunnel leading to the Pool of the Shiloah.

722 B.C.   Fall of the northern kingdom (Israel) to Assyria. Inhabitants taken into captivity.

586 B.C.   Fall of the southern kingdom (Judah) to Nebuchadnezzar of Babylon. Inhabitants exiled.

538 B.C.   Persians under Cyrus the Great defeat Babylon and permit exiled Judeans to return to Jerusalem. Return to Zion movement.

515 B.C.   Second Temple completed.

332 B.C.   Jerusalem surrenders to Alexander the Great.

301–200 B.C.   Jerusalem under the rule of the Ptolemies, Alexander's successors in Egypt.

200–152 B.C.   Jerusalem under the rule of the Seleucids, Alexander's successors in Syria.

175–168 B.C.	Antiochus IV Epiphanes ascends the Seleucid throne. Aims at complete Hellenization of Jerusalem. Desecration of the Temple.
168 B.C.	The priestly Hasmonean family (the Maccabees) organizes a revolt against the Seleucids.
165 B.C.	The Maccabees seize the Temple Mount and cleanse and rededicate the Temple (commemorated in the festival of Hanukah).
152–63 B.C.	Rule of the Hasmoneans—first as governors, then as kings and high priests.
63 B.C.	Capture of Jerusalem by the Romans under Pompey.
47 B.C.	Antipater, father of Herod, becomes procurator of Judea.
40 B.C.	Roman senate names Herod king.
20 B.C.	Herod rebuilds the Temple and extends the Temple Mount.
6 A.D.	Judea becomes a Roman province.
26 A.D.	Pontius Pilate becomes procurator.
27–30 A.D.	Ministry of Jesus.
66–70 A.D.	First Jewish War against Rome.
70 A.D.	Destruction of Jerusalem and its Temple by Titus, son of the emperor Vespasian.
73 A.D.	The fall of Massada on the Dead Sea.
132	Second Jewish War (Bar Kochba rebellion) against Rome.
135	Rebellion suppressed and Jews banished from Jerusalem on pain of death.
135	Emperor Hadrian builds the Roman provincial town of Aelia Capitolina on the destroyed remains of Jerusalem.
313	Emperor Constantine issues the Edict of Milan granting religious freedom to Christians.
330	Constantine inaugurates his new capital, Constantinople, on the site of the Greek city of Byzantium.
335	Dedication of the Church of the Holy Sepulchre. Era of church-building in Jerusalem.
361–363	Reign of the emperor Julian (the apostate). Julian repudiates Constantine's association with Christianity and gives permission to rebuild the Jewish Temple. He is killed before the plan can be carried out.
527–565	Rule of the emperor Justinian. Intensive church-building (the Nea Church, 543), and persecution of Jews.

614	Persian capture of Jerusalem under Chosroes II. City's churches destroyed.
628	Emperor Heraclius retakes Jerusalem. Begins systematic dismantling of the Temple Mount in revenge for Jewish role in the Persian invasion.
638	Muslims capture Jerusalem. The caliph Omar negotiates its surrender and prays at the site of Solomon's Temple.
661–750	Muawiya proclaimed caliph in Jerusalem and establishes the Umayyad dynasty, which rules from Damascus in Syria.
685–705	Reign of Abd al-Malik. Building of the Dome of the Rock.
705–715	Reign of al-Walid. Building of al-Aqsa mosque and Umayyad palaces.
750–969	Abbasid caliphate (House of Abbas), which rules from Baghdad in Iraq. From mid-ninth century Muslim interest in Jerusalem declines.
969–1071	Rival caliphate, the Fatimids of Egypt (Cairo), captures and holds Jerusalem.
1009	The Fatimid caliph al-Hakim orders all Christian churches destroyed.
1071–1099	Seljuk Turks in Jerusalem. Their acts of brutality against Christians cause Pope Urban II to call for a holy war to recapture Jerusalem.
1099	The Crusaders take Jerusalem and establish the Latin Kingdom of Jerusalem. The city's Jews and Muslims are slaughtered.
1187	Salah a-Din (Saladin) the Ayyubid recaptures Jerusalem. Ayyubid rule.
1229–1244	Partial renewal of Crusader presence in Jerusalem.
1244	Khwarismic Turks (Tartars) sack Jerusalem. End of Crusader presence in the city.
1260–1517	The Mamelukes, former royal guards of the Ayyubids, overthrow them and rule in their place.
1267	The Ramban arrives in Jerusalem.
1517	The Ottoman Turkish sultan Selim I defeats the Mamelukes of Egypt and Syria.
1517–1917	Rule of Ottoman Turks.
1520–1566	Reign of the sultan Suleiman the Magnificent. Rebuilds Jerusalem's walls. These are the walls we see today.
1917	Jerusalem surrenders to the British.
1947	The United Nations partitions British-mandated Palestine into a Jewish and an Arab

state. Jerusalem is proclaimed an international city. Arabs reject the resolution.

1948   Proclamation of the State of Israel. In the ensuing fighting Jordan takes and holds the Old City of Jerusalem. Jews in the new city (under Israeli rule) are forbidden access to the Old City's holy sites.

1967   The Six Day War. Israeli forces reunite divided Jerusalem. For the first time in its history, Jerusalem is freely open to all faiths.

FOR FURTHER READING

Avigad, Nahman. *Discovering Jerusalem*. Jerusalem: 1980.

Bagatti, Ballarimo. *The Church from the Circumcision*. Jerusalem: 1984.

Bagatti, Bellarimo. *The Church from the Gentiles in Palestine*. Jerusalem: 1984.

Bagatti, B., M. Piccirillo, and A. Prodomo. *New Discoveries at the Tomb of the Virgin Mary in Gethsemane*. Jerusalem: 1975.

Bahat, Dan. *Carta's Historical Atlas of Jerusalem*. Jerusalem: 1980; Milwaukee: 1983.

Bahat, Dan. *Jerusalem: Selected Plans of Historical Sites and Monumental Buildings*. Jerusalem: 1980.

Ben-Dov, Meir. *In the Shadow of the Temple*. Jerusalem: 1982.

Ben-Dov, M., Z. Aner, and M. Naor. *The Western Wall*. Jerusalem: 1981.

Cook, Roger. *The Tree of Life*. New York: 1974.

Coüasnon, Charles. *The Church of the Holy Sepulchre in Jerusalem*. London and Wolfeboro, N.H.: 1972.

Creswell, K. A. C. *The Origin of the Plan of the Dome of the Rock*. London: 1924.

Creswell, K. A. C. *A Short Account of Early Muslim Architecture*. London: 1958.

Cust, L. G. A. *The Status Quo in the Holy Places*. Jerusalem: 1980.

Daniélon, J. *Primitive Christian Symbols*. London: 1964.

Duncan, A. *The Noble Heritage: A Portrait of the Church of the Resurrection*. London: 1974.

Eliade, Mircea. *Cosmos and History: The Myth of the Eternal Return*. Chicago: 1959.

Eliade, Mircea. *Myth and Reality*. Chicago: 1963.

Eliade, Mircea. *The Sacred and the Profane*. Chicago: 1961.

Ginsberg, Louis. *Legends of the Bible*. New York: 1956.

Hamilton, R. W. *The Structural History of the Aqsa Mosque*. London: 1949.

Hintlian, Kevork. *History of the Armenians in the Holy Land*. Jerusalem: 1976.

James M. R. *The Apocryphal New Testament*. Oxford: 1955.

Jerusalem. Jerusalem: 1973. (Material originally published in the *Encyclopedia Judaica,* 1971.)

Kasher, M. *The Western Wall: Its Meaning in the Thought of Sages*. New York: 1972.

Klein, M. C., and N. A. Klein. *Temple Beyond Time*. New York: 1970.

Le Strange, Guy. *History of Jerusalem Under the Moslems from A.D. 650 to 1500*. Jerusalem: 1975. (Reprinted from *Palestine Under the Moslems*. London: 1890.)

Mazor, Benjamin. *The Mountain of the Lord*. New York: 1975.

Moore, Eliron A. *The Ancient Churches of Old Jerusalem*. London: 1961.

Nicoll, Maurice. *The New Man*. Boston: 1984.

Peters, Frances E. *Jerusalem: The Holy City in the Eyes of the Chroniclers, Visitors, Pilgrims and Prophets from the Days of Abraham to the Beginnings of Modern Times*. Princeton: 1985.

Prawer, Joshua. *The Latin Kingdom of Jerusalem*. London: 1972.

Quartertour—Walking Tour of the Jewish Quarter. Jerusalem.

Schaffer, Shaul. *Israel's Temple Mount*. Jerusalem: 1975.

Shur, N. *Jerusalem in Pilgrims' and Travelers' Accounts*. Jerusalem: 1980.

Sperber, Daniel. *Midrash Yerusalem: A Metaphysical History of Jerusalem*. Jerusalem: 1982.

Storme, Albert. *Gethsemane*. Jerusalem: 1972.

Storme, Albert. *The Way of the Cross*. Jerusalem: 1976.

Vilnay, Zev. *Legends of Jerusalem*. Philadelphia: 1973.

Ware, Timothy. *The Orthodox Church*. Harmondsworth and New York: 1963.

Wilkinson, John. *Egeria's Travels to the Holy Land*. Jerusalem: 1981.

Wilkinson, John. *Jerusalem Pilgrims*. Jerusalem: 1977.

INDEX

A Note About the Author

Martin Lev, a writer, lecturer, and guide, was born in New York City, and has a Ph.D. in archeology from the Institute of Archeology of the University of London. He lived for many years in Israel, first on a *moshav* and then in Jerusalem, where he studied sacred traditions and explored the essential question of this book: What is a sacred place?

A Note on the Type

This book was set on the Linotype in a face called Primer, designed by Rudolph Ruzicka (1883–1978). Mr. Ruzicka was earlier responsible for the design of Fairfield and Fairfield Medium, Linotype faces whose virtues have for some time been accorded wide recognition.

The complete range of sizes of Primer was first made available in 1954, although the pilot size of 12-point was ready as early as 1951. The design of the face makes general reference to Linotype Century—long a serviceable type, totally lacking in manner or frills of any kind—but brilliantly corrects its characterless quality.